LETTERS FROM
A YANKEE DOUGHBOY:
PRIVATE 1ST CLASS
RAYMOND W. MAKER
IN WORLD WAR I

BRUCE H. NORTON

LETTERS FROM
A YANKEE DOUGHBOY:
PRIVATE 1ST CLASS
RAYMOND W. MAKER
IN WORLD WAR I

BRUCE H. NORTON

ACADEMICA PRESS
WASHINGTON - LONDON

Library of Congress Cataloging-in-Publication Data

Names: Norton, B. H. (Bruce H.), author.
Title: Letters from a Yankee doughboy : Private 1st Class Raymond W.
Maker in World War I / Bruce H. Norton.
Other titles: Letters from a Yankee doughboy, Private 1st Class
Raymond W. Maker in World War I
Description: Washington : Academica Press, [2019] | Includes
bibliographical references. | Summary: "This is an edited collection of
letters from a U.S. Army infantryman during World War I."-- Provided
by publisher.
Identifiers: LCCN 2019035649 | ISBN 9781680531985 (hardcover) |
ISBN 9781680532012 (paperback)
Subjects: LCSH: Maker, Raymond W. (Raymond Whitney),
1892-1964--Correspondence. | United States. Army. Infantry Division,
26th--Biography. | Soldiers--United States--Biography. | World War,
1914-1918--Campaigns--Western Front. | World War, 1914-1918--
Regimental

DEDICATION

This work is dedicated to my wife, Helen.
With my sincere love and my most grateful appreciation in helping to
bring this story of Private First Class Raymond Whitney Maker to life.

Doc

CONTENTS

ACKNOWLEDGEMENTS vii

PREFACE ix

INTRODUCTION 1

RAYMOND'S LETTERS FROM 1917 21

FIRST COMBAT ACTION AT
CHEMIN-DES-DAMES (JANUARY – FEBRUARY 1918) 37

RAYMOND'S LETTERS DIARY ENTRIES 39

ACTIONS IN LA REINE (BOUCQ) SECTOR – BOIS BRÛLE,
SEICHEPREY, XIVRAY, HUMBERT PLANTATION
(MARCH 1918) 61

THE DIVISION REST AREA
(JULY 1918) 105

THE ST.MIHIEL OFFENSIVE
(SEPTEMBER 12-15, 1918) 145

THE MEUSE-ARGONNE OFFENSIVE
(SEPTEMBER 26 TO NOVEMBER 11, 1918) 151

THE KEY TO VERDUN 239

THE FINAL CHAPTER 241

THE MAKER FAMILY 247

ACKNOWLEDGEMENTS

Rosalba H. Norton; Marilyn B. Nardone; Mr. Raymond W. Maker, III; Master Sergeant Phillip R. Gibbons, USMC (Ret); Col. Raymond C. Damm, Jr., USMC (Ret); James and Connie M. Simons; Bruce H. Norton, Jr.; Major Greg W. Dyson, USMC; Monsieur Thierry Hubscher, Director, Mémorial de Verdun; Ms. Gabrielle Perissi; Natacha Glaudel, Head of Collections, Verdun War Memorial; and the Honorable Monsieur Samuel Hazard, Mayor de Verdun; and Mr. Greg Norman, Fox News.

Other books by Major Bruce H. "Doc" Norton, USMC (Ret.)

Force Recon Diary, 1969

Force Recon Diary, 1970

One Tough Marine:
The Biography of 1ˢᵗ Sergeant Donald N. Hamblen, USMC

Sergeant Major, U.S. Marines:
The Biography of Sergeant Major Maurice J. Jacques, USMC

Stingray: The History of Reconnaissance Marines Vietnam - 1965-1972

Encyclopedia of American War Heroes

I AM ALIVE! -
A United States Marine's Story of Survival in a Japanese POW Camp

Grown Gray in War:
The Biography of Master Gunnery Sergeant Len Maffioli, USMC

PREFACE

Raymond Whitney Maker was my grandfather. Born on November 15, 1892, in Weston, Massachusetts, he was the son of Winfield Scott Maker and Rosalba Maker (Peck), of Framingham, Massachusetts. Raymond had a brother Clifford (Kip), a sister Eva, and a half-sister, Harriet. His mother, Rosalba (Peck) Maker died when Raymond was twenty-three and he, Kip, and their sister Eva, helped their father manage a general store and horse stables in Framingham to keep the family together and supplement their combined incomes. He was proud of his "Yankee" lineage, as his mother, Rosalba Peck, was a direct descendant of Mary Allerton (Cushman), the youngest passenger aboard the *Mayflower*.

I remember my grandfather as a quiet, slim-built man, five foot six-inches tall, with thinning white hair, who enjoyed sitting in his Morris chair and listening to the radio, smoking Half & Half tobacco from an old corn-cob pipe, and sipping a cold Ballantine beer from a small juice glass as the Boston Red Sox played baseball every Saturday or Sunday afternoon at Boston's Fenway Park.

In 1960, he retired after forty-two years of working for the New England Telephone and Telegraph Company as a telephone installation specialist. He enjoyed a few of the simple pleasures of retired life: working with wood in his basement workshop, fishing, and hosting the traditional Saturday night "beans and franks" dinner at his home in Cranston, Rhode Island, with his wife, Gladys.

Raymond and Gladys had four children: two sons, Raymond (junior) and Donald, and two daughters, Rosalba (my mother) and her sister Marjorie. A man with a dry sense of humor, he was very proud of his sons and daughters and tolerated his eight grandchildren as well as could be expected.

I believe he found some degree of pleasure in my company as his young "fishing buddy," but that was challenged on the day that I thought I would help him by scrubbing his dentures with Ajax powder while he was taking his afternoon nap. Upon waking and positioning his upper and lower dentures, his facial expression suddenly changed with the unnatural taste of grit and chlorine from my shoddy job of properly rinsing his teeth. I suddenly heard words I had never heard before, and not understanding what they meant, there was no doubt from his rapid-fire delivery of swearing, that I had done something very wrong. My grandmother quickly removed me from his presence and probably saved my life.

Raymond Whitney Maker served in the Massachusetts Volunteer Militia (National Guard) for three years before enlisting in the U.S. Army's 26th Infantry Division. He saw the very worst of what war had to offer a young man from rural Massachusetts and, in my presence when I was very young, never spoke about his experiences during the war in France with the "Yankee" Division.

Private 1st Class Raymond W. Maker was the unsuspecting recipient of mustard gas fired by German artillery into his dugout position on July 20, 1918, at the Battle of Château-Thierry. As a horrific chemical agent, it caused severe burning of the skin, eyes, and respiratory tract. The Germans used this gas as an effective method of incapacitating victims *en masse*.

He was hospitalized and treated at Base Hospital #31, in Contrexeville (Vosges), where the U.S. Army had taken over nine hotels for use as hospitals to treat thousands of wounded American soldiers. After a month of hospitalization, in late August 1918 he rejoined the 104th Infantry Regiment.

He was wounded by enemy artillery fire at Verdun on November 9, 1918, during the Meuse-Argonne offensive and was awarded a second wound stripe and the Purple Heart. In December 1918, he went into the city of Verdun and as a "keepsake" took the key from the North Gate of Verdun. He wrote about acquiring his "souvenir" to his sister and mailed the key to Eva, telling her to take care of it as it could someday "be of value."

I believe Raymond's daily pocket diary entries and letters to his family accurately describe the day-to-day boredom and sufferings not unlike those of millions of American infantrymen who, since our early colonial days, have taken up arms against other enemy combatants. There is an unmistakable change in his letters from routine and mundane to more heart-felt and foreboding, after he had survived numerous incoming enemy artillery barrages, "going over the top," and meeting enemy machinegun and rifle fire.

One aspect of Raymond's character which I believe is most telling is that his eldest son, Raymond W. Maker, Jr., married a girl whose parents, Mr. and Mrs. Ludwig Britsch, came to the United States from Germany after the First World War. It was during a Thanksgiving Day dinner at Raymond's home, in the late 1950s, when it was revealed that Mr. Britsch had served in the German Army and had fought against Raymond during the Meuse-Argonne Offensive in the fall of 1918. Mr. Britsch had been wounded by American artillery fire and was immediately taken as a prisoner of war. He credited his survival to the care given to him by American infantrymen and the U.S. Army's doctors and nurses. Mr. and Mrs. Britsch and Raymond and Gladys became close friends and were together at numerous family gatherings.

In 1990, I visited with my uncle Donald Maker, Raymond's youngest son, who lived with his wife Ruthie, in North Scituate, Rhode Island. I was presented with Raymond's Colt .45 pistol, with serial number 274084, the very sidearm he carried throughout his time in France. Uncle "Donnie" wanted to make sure that the pistol would be cared for long after he was gone and, knowing that I was military historian, thought I would cherish such a gift. Raymond's Colt .45 holds a place of honor in our home and is one of my most prized possessions.

He told me that Raymond had used the pistol in the Battle of Château-Thierry when he was pinned down my German machinegun fire. He was unable to move from a large shell hole as he laid out communication wire. He remained motionless as four German infantrymen slowly approached his position. Raymond waited for the right moment and fire his Colt into the group, killing all four of them.

Uncle Donnie went on to explain that at the time soldiers were forbidden to write about the actions in combat. The could not record where they were, where they we going, and what actions they had been involved in. Raymond's letters, written during the month of July 1918, mention how horrible the experience was, but he did not describe his actions in his letters to his sister and father for fear of worrying them.

What follows are Raymond's short pocket diary entries, from January 1 to December 30, 1918, and his letters from October 1917 to April 1919, which he wrote to his sister, Eva and other family members and friends. His sister saved these letters and passed them along to his wife Gladys, who gave them to my mother, Rosalba. I ultimately received them in 1992.

This story is a personal record of one Yankee Doughboy, Private 1st Class Raymond Whitney Maker - who he was, how he lived, his fears and hopes and joys, and how he fought to survive the many hardships he endured in the "War to End All Wars."

Major Bruce H. "Doc" Norton, USMC (Ret) - 2019

"You smug-faced cowards with kindling eye,
Who cheer when soldier lads march by
Sneak home and pray you'll never know,
The hell where youth and laughter go."

-Royal Welsh Captain Siegfried Sassoon - 1918[i]

INTRODUCTION

When World War I erupted in 1914, President Woodrow Wilson declared neutrality for the United States, a position the vast majority of Americans favored. Britain, however, was one of America's closest trading partners, and tension soon arose between the United States and Germany over the latter's attempted quarantine of the British Isles. Several U.S. ships traveling to Britain were damaged or sunk by German mines, and in February 1915 Germany announced unrestricted submarine warfare against all ships, neutral or otherwise, that entered the war zone around Britain. One month later, Germany announced the sinking of the *William P. Frye,* a private American vessel. President Wilson was outraged, but the German government apologized and called the attack an unfortunate mistake.

On May 7, 1915, the British-owned *Lusitania*, a large ocean liner, was torpedoed without warning just off the coast of Ireland. Of the 1,959 passengers, 1,198 were killed, including 128 Americans. The German government maintained that the *Lusitania* was carrying munitions, but the U.S. demanded reparations and an end to German attacks on unarmed passenger and merchant ships. In August, Germany pledged to see to the safety of passengers before sinking unarmed vessels, but in November it sank an Italian liner without warning, killing 272 people, including 27 Americans. With these attacks, public opinion in the United States began to turn irrevocably against Germany.

On January 31, 1917, Germany, determined to win its war of attrition against the Allies, announced the resumption of unrestricted warfare. Three days later, the United States broke diplomatic relations with Germany, and just hours after that, on February 6, 1917, the

American liner *USS Housatonic* was sunk by a German U-boat. On February 22, Congress passed a $250 million arms appropriations bill intended to make the United States ready for war. In late March, Germany sank four more U.S. merchant ships, and on April 2, President Wilson appeared before Congress and called for a declaration of war against Germany. Four days later, his request was granted.

On June 26, 1917, the first 14,000 U.S. infantry troops landed in France to begin combat training. After three years of bloody stalemate along the Western front, the entrance of America's well-supplied forces into the conflict marked a major turning point in the war and helped the Allies to victory. When the war finally ended, on November 11, 1918, more than two million American soldiers had arrived in Europe, and some 50,000 of them had lost their lives in combat.

War is built around long periods of boredom, the daily repetition of events, and meaninglessness. To write honestly about war, readers need to feel that they have endured those things as well. Yet, no sane novelist wants to inflict that much pain and discomfort on his audience. And so, we read novels and watch movies filled with the kind of bravery and drama that make war look at least entertaining, if not admirable. Many of these works are tremendous artistic achievements. But they are not war.

America's official participation in World War I began, as the history books tell us, on April 2, 1917. Before a joint session of Congress, attended by the justices of the Supreme Court and a gallery of distinguished spectators, President Woodrow Wilson asked the Congress of the United States for a declaration of war against Germany and her allies. Congress, composed largely of men who had little idea of what a large-scale war was like, eagerly granted his request, and the United States, after 134 years of studious disengagement from the affairs of Europe, committed itself to its first adventure in the hemisphere which its founding fathers had left and avoided.

Goaded by greed and suspicion, the great powers of Europe had been girding for war and choosing up sides for years before it began. Yet when war came, it was a complete surprise to most Americans, and a shock to many Europeans as well. The spark that "ignited the timbers of a rotting world" was a Bosnian Serb assassin's bullets, which killed the Archduke

Francis Ferdinand, heir to the Austrian throne, with a pistol presented to him by a Serbian intelligence officer. In the two and a half years of slaughter that followed, the United States maintained a precarious neutrality that had split German-American communities and families and created a breach in public sentiment that could be resolved only in the general enthusiasm with which the declaration of war was received. For a decade, the advocates of peace had kept the country armed to the bare minimum necessary to preserve civil order and peace in neighboring Latin American nations. The regular U.S. Army was hardly large sufficient to be of use on the Western Front in Europe. The senior military staff was unorganized for active warfare. There were not enough rifles to arm half of the proposed army, and there were scarcely any plans even on paper for providing more. Yet, congressional leaders and an uninformed public thought that six weeks of American action would suffice to defeat the most formidable military machine ever created, and that American troops would be home by Christmas. It took six weeks for the Draft Act to become law, and it was only in June 1917 that the first American soldiers set foot on French soil.

"The raw American recruits who were rushed to Europe were called the Doughboys. There can be little dispute as to the derivation of the name. In Texas, the U.S. Infantry, patrolling along the Rio Grande, were powdered white with the dust of the adobe soil, and hence were called "adobes" by mounted troops. It was a short step to "dobies" and then, by metathesis, the word was Doughboys. The weight of their masses, the Allies hoped, would turn the scales, making anything less than a looter's victory implausible. The Doughboys entered the tragedy at the beginning of the fifth act, with millions of men already dead, like off-stage soldiers in a play; and they entered singing. Woodrow Wilson had given them their simple theme; Kaiser Bill was a villain and they marched to make the world safe for democracy."[ii]

The Doughboys' battlefields ranged as far as Arkhangelsk in northern Russia and the Italian Piave, but they were centered in France, from the Swiss border to the English Channel. To treat their endeavors in detail, it is necessary to pass over briefly the great tragedies of the Allies and their enemies that preceded them. In 1916 alone, a million men were casualties at Verdun, another million in Flanders, and another million casualties on the Eastern Front.

The Doughboy losses in 1918 were a pittance in comparison with these figures. Yet it was the Doughboy who held the line at the critical Marne in 1918, broke the back of Ludendorff's offensive spirit at Soissons, wiped out the four-year torment of the Saint-Mihiel salient, cracked the Saint-Quentin Canal complex of the Hindenburg Line, destroyed the great German bastion of Blanc Mont behind Rheims, fought across the rain-swollen Scheldt River to give Belgians a bridgehead to Brussels, and most notably plunged into the maze of the Meuse-Argonne sector to cut the broad highway of the Sedan-Mézières railroad network, forestalling any German hope of a last ditch effort on the Rhine.

The strategy of the Doughboy was never dictated by his own high commanders – who were good – but by Allied generals who had never been conspicuously successful in any offensive operations over a three-year period of war. However, the Doughboys' strategy to seize strategic areas was vetoed by overall Allied commander Marshal Foch at the insistence of the British ground commander, Field Marshal Haig. For reasons of European *Weltpolitik* that are not a part of this story, the only war the Doughboy was permitted to wage was tactical – the science of killing your enemy without getting killed yourself. Two million Doughboys reached France, most of them deficient in the basic school of the rifleman. But in the savage clinics conducted by the veteran Germans, the Doughboy progressed and by war's end, he and his officers had become superior fighters.[iii]

A BRIEF HISTORY OF THE FIGHTING "YANKEE" DIVISION A.E.F.

On the Battlefront February 5 – November 11, 1918

THE 26th DIVISION: "SAVIORS OF PARIS"

The record of the New England Division, the 26th Division of the United States Army, will live forever as one of the most glorious in the annals of American military history. No division in any army has ever fought with greater gallantry and skill in arms, with greater endurance and grit and bulldog tenacity, with greater cheerfulness in morale than the

Yankee Division, the Sacrifice Division, or the to use the full-hearted sobriquet bestowed by the grateful French people, "the Saviors of Paris."

No New England heart can help but leap at the thought of these splendid representatives of American manhood who were chosen by General Pershing to march to the Rhine as a part of the Allied Army of Triumph.

But the gallant regiments had losses to mourn. Cut to pieces in the frightful battles on the Meuse, in the Argonne, and around Verdun, 10,000 men lost their lives in the last weeks of the fighting. The remnants were worn out by the cumulative fatigue of months of incessant campaigning, their horses exhausted or dead, their clothing reduced to rags. The spirit willing but the flesh weak, but the honor and glory remained theirs.

The Yankee Division is one of four divisions of the American Army which are grouped as the veterans of the American Expeditionary Force, along with the 1st, 2nd, and 42nd Divisions. Other American divisions fought as valiantly, but none saw the same intensity of frontline combat. Military experts French, British, and American alike all agree with this assessment. The 1st and 2nd Regulars and the 26th and 42nd National Guardsmen are the premier divisions of the U.S. Army. Much of what is here written about the Yankee Divisions could be said as truthfully of any one of the others, but only of them.

THE YANKEE DIVISION'S CITATIONS AND DECORATIONS

The 26th Division has to its credit nearly 150 citations from the French nation. Fully 7,000 of its men were cited for bravery, and over 500 won the Distinguished Service Medal of the American Army or the French Croix de Guerre.

The 104th Infantry was until recently the only regiment in the United States Army whose colors were decorated by a foreign government. On April 26, 1918, after the battle of Bois Brûle, at Apremont, the 104th was cited by the headquarters of the 32nd French Army Corps, and its colors were decorated with the Croix de Guerre.

The 104th Infantry - with its Companies A, C and H of Worcester, the Light Infantry, the City Guards, and the Wellington Rifles - was decorated as a regiment with the Croix de Guerre, the only American regiment thus honored by the French. The 101st Infantry - including Company G, the old Emmet Guards - has likewise covered itself with glory and won citations for gallantry. As with the 104th, a large number of its men wore decorations bestowed for valor. So, too, did honor come to the Worcester batteries, B and E of the 102nd Field Artillery, for brave and effective work on many a bloody field, and the same was true of the 101st Engineers, the 101st Field Artillery, and every other unit of the division.

GENERAL EDWARDS
AND THE YANKEE DIVISION

Major General Clarence R. Edwards and his Yankee Division will forever remain in intimate and loving association. This fighting general of the regular army organized the Division and took it overseas. He oversaw the training which formed it into a combat division of the highest class. He commanded it at Chemin-des-Dames, Toul, Château-Thierry, the Second Battle of the Marne, St. Mihiel, on the Meuse, and at Verdun, until the final fortnight preceding the Armistice. He was more than a friend - he was a father to his boys, and they knew him as such and as a leader of rare military skill. His departure just before the end of the war caused them great grief despite the fact that he was relieved of command. Among the men of the Yankee Division, he always remained "Our General."

General Edwards was succeeded on October 25, 1918, by Brigadier General F. E. Bamford, who in turn, on November 19, was relieved by Major General Harry C. Hale.

THE FIRST NATIONAL GUARD
DIVISION IN FRANCE

The 26th was the first National Guard division. Among American fighting men in France, it was preceded only by a part of the 1st Division of regulars. Its men are numbered in the first 50,000 of the American Expeditionary Force to arrive in Europe. No other American division saw such long and continuous service on the front. None sustained so many casualties, and, for that reason, none has had so many names on its rolls. When the armistice was signed, and the guns ceased to roar, the Yankee

Division had gone through nine months of incessant fighting, interrupted only by transfers from sector to sector of the front, always, as it happened, in adverse weather conditions. Back and forth across northern France the regiments were shuttled, always promised rest but never getting it, for no campaign could begin without them. The Yankees traveled some 1,200 miles in France, always on grim business, never on pleasure.

The Division was the first American unit to take up a sector at the front. They fought at Chemin-des-Dames, at Toul, at the Second Battle of the Marne, where they delivered the blow that sent the Germans reeling back from the salient, the apex of which was Château-Thierry. They fought at St. Mihiel, where they were manned the most difficult sector, and they fought in the bloodiest of battles, before Metz, on the Meuse, in the Argonne, and at Verdun.

The 26th was always assigned the most difficult tasks, for they were certain to do it right. The post of honor was always theirs, and in war the post of honor is where the hardest, most resolute, most desperate fighting is to be done. The Yankee Division earned the name given it by the Allied armies, the "Sacrifice Division." Its men never complained. Incessant, nerve-straining danger, terrible suffering from exposure, hunger and thirst, endless want of sleep, the disappointment of promised rest and pleasure again and again deferred - none of these afflictions dampened the cheerfulness and fighting spirit of the Yankee lads. One has but to read their letters home to know this. When the full history is written of the Minutemen, as they came very near being called in homage to the militias of the American Revolution, there will be no more inspiring tale for future generations. Because the Yankee Division had longest service of any American division in France, President Wilson selected it for his Christmas visit to the soldiers.

The 26th Division was originally made up entirely of National Guard troops from New England. When it left the United States, every man was a volunteer. Tens of thousands of replacements were made from the National Army, but most of these men were from Western states. And of course, many of the new officers hailed from other parts of the country. But every one of those New England boys who went overseas with the Division was a volunteer. When hostilities ceased hardly fifteen percent of them remained in the field. The names of most of the others are in the casualty lists.

The Division was called into service on July 25, 1917. The infantry mobilized at Framingham, Worcester, Westfield, and other camps, and the artillery at Boxford, Massachusetts. The National Guard replacements had to be consolidated and readjusted in order to attain the full strength of four infantry regiments on the basis of organization, and to expand the artillery from fractions of regiments to three full regiments of six batteries each.

Another unit, the Rainbow Division, was organized to go over first; its composition of National Guard units from thirty-eight states had that end in view. But it was not ready, and the better prepared Yankee Division beat the Rainbows overseas by several months.

FORMING A GREAT COMBAT DIVISION

Training progressed rapidly until, in early September 1917, the first contingent, consisting of the 101st Infantry and the 101st Field Artillery, left camp for Hoboken, New Jersey, to sail to Liverpool. The transports stopped at Halifax, Nova Scotia, to join a convoy to be safe from German U-boat attacks. Without delay, the regiments crossed England to Southampton and immediately embarked for France, landing at Brest on September 21. The Division's other regiments followed in quick succession.

The infantry training camp was at Neufchâteau, in eastern France, while the artillery units were stationed at Coëtquidan, near Rennes in Brittany, an ancient artillery training camp established by Napoleon. The daily routine was tough and relentless, but the results showed the wisdom of the hard, well-directed training, in which experienced French officers played important parts as instructors.

The artillery had won a name for itself for the rapidity and accuracy of its fire even before it left Coëtquidan. The American army guns had been left at home, and the task was to master the French 75mm guns and the heavier 155s, and to equal the French standard of fire. No greater accuracy than that of the French could be achieved, but for speed the Yankees went them one better, by mastering the difficult and dangerous method of loading on the recoil. In fact they could perform the operation so rapidly that German officers believed the Americans were using a 3-inch machine gun. The artillery of the 26th won such high encomiums from the officers of the Allied armies, but best of all was the praise from their own infantry: "We would charge into the jaws of hell behind a barrage from our batteries."

The Division's engineering battalion, the 101st, won enduring fame, not only for its specialized work, but for its fighting ability as well. The deadly skill of the machine gun and trench mortar battalions also won laurels. The 101st Field Signal Battalion, ever alert and efficient, often operating under most difficult and hazardous conditions, rendered conspicuous service. The Ammunition Train Supply and Sanitary Train functioned smoothly in the divisional machine, despite insuperable difficulties and grave peril. The Military Police were the pride of General Edwards. Of the Ambulance Companies and Field Hospitals of the Division, no praise could be too great. As noncombatants, in action they faced punishment from the enemy but were never permitted to retaliate. They had perilous work to do, and they did it well.

ON TO CHEMIN-DES-DAMES

After four solid months of training, the 26th moved up to Chemin-des-Dames, leaving camp on February 1, 1918. On the afternoon of February 5, the guns of Battery A, 101st Field Artillery, took the line, and at 3:45pm, one of its 75s barked forth the first shot fired by the National Guard in World War I. The shell casing is preserved to this day in the Massachusetts State House. That night, the 101st Infantry went through the artillery lines and became the first National Guard contingent to enter the trenches. There was plenty of fighting at Chemin-des-Dames, though none on a large scale.

While manning this sector, the Yankee Division was associated with the 11th French Army Corps. General Edwards issued an order stating that he was pleased to consider the 11th Corps the godfather of the 26th Division. General Maud Huy, commander of the 11th, replied: "The 11th corps feels proud of the marked honor, being sure that, wherever he may be sent, the godson shall do credit to the godfather."

After forty-six days at Chemin-des-Dames, the Division entrained at Soissons under heavy shell fire and proceeded to Rimaucourt, in Haute Saône, not far from Neufchâteau. Much of the journey from Soissons was over the road, and it was still winter, with rainy weather and exceedingly muddy roads. But the Division was not unhappy, for a rest period was promised, and the men needed rest and a little play. But they got neither.

THE FORCED MARCH TO TOUL

The great German offensive of March 21, 1918 had just started, sweeping over the very positions that the 26th had just vacated, and which the Germans might not have taken quite so easily had the Yankee Division been there to help their French comrades. The Division had hardly arrived at Rimaucourt when orders came to proceed to the Toul sector, to relieve a French division. The Toul sector was comparatively quiet but vitally important. Good troops were needed to hold it against the possibility of serious German attack.

With scant warning, the men started on a ten-day march northward, through Neufchâteau, 125 miles as the crow flies and much longer on the road. It rained and snowed steadily and was very cold. Every man, from colonel to private, was soaked to the skin day and night. Food and water were scarce. The Division's sudden move was wholly unexpected, and precautions for supplying so large a body of troops could not be made without advance planning. Everyone suffered from exposure, scanty diet, and the lack of sleep. Many horses gave out under the strain. Mounted men walked to spare their animals. But, strange to say, very few men were put on the sick list. They were too well conditioned.

On the battle line north of Toul, the Division took over a sector of eighteen kilometers, the longest held by an American division on the Western front. The Germans gave them a warm welcome; the arrival was marked by a terrific bombardment, which compelled a quick shifting of artillery positions, for the Germans had by then developed capable airplanes for observation. There followed a long series of actions, some of them battles of considerable proportions. Of these, Bois Brûle at Apremont and Seicheprey were the first real battles in which American troops engaged. The 26th never failed. The Germans had their first real taste of the kind of fighters the United States breeds and, when aroused, sends to war. Of the Yankee Division's record at Toul, General Passaga stated in General orders:

> At the moment when the 26th Division of the United States is leaving the 32nd French Corps, I salute its colors and thank it for the splendid services it has rendered here to the common cause ... Under the distinguished command of their Chief, General Edwards, the high-spirited soldiers of the Yankee Division have taught the enemy some bitter lessons, at Bois Brûle, the Seicheprey, at Xivray-Marvoisin; they have taught him to realize the staunch vigor of the sons of the great republic; fighting for the world's freedom ... My heartiest good wishes will accompany the Yankee Division always in its future combats.

CHÂTEAU-THIERRY

Late in June, the glorious word went about the regiments: "Rest billets a short distance from Paris." The Division left Toul, traveling first over the road, then by train, in the usual cattle cars. Five months of trench warfare and suffering were forgotten. They were going to Paris! The rumor was a fact, too. The orders were to take station at Panton and neighboring villages, in the suburbs of the French capital. Furloughs were to be expected, but there was no rest for these war-torn soldiers. They reached Panton, in sight of the Eiffel Tower, but never disembarked. The trains suddenly reversed their direction and proceeded back, eastward, to the Marne front at Château-Thierry. They were to relieve the 2nd Division, including the Marines, who had won immortal glory at Belleau Wood by halting one of the most menacing German drives.

"THE SAVIORS OF PARIS"

The world knows what the Yankee Division did at Château-Thierry; how it earned the French name of "Saviors of Paris," and from the famous General Degoutte of the French Sixth Army these thrilling words: "The 26th Infantry Division alone is responsible for the whole Allied advance on the Marne. They are shock troops, par excellence!" A sweet compliment this must have been to those brave soldier boys.

The division took its position on July 9, 1918. It relieved the 2nd Division, which hurled back the German advance on June 2. The 2nd Division fought the first battle of Château-Thierry; the Yankee Division fought the second battle of Château-Thierry. The New England boys broke the final thrust of the last German drive, and their counterattack was the initial blow in a series that hurled the Germans back for the next four months until they finally surrendered.

When the 26th went into position at Vaux, the German armies were massing for the fourth great drive of their grand offensive, which started in March. The sector had been comparatively quiet, but almost immediately upon arrival of the Yankee Division, enemy artillery fire became intense. The Yankees had neither trenches nor shelters of any kind. The forest, including Belleau Wood, was shattered to pieces.

On June 15, following a bombardment more severe than the war had previously known that deluged the Allied lines even to the rearmost positions with gas and high explosives, the Germans struck in massed formations and in overwhelming superior numbers. The French were forced back across the Marne.

THE YANKEE DIVISION
TURNS THE TIDE OF WAR

The 26th's artillery was instructed that an attack against their positions was inevitable. Their orders were to meet the onslaught with the most intense fire possible and to keep firing until about to be engulfed in the advancing masses, then blow up their guns and retreat. The attack did not come at the moment expected, but finally, on July 18, a dense body of Germans was discerned preparing to attack. Before they had even started, the guns opened a drumfire of such intensity and accuracy that the enemy was thrown into complete confusion. At that moment the tide turned, and the gallant infantry of the 26th went over the top. From that instant, the 26th chased the enemy northward, licking him time and again.

As General Edwards stated in General orders, "In those eight days you carried your line as far as any part of the advance was carried. Torey, Belleau, Givry, the Bouresches Woods, Rochet Woods, Hill 190 overlooking Château-Thierry, Étrépilly, Épieds, Trugny, and finally La

Fère Woods and the objective, the Jaulgonne-Fère-en-Tardenois Road, belong to your arms."

And this fighting was against the picked troops of the German army, the famous Prussian Guards and the Bavarians. They could not withstand the doughboys from New England. No troops could have withstood them. They suffered heavy losses, but they kept going. At times the artillery, racing after, could hardly keep up with them.

On July 25, the Rainbow Division went through the Yankee Division's infantry, who had done their stint. When the Rainbow infantry went out, the guns of the 26th kept on with the 5th Division of regulars, and in tandem with a French division, until they were overlooking the Vesle River at Fismes, sweeping the German positions on the plateau beyond. The artillery had fought so far forward that it took them two days to get back to the Marne where they arrived August 8.

General Degoutte, commander of the 5th French Army, issued general orders in which he said:

> The operations carried out by the 26th American Division
> from July 18 to July 24 demonstrated the fine soldierly
> qualities of this, and of its leader, General Edwards. Co-
> operating in the attack north of the Marne, the 26th
> Division fought brilliantly on the line Torey-Belleau, at
> Molthiers, Épieds and Trugny and in the forest of Fère,
> advancing more than 15 kilometers in depth in spite of the
> desperate resistance of the enemy … I take great pleasure
> in communicating to General Edwards and his valiant
> Division this expression of my great esteem, together with
> my heartiest congratulations for the manner in which they
> have served the common cause. I could not have done
> better in a similar occasion with my best troops.

THE BITTER CUP OF DISAPPOINTMENT

The division had done its share, and much more, in the Second Battle of the Marne. The men went into camp in the little villages of the Marne valley, tired lads when they left the battlefield, their horses in pitiable shape. Then the regiments moved to the vicinity of Châtillon, on the headwaters of the Seine. First in pup tents, then in billets in the villages, the boys rested a little while, in preparation for their furloughs, promised twice before but of necessity withheld. It was a jubilant camp for each man was to have seven days all his own, away from exacting commanders and grating disciplione. But again, there was the slip twixt cup and lip. Imperative orders arrived to proceed back to the front. Furloughs were cancelled, the soldiers said "*C'est la guerre*," and the 26th started on its way to take a vital part in the sudden snapping off the St. Mihiel salient.

ST. MIHIEL

The preparations for this campaign were conducted in the utmost secrecy. The last stages of the advance were made at night. It rained constantly. In the long dark hours of the onset northern autumn, the companies and batteries plodded along in the damp cold, sometimes hungry, and forbidden to smoke for fear of the betraying light. And when each day dawned, the men slept, somewhere, anywhere, wrapped in soggy wet blankets. Finally, they were in the forest on the western side of the salient, where in 1915 some 30,000 French soldiers laid down their lives to stem the German tide.

Troyon, as the French called it, or the New England Sector, as the men of the 26th called it, is about half way between St. Mihiel and Verdun, on the heights of the Meuse, and was regarded as the most difficult section of the line of attack. After an artillery bombardment of almost unprecedented ferocity, the Division went over the top on September 12. Within twenty-four hours, the salient had ceased to exist and the 26th had its full share of the vast numbers of prisoners and enormous booty that fell to the American army. The Yanks at St. Mihiel took 2,400 prisoners and many field guns, much ammunition, and stores of every kind. The gratitude of the liberated people was expressed in a letter from the Catholic priest of Rupt-en-Woëvre after the boys had driven off the Germans:

> Sir, your gallant 26th American Division has just set us free. Since September 1914, the barbarians have held the heights of the Meuse, have murdered three hostages from Mouilly, have shelled Rupt, and on July 23, 1915, forced its inhabitants to scatter to the four corners of France. I, who remain at my little listening post upon the advice of

my bishop, feel certain, sir, that I do but speak for Monseigneur Ginisty, Lord Bishop of Verdun, my parishioners of Rupt, Mouilly and Genicourt and the people of this vicinity, in conveying to you and your associates the heartfelt and unforgettable gratitude of all ... Several of your comrades lie at rest in our truly Christian and French soil. Their ashes shall be cared for as if they were our own. We shall cover their graves with flowers and shall kneel by them as their own families would do with a prayer to God to reward with eternal glory these heroes fallen on the field of honor and to bless the 26th Division and generous Americans. Be pleased, sir, to accept the expression of my profound respect.

Of the 1st Battalion of the 102nd infantry, General Blondiat, commander of the 2nd Colonial Army Corps, asked that it be cited for the heroism of its men at Bois de Chauffor to Mesnil, stating: "The spirit of sacrifice and magnificent courage displayed by the troops of the 26th United States Division on this occasion were certainly not in vain; they seem to me worthy of recompense."

THE BATTLES OF THE MEUSE

Following St. Mihiel, the 26th had little rest, and what it did have was under shellfire. On September 25 the New England boys were in the thick of the fighting again, and they stayed there until the clock struck 11am on November 11, 1918, announcing the armistice. Their first task was to create a diversion, in conjunction with French units, in order to befog the enemy as to the Allies' true intentions and keep as many German divisions as possible away from the sectors where the great American offenive was to ne concentrate.

Accordingly, the Yankee Division and its French comrades made a feint in the vicinity of Dommartin, on the plain of the Woëvre. The action of September 25, the day before the First Army started on its victorious drive northwest of Verdun, was a battle of a magnitude which would have attracted world-wide attention had it not been coincident with bigger doings on other parts of the French-Belgian front. Harassing attacks continued for some days.

The Germans began massing troops to stay the northward rush of the American army west of the Meuse, and the Yankee Division was ordered to frustrate them in the region of Sivry-sur-Meuse, fifteen miles north of Verdun and just east of the river. It arrived there on October 8, and two days later it took over the sector from the 18th French Division and a part of the American 29th. The fighting there was serious enough, but it was child's play when compared to what was to follow.

The Division set out from Sivry October 21, advancing southeast through a hill and valley country, covered with what once had been forest but now reduced to a wilderness of scraggly chunks of trees which rose from a honeycomb of shell holes - a ghastly waste that included the German point of departure for their drive against Verdun in 1916, which cost them more than half a million casualties.

THE BLOODY CLOSING DAYS

On November 7, the Yankee Division opened the final phase of the battle, which can ever be remembered without a shudder and a tear. In the four shorts days of war that remained before the last shot was fired, more than 10,000 splendid lads of the 26th were killed or wounded. Swinging sharply from southeast due east, the Division's embattled regiments headed straight for the Briey coalfields. Here, near Belleau Wood, the Division formed the pivot of the attacking armies.

This time it was the Germans who cried, "They shall not pass!" But the Yankee boys did pass. Division after division, the German commanders threw into the battle, the best troops they had in a desperate effort to check the onrush of the irresistible 26th. The odds were against the Americans. They went forward against thousands of machine guns, massed artillery of every caliber, numerically superior defending infantry, and carefully prepared defenses. But the Yankees carried on, surely, relentlessly.

They sustained shellfire that no soldier present had even seen equaled. From the time they left Sivry, they were under continuous savage cannonading. But the climax arrived between Bois d'Ormont and Belleau Wood, where a bombardment of indescribable ferocity raged for two days. The forward lines and gun positions were deluged with high explosives and poison gas. The woods were literally hidden in the clouds of mud and dirt thrown up by high explosive shells. An inspection of the territory by officers following the armistice proved that not even the many months of intensive shelling of Douaumont, in front of Verdun, had wrought so complete a destruction as that of the few days at Belleau and d'Ormont.

There were hellish frontal charges into jungles of trees and barbed wire entanglements, through hurricanes of shrapnel, into the muzzles of thousands of machine guns. For four days this continued. Each day won a mile. The cost was terrible. In those hideous hours, the Division lost thousands and thousands of men. Those others of whom neither shell nor bullet, grenade nor gas had taken toll were almost dead from fatigue, lack of sleep, intolerable nervous strain, and hunger and filth. It was thus that the Yankee Division completed "doing its bit."

General Bamford, on November 18, the day he was relieved of his command one week after the armistice, issued the following order:

> Officers and enlisted men of the 26th Division, I congratulate you upon your success in the war which has been fought to a victorious end. From your entry into the battle line on February 5, 1918, at Chemin-des-Dames, as a division of recruits, until the cessation of hostilities on the 11th of November 1918, when you laid down your arms fighting in the front line as a veteran division, you have shown yourselves worthy sons of the country that gave you birth. Bois Brûle, Xivray-Marvoisin, Torey, Belleau, Givry, Bouresches, Hill 190, Epieds, Trugny, St. Mihiel salient, Bois d'Haumont, Bois de Belleau, Bois d'Ormont, Bois de Ville, are indelibly written on your banners.

And so, the Army of Occupation marched away, without the 26th Division. Certainly, that army would never have set foot on German soil had it not been for the patriotic, self-sacrificing men, who hurried to the recruiting offices and offered themselves to Uncle Sam for his army. They went early, and therefore were trained early, and, because they were ready, stepped into the breach whenever there was a breach, until the days when they themselves made the breaches. The 26th Division, as much as any division serving in any army in all the war, has had full share in bringing the German beast, crawling and whining, praying for mercy and peace. It was fitting that the Yankee Division should celebrate, as it did, the announcement of the armistice in the ruined city of Verdun, around which are buried half a million soldiers - the city which symbolizes for France the sacrifice and the victory.[iv]

26TH DIVISION'S TABLE OF ORGANIZATION - 1917

51st Brigade of Infantry

101st Regiment of Infantry
102nd Regiment of Infantry
102nd Machine Gun Battalion

52nd Brigade of Infantry

103rd Regiment of Infantry
104th Regiment of Infantry
103rd Machine Gun Battalion

51st Brigade of Field Artillery

101st Regiment of Field Artillery
102nd Regiment of Field Artillery
103rd Regiment of Field Artillery (Heavy)
101st Trench Mortar Battery

Engineer Corps

101st Regiment off Engineers

Signal Troops

101st Field Signal Battalion

Divisional Units

26th Division Headquarters Troop
Headquarters Train and Military Police
101st Machine Gun Battalion
101st Ammunition Train
101st Supply Train
101st Sanitary Train

Ambulance Corps

101st Ambulance Company
102nd Ambulance Company
103rd Ambulance Company
104th Ambulance Company

Hospital Corps

101st Field Hospital
102nd Field Hospital
103rd Field Hospital
104th Field Hospital

"I love the infantry because they are the underdogs. They are the mud-rain-and-wind boys. They have no comforts, and they even learn to live without necessities. And in the end, they are the guys that wars can't be won without.

Ernie Pyle, *New York World Telegram*

THE 26TH INFANTRY DIVISION'S TRAINING PERIOD IN FRANCE - 1917

Prior to the American declaration of war on April 6, 1917, most of the Division's troops had been in active service, on guard duty, or in training. Mobilized at state or other training camps, at Framingham, Westfield, and Boxford, Massachusetts; New Haven and Niantic, Connecticut; and Quonset Point, Rhode Island, the units were held for further training and provisioning until it was time to send them overseas.

The first elements of the 26th Division to arrive abroad were Headquarters, 51st Infantry Brigade, and 101st Infantry, which sailed from Hoboken, New Jersey, on September 7 and landed at St. Nazaire, France two weeks later, on September 21, 1917.

The remainder followed rapidly, until by the end of October all units had arrived in France. The 26th was the second full division to arrive in France (the 1st Division had preceded it), and it was the first division of the National Guard or the National Army troops to be organized, equipped, and sent overseas. The 51st Field Artillery Brigade was assembled for training at Coëtquidan; the infantry brigades, machine gun battalions, engineers, field signal battalion, and trains were assembled in the area just south of Neufchâteau, where Division Headquarters was established on October 31.

Private Raymond Whitney Maker was assigned to the 101st Field Signal Battalion, commanded by Major Harry G. Chase. The 101st was one of approximately eighteen battalions – including infantry, field artillery, machine gun battalions, engineers, and supply -- that made up the 26th Infantry Division.

Intensive training for trench warfare began at once, following a thorough, progressive course. At the same time, however, large details from all units were employed for construction work on barracks, telephone lines, quartermaster storehouses, hospitals, and other buildings.

To demonstrate the latest methods of trench warfare, the 162nd and a detachment of the 151st Regiment of the French Infantry attend to the Division. Daily instruction was given in grenade throwing, machine gun and automatic rifle practice, mortars and 37mm field guns, and in formations of approach and attack.

A school for officers and NCOs was established at Bazoilles, and many officers were sent to the First Corps School at Gondrecourt for infantry instruction. Others were sent to the Army General Staff College at Langres for training as staff officers. Machine gun officers and NCOs attended training courses conducted by the British or the French, and other detachments took courses as signalers and liaison officers in schools at Neufchâteau.

At their station at Coëtquidan, officers and men of the artillery brigade received intensive special training courses, while many received advanced artillery instruction at French or British instructional centers. Infantry and engineer instruction at Neufchâteau included the construction of a model system of fire, cover, and support trenches, suitable for a battalion front, in which practical problems of attack and defense were worked out. Units in turn occupied this "Noncourt Sector," as the trenches were called, and all had the opportunity to become accustomed to trench warfare methods.[v]

RAYMOND'S LETTERS FROM 1917

OCTOBER 1917

October 6th 1917

Somewhere in France

My Dear Eva & all the folks,

We are safe and sound in France, but we are not allowed to tell the name of the port [St. Nazaire], but believe me it was some trip and about all the fellows were glad to see land after almost two weeks on the water and most of the boys were all sick, but I was not sick a minute. We did not even see a submarine and we got a great hand when we went through to the Port. Where we are, we are still on the ship and will not go ashore until tomorrow as near as I understand. You want to write to me every chance that you get and tell the folks at home to do the same. Ed Collins is on the same boat. Tell the boys I was asking for them and tell Grandma and Gramps and everybody. I hope that it won't be so very long before I see you all again and do not lose heart if you do not hear from me very often because I may be in places where I cannot get a chance to write but will every time I can. You got my address. Tell Pa not to worry about me because I am all okay and never felt better but would like a ride in the Hudson. I will close for now with love to all.

Private 1st Class Raymond W. Maker

October 24th 1917

Somewhere in France

Dear Dad,

I thought you would be glad to get a few lines from me but as you know it is hard to write just what I want because they (sensors) must read all of the mail and if it is not just right they send it back and all that stuff. I am fine and hope that you are all well. It rains here most of the time. I wish I could tell you where we are. It is a very old farm and goes back as far as 800 years ago.

We have a YMCA here and it makes it a little bit better because it takes the dull moments away and believe me there are a few. But I can take care of myself and watch my step and will see you all soon.

I saw Dan Callahan this morning. He was up to our camp. There is not much more to say, only just drop me a line once in a while even if you don't write very often. I think of you all the same.

With the best of love to all,

Private 1st Class Raymond W. Maker

October 28th 1917

Somewhere in France

Dear Eva,

It snowed here last night, and all the hills are covered with it, but there is no more here where we are. We are in a valley like place, and it is cold. There is a village here and we are all sleeping around in the barns and houses.

I am in a hay loft and we have got it all fixed up just fine. The only trouble is the rain. It rains almost every day and that is to say nothing of the mud. I would like to see the papers and know what's going on in God's country, but I guess we will all be home before too long.

There are a lot of things I would like to say but you know how it is. If we have turkey here next month and mince pie, why we will all go mad. We are going to have a time here Wednesday night singing and things like that. We have a YMCA here and can buy different things to eat.

I am waiting for the time to get home and drive that Hudson and tell Dad that is to be an old soldier's job. The sun is out now, the first time in three days. I was talking to Dr. Mannow and he said that he would like me to be up to the counter now. I am feeling fine and dandy.

I sure will be glad when I hear from you folks. I will close now and give my love to everybody.

With love,

Private 1st Class Raymond W. Maker

NOVEMBER 1917

November 4th 1917
Somewhere in France

Dear Eva and all the folks,

I thought it was about time that I wrote you a couple of lines. I am still waiting for a letter from home and believe me I would rather get that than anything else I know of. I know of a surprise that you received – Jack Nelson's letter. I am going to see if I can find Walter Chase. He is here somewhere. I'm feeling fine and guess that I am getting fat. Tell Gus and Kip to write to me. All the fellows here have gotten mail but me. Dr. Morrow said something about his mother and some other people sending a box of stuff to me. Did they tell you? You can find out by Dr. Owen's wife. Everything is so high here that out pay does not last very long. We cannot get any real smoking tobacco and cigarettes are one and two francs or about 20 to 40 cents for 5 and 10 cent boxes.

How are all the folks? You will want to let Grandma and Grandpa read the letters I send because it is so hard to know what to write and I would have to write the same thing to them all. We have a little YMCA here all by ourselves and we have French lessons here two times a week, but it is like going to school all over again and believe me they will never make a Frenchmen out of me!

We are going to have a football match this PM and Framingham will be there strong. Fat Bradway, Avery, Ames and I are four of the eleven players. We are playing B Company. Eggs, or oeufs, as they are called here are $1.00 a dozen. Well, Eva, I do not know of much more to write about and will write again in a few days.

Love to all the folks,

Your brother,

Private 1st Class Raymond W. Maker

November 6th 1917

Somewhere in France

My Dear Dad,

I thought that it was about time I wrote, but when I write to Eva it is meant for you all. I wish you could see the country here and the way they drive the horses and see the wagons. This is a very old town here, where we are, and it is quite a site to see. It is a small town. The weather here is very unsettled; cold some days and rain and one day it snowed. I am feeling fine and getting fat and I am waiting every day for a letter from home and when I get one believe me it will receive some welcome.

We are sleeping around in houses and barns and it is a lot better than sleeping outdoors. We have a YMCA here and that helps quite a bit, but everything is so high that it keeps a few of us broke near the last of the month and payday does not come once a week. I told Eva to send me some tobacco and cigarettes and matches. We had a great trip coming over on the boat; days and days we sailed and never saw land and believe me it was rough, but I was not sick a single minute.

Tell Uncle Ed and Jap and Grandpa and Kip to write to me. I will try to write a couple of time s a week, but it is hard to write a letter because they all are read over twice. Once by our officers and censors and we are not allowed to give out any news at all. Can you drive the Hudson yet? I am just waiting to get back and have a good ride. Tell the folks up to Concord that I was asking for them and Barbara Joyce. I would have like to see you before I left, but we left so quickly that I did not know myself, but I guess that it won't be very long before I see you all again. Well Dad, I guess that this is about all that I will write now and don't worry about me because I will come through this all ok.

Love to all the folks,

Private 1st Class Raymond W. Maker

November 14th 1917

Somewhere in France

Dear Eva & Folks,

I suppose you are waiting for a few lines and I suppose it is about time that I did write. First of all, I am feeling fine and dandy and I am beginning to like this country more. We had a speaker here at the YMCA last night, a Dr. Anderson, and he gave a good talk and he is going back to the States – God's Country, the first of December and he said that he would write to you. In fact, he is going to do this for all the boys and tell you I was okay. Major General Clarence Edwards (the 26th Infantry Division Commanding General) was here this morning and talked to us.

It has started to get cold here, but they are still working in the fields and ploughing. We don't see many men here; they are all away fighting and the women folk so all the work around the farms. I hear there is going to be another draft of men 18 to 40-years-old. I hope that they won't get Kip for one of us boys are enough to go through this stuff. I suppose that you know that I am having a birthday tomorrow the 15th, and I think that we are to be paid that day.

I am going to start the first of the year and send home about $15.00 a month. Do you understand about getting the money from the State? I don't know if you must go to the State House or not and put it in the bank for me with the money I send home and in case I should not come home there will be money from the Government and you and Kip are to fix it up. But I guess there will not be any trouble doing that because I will be back, and you can bet on that. Well, Eva, I guess that I will close now.

Love to all the folks,

Private 1st Class Raymond W. Maker

November 20th 1917

Somewhere in France

My Dear Eva,

I received your letter a couple of days ago and believe me I was never so glad to get anything in all my life. I have not received the box you have sent to me yet and I am waiting with good hopes. You know mail is very slow to arrive in getting here and it is quite a job to get it all fixed up.

Please tell Kip & Pa to write and Jap and tell E. C. Esty that I thank him very much for the tobacco and he can keep it coming as long as he wants to because tobacco is very hard to get over here. I do hope that Pa came home alright with the machine without running over anybody. Believe me, I would like to stand on the running board when he was driving it but tell him that he can run over here anytime and get me.

Well Eva, I am fine, and I hope you are all well. You wanted to know what I wanted. I would like a good pair of warm leather gloves about the best of all and strong stockings. I understand that we are all going to have quite a feed; Thanksgiving turkey and all the fixings and a football game, and I am playing end on our team.

It is starting to get cold here, but there is no snow here to speak of - a couple of inches and then it is all melted in an hour. Eva, I wish you could see the way that the women have to cook here with old fire places that are hundreds of years old. Tell Nucker and Joe Barrette that I was asking for them and to write to me. Give them my address and tell Bessie, my Red, that I have not forgotten her either and one of her hot rolls would make a fellow about leave the army. Please tell her to write too because mail is about the only thing worth living for over here.

I guess that we will have some time when we come back. Well, Eva, I think that I have done very well and will write again soon.

Love to you and all the folks,

Private 1st Class Raymond W. Maker

November 23rd 1917

Somewhere in France

My Dear Eva,

Just a couple of lines to let you know that I am well. I have not received the box yet, but I am waiting every day for it and the eats. I don't think it will last very long after I get it. Did you get Jack Nelson's letter that he sent to you? When you write, I wish that you would number your letters and then I can tell if I get them all. Everything is about the same here and every once in a while, we hear a big gun go off. If only for that we would never know there was a war on here, at all. Mullens and I are hanging around the YMCA this afternoon. It is kind of cold here today, and about the first day that I had to wear my overcoat. I don't know how long it will last. The people say there is very little snow here and we don't want it either.

Tell Kip to write to me and tell Bessie too. You know that when I write to you it is meant for all of you, Grandma and Grandpa as well as anyone. There is not much that I want but you can send anything that you want to, and they will be taken care of and so will the tobacco. Did I tell you much about our trip over here? You know I always wanted to go out on the water, but the only time I ever want to go on it again is when I come home. Believe me, it was no fun sailing around a couple of weeks without ever seeing land and never knowing if we were going to be sunk or not. Well, we fooled them at that. Well, Eva, I think that I will close now, so please give my love to all the folks and the best of love to you.

Your loving brother,

Private 1st Class Raymond W. Maker

DECEMBER 1917

December 2nd 1917

Somewhere in France

My Dear Eva,

I suppose that it is about time that I wrote to you and the rest of the folks. We had quite a dinner here, Thanksgiving Day. We had turkey and sweet potatoes and apple pie and all that we wanted of it. I have not received any more mail yet and have not received the box, but I am waiting and that's all. We had a great game of football Thanksgiving Day and neither side could make a point. I played end and caught a pass and got to the one-yard line, but we could not put the ball over.

How are all the folks and I hope that you all had a nice dinner on the 30th. I am feeling fine and dandy. The sun is out here today, and it is about the first time that I have seen the sun for about a month. How are things going on in the States and the old town? Has Dad learned to run the machine yet, and have you gotten any of my letters yet?

I wish that you would send me some tobacco and cigarettes and matches because you don't know how hard it is to get them over here. They have them in a YMCA, but they don't last very long because they only get a few at a time. I hear that things are priced very high in the States. Is bacon high? I wish the Lord that you could have some of it that we have. It is very good, but it is bacon, bacon and bacon all the time. We had some great beans last night and this morning and they were just like the ones we have at home.

As I told you before, it is difficult to write a letter because I must think about what to write to pass the censor. I don't believe that your letters are censored. Your letter was not opened. Mullens is writing a letter here with me and he is as bad off as I am. If anyone just came around and said a dollar for a match so you know how it is.

Dr. Owen has been promoted to a Major. We had a nice pair of woolen stocking given to us from the Red Cross the other day. The only trouble with me is that I cannot learn to wash my clothes and I must send them to a china man. I have a woman next door to wash them for me and she does them fine. Mullens has only one page written now. I think that he is homesick, but I don't blame him. I do get homesick myself sometimes, but I have it on them because I have been away so much. I would like to send you some things, but I will bring you back the things that I have gotten when I come home.

We are going to have movies tonight. We have had them a couple of times but we cannot get any electric lights and so we have to make our own.

Well, Eva, I think that I have done very well this time, so I will close now and wish you all a very happy Xmas and New Year, and hope you hang up my sock for me. I don't dare to hang one up here because someone would probably steal it. Give my love to all the folks and the best of love to you.

Private 1st Class Raymond W. Maker

December 5th
My Dear Sister, Eva,

I was about the happiest boy in the company yesterday when I receive the box and the letter from you and a letter from Grandma and the newspapers, and believe me Eva, I was so thankful to you and the rest of the folks. I thank everybody, and the cake! Oh boy! I will sleep over it and have a loaded gun and that little diary book was just what I wanted. The sardines I have not opened yet. They are too good. If you happen to notice, they came from France and we went through there. Oh, Eva, everything was just great.

Do you know anything about the club that Major Chase's wife has got up? They are all mothers and sisters of the boys over here. If you look it up I guess it is a good thing and a great help to the boys.

That money that you received is State pay. You are supposed to get $8.00 a month. Please tell Jap to write and Bessie and Kip and tell Charlie Esty that I thank him and to keep up the good work.

I was glad to get a letter from Grandma and I will write to her today. We don't have to use stamps, so please don't send me any. It is getting quite cold here now and the ground is all frozen up and it is good and clear weather. It used to be just mud all of the time. When Uncle Ed goes down to the river tell him to look out that he does not go over.

It is after supper now and I just got a letter from Jap and I was very glad to hear from him. He said that Nucker sent me a letter. Well, I did not go to supper tonight. We have a stove in our billet and we had a few small pieces of bread and we had some of the sardines and they were great.

Tell Dad that they make a fellow want more of them, but tobacco is the main thing we want here, Eva, and matches.

Well, Eva, I want you to know and remember that I will take care of myself and I will watch my step all of the time and I will come home just the way I went away. For the sake of our Mother, for the one who does not know that, I am here, and I wish to God that she was alive now most of all.

Well, I will say good night. Write as often as you can.

Love to all.

Your loving brother,

Private 1ˢᵗ Class Raymond W. Maker

December 6ᵗʰ 1917

My Dear Sister, Eva,

I received another letter this morning and I was glad to get it. There is a café here where we are, and they sell beer and wine. I have a bottle before dinner and supper and the old lady that runs it is my best friend. She is teaching me French and I give her different things and I gave her some candy and she was tickled.

The water is not very good here, so I have a little beer once in a while and I guess that is what makes me feel good all the time and fat. I suppose Pa will kick on that but that is my only bad habit and believe me, Eva, there are a lot of other worse things.

I suppose that Louie felt bad when he found that he did not have much of a fire. Well, Eva, it sure makes a fellow great to think that he has a sister like you and when he is away in a country like this, is when he wakes up and finds it out and especially one who takes the place of a mother. Tell Kip not to get foolish and to stay at home and to help out all he can because it is his place. Tell him to send me some Edgeworth tobacco and the makings.

We are going to get two month's pay in a day or so (most welcomed). I have been broke for a month.

We have got a very fine billet as they call them. That is where we live. We have a stove and a wooden bunk and a bed sack that we fill with straw and Mullen and I take our blankets and put one under us and then we have five over us (we take the two bunks and put them side by side). It is very cold here now.

I wish that they did not have a censor because I could tell you many different things, but I will save them all until I get home. I feel that the drafted ones are having quite a good time, but I would hate to tell you what we think of them.

I have written a poem that you ought to send to the newspapers and it goes like this...

> Oh, why didn't I want to be drafted
> And be led to the train by a band
> And put in a claim for exemption
> Oh, why did I put up my hand—
> Oh, why didn't I wait for a banquet
> Oh, why didn't I wait to be cleared
> For the drafted one gets all the credit
> While I only volunteered—
> And nobody gave me a banquet
> And nobody said a kind word
> The grind of the wheels of the engine
> Was the only good-bye that I heard—
> And then off to France we were hustled
> To be billeted in barns for a year
> And then in the scuffle forgotten
> For I was only a volunteer—
> And maybe someday in the future
> When me little boy sits on my knee
> And asks what I did in the conflict
> And his bright eyes look up at me
> I will have to look back as I'm blushing
> To the eyes that so trusting do peer
> And tell him that I missed being drafted
> For I was only a volunteer—

Well, Eva, I have gone my limit in writing, so I will say love to all.

Private 1ˢᵗ Class Raymond W. Maker

December 17th 1917
My Dear Sister, Eva,
Somewhere in France

I think that it is about time that I write to you. I have not heard from you in quite a few days, but when the mail comes in it all comes in a bunch. I did not get Nucker's letter yet, but I did get a letter from Walter Chase and he was very much surprised to know that I was over here. I will write to him after I write this letter.

Have you had any snow there yet and what is the news around the town? I hear that there is going to be another draft. They cannot take many more men out of the town. I paid 50 cents a can for the condensed milk here. What do you know about that? I make cocoa quite a lot. Did I tell you the socks would come in handy now?

How is Bessie? Is she still with you? I hope that she will be there when I come home because I kind of like her myself. Well, Eva, I don't know of much more to write about, only to say that I wish you all a very Merry Christmas and a Happy New year.

Love to all and write often.

Private 1st Class Raymond W. Maker
PS: I am going to start and keep my book the first of the year that you sent to me and I also expect to get a non-com's job soon.

December 24th 1917
Somewhere in France

My Dear Sister, Eva,
Well here it is, the day before Christmas and I am many miles from home. I received your letters, #5 and #6 and the cards yesterday. I think that when I receive your mail it all comes in a bunch. The Christmas box is here, but I have not opened it yet. They are keeping them all until tomorrow. I do not know how many more I have received but I will write in a day or so.

You wanted to know how I was, Eva. I am fine and am fatter than I ever was. It is hard to know what to write because I don't want to spoil them by putting in something that won't go by the censors. I have read over your letters about five times and I would like to tell you what we are doing but some other time.

I received a letter from Walter Chase. Did you receive my Cablegram? I miss a lot of the boys from home around here and I am going to take a chance and send some things home because I do not want to keep them here. I hope that you all had a good Christmas and I guess I will too.

Tell everybody that I was asking for them. I received a letter from Gladys and one from Gap, Bessie's card and all. Why doesn't Kip write to me? Please tell Bessie to write, too. I want to hear from everybody. I will write to Miss Emerson soon, but it is so hard to write to so many people because I want to have you get all the letters that I write. I will write again in a few days and let you know what I received in the box.

All the boys here are well and want to be remembered to you. I let some of the boys read your letters and they are about the best that any of them have read and I think so too. I have not heard from Nucker yet. I must write to him and wish that he was with me. Well, Eva, I will close now and write in a day or so. Love to you all and the best of love to you.

Private 1st Class Raymond W. Maker

December 27th 1917
Somewhere in France

My Dear Dad,
I thought that you would be glad to get a letter every now and then. I write to Eva very often, as you know, and I am sure they are meant for you all. The weather is quite cold and there is a little snow. You made a fine box and I keep it locked up so to keep the mice out. I hear that you are up to your old tricks but never mind Dad, there is a lot of fun in it and something to take up your mind. They have some nice-looking houses here, but they are all full of hay and turnips. They mix the hay with the turnips. I suppose that you will have a garage when I come back. Why don't you write me a few lines once in a while? I saw 24 flying machines up in the air at one time here. I suppose it seems kind of strange to see poor Kip going to work but more power to him. You all know by this time that it is hard to write because we do not want to have our letters all cut up.

How are things – normal! I had to laugh when Eva wrote about that. Well Dad, how you feel these days, and please tell Uncle Ed that someday I am going to write to him, too. Did you all have a good time at Christmas? I will close for now and give my love to all the folks.

From your loving, son,

Private 1st Class Raymond W. Maker

December 28th, 1917

Somewhere in France

My Dear Sister, Eva,

Well Christmas is all over and I received the box that Dad made and 6 letters and the newspapers. I have not gotten any more boxes, but I am waiting. It is a hard job to handle all the Christmas boxes because there are a lot of boys here in this country. I want to thank you and everybody else that put things in the box. And, the stockings, as they say here, are the "Darb." We have quite a little snow here now and it is quite cold. I am going to send you a box in a day or so and hope that you get it all right. You want to know what I am doing? Well it is hard to say, Eva. We are getting a lot of schooling and other things. We are dry and do not have much trouble with colds. It must be a joke to see Kip go to work and I hope that he keeps it up. I suppose Dad will be in the auto business before long, if he takes the stable back. I would have liked to have seen the time they headed up to the church. It must have been very nice.

All the boys are fine and me too. Please thank Mrs. Clarke and Miss Ferry for me. Who is this Mrs. Hall and what did she send to me? I found the tag in the bottom of the box. Please tell Miss Ferry I was talking to R. Newton the other day. I received a letter from Gladys yesterday. Ask Jap what he is going to run the machine with and tell him to drive over and see me sometime.

We have a stove in our place here and we have a spider and a pan to make stuff in and we have a lot of hot chocolate nights and corn – oh boy – it is great. We buy canned corn for a franc (20 cents) and milk for 12 cents a can. It is very hard to get sugar here, but we get along some way, believe me. We see a lot of French soldiers going through here all the time. We do not ride, but we are going to have machines. You knew that before we left.

How are all the folks and please tell them that I was asking for them. Thank Bessie for the book, in fact you know I thank everybody. I must write to Granddad soon. Have you any idea where we are yet? Some of the people know but we do not know how they found out. How are things going on and how does Kip like his job? I think that I have done a very good job this time and I will write again soon.

Love to all and the best of love to you.

Private 1st Class Raymond W. Maker

PS: I just received the box with the candy and the peanut brittle, and it was great! Everything was great. I suppose that the other boxes will come later.

FIRST COMBAT ACTION
AT CHEMIN-DES-DAMES
(JANUARY – FEBRUARY 1918)

Preliminary training came to an end during the first week in February 1918. The 26th Division was placed under the tactical direction of the commanding general, 11th Army Corps (French), to give all elements, by way of a month's experience in the front line, a finishing course of practical instruction.

Between February 5 and February 8, 1918, the Division entered the line north of Soissons, in the famous Chemin-des-Dames sector, between Pinon Forest and Pargny-Filain. At first, the Division's infantry companies (with two platoons on the line and two in support) were alternated in the line with French companies. The artillery batteries were also limited at first to take over only a few positions. Experienced French officers and NCOs were detailed to all headquarters, where they gave minute personal instruction to all units, down to the smallest.

Confidence and proficiency obtained rapidly. By degrees, larger stretches of the front line were entrusted to the American troops, and the French were withdrawn, until practically the whole sector was occupied by American infantry regiments, each with one battalion in the line, one in support, and one in reserve. In a similar way, the artillery and machine guns occupied an increased number of positions. Although the sector had been considered quiet, it was only a very short time before the enemy tested the new arrivals, whom they took at first to be British.

On February 19, near the Bois Quincy, the enemy attempted to raid the sub-sector occupied by Company B, 104th Infantry, and the 104th's machine gun company. The German assault was repulsed with significant losses, including prisoners of war. On February 28 the Germans launched a second assault, this time against the 2nd Battalion, 102nd Infantry, near Chavignon, and enjoyed no better success. On March 16-17 they put down a heavy and continuous gas bombardment, mainly directed at the segment of the Division's front occupied by the 101st and 102nd Infantry, between Pargnv-Filain and Chavignon, as well as on the battery positions. This caused some losses, especially in the 3rd Battalion, 102nd Infantry, but the return fire by the 51st Brigade was exceedingly severe and inflicted much damage. Raids to take prisoners, and to give the American troops experience in trench warfare, proceeded against the enemy in conjunction with the French. Thus, on February 23, a volunteer detachment of the 101st Infantry, supported by the 103rd and Company B, 101st Machine Gun Battalion, raided the German lines at Grand Pont, bringing back twenty-two prisoners, including two officers. This affair was doubly noteworthy: it was the first raid in which American infantry had engaged, and the first time that an attacking force advanced behind a rolling barrage laid by American artillery. Similar raids were carried out by the 102nd and 104th Infantry.

RAYMOND'S LETTERS DIARY ENTRIES

JANUARY 1918

(The pocket diary entries are normally two or three sentences):

1 January

Today, I started to keep this book. The weather is cold, but I'll pull through. I don't know how long I will keep this book up.

2 January

Cold is the same, can hardly speak. The weather is cold, no news of any kind. Went to bed early, am not feeling very well.

3 January

Cold the same. Walked over to the trenches and believe me it was cold and windy. No news. Go to bed early.

4 January

Today I stay in bed and the weather is cold. Tonight, I am fine. Cold is better. 120 men came to our company.

5 January

Today in bed, cold is better. Cold outside. Go to work tomorrow, but I am feeling well. I am waiting for a good feed.

January 5th 1918
Somewhere in France

My Dear Sister,

A few more lines today to let you know that I am alive and well. I am working in the cookhouse, it is quite a hard job, but I guess that it won't hurt me any. I am having a $10 a month allotment sent to you out of my pay and it will come from the government and not from the state. If you see Mr. Hillard please tell him that I always liked his peanut candy. I received a couple of cards from Dr. Perry and will write him and say that I have not received his letter yet, and please tell Jap that just because he sent me one letter he did not have to stop writing any more.

All the boys want to be remembered to you. I wish that you could see the way the people live, just about 100 years behind the times and I guess they will never catch up with us. How is everyone and what you all doing these days? There is so much noise around here now and I'll write again in a few days.

Love to all and best of love to you.

Private 1st Class Raymond W. Maker

7 January

Today it rained all day and much warmer. Got our gas masks and it is some job to get used to them and we can't stand the water.

8 January

Today it snowed but is all cleared up now. Worked all day. River all overflowed and feeling very well. A shack on the river washed away.

January 8th 1918
Somewhere in France

My Dear Sister,

I thought that it was about time that I sent you another letter. I am feeling fine and I hope that you all are, too. The weather here is quite cold now, but we are all very well fixed for clothes. The boys are starting to come back from supper and it is starting to get a little noisy here.

This is my afternoon off today and I went for a little ride with a fellow in a car. I have not seen an electric car since I left the states and the French trains are so funny. I thought that this was a country like the states, but I am sending you some post cards of the place that we are staying in, but I have to cut the name off, but you can see what the place looks like. I am starting to learn to speak French fairly well now. I received some more newspapers tonight; the Evening News. We have moving pictures here about every Sunday night and there is a kind of a church meeting led by a YMCA man and he is a good fellow. Take it as a whole, we don't have it so very hard and we have to remember that we are at war and believe me as the boys say, "This is the hardest war I was ever in."

I found a picture in my bag of you, Kip and myself. Do you remember the time that we had them taken? Tell Bessie that I have not received her letter yet and I guess that I never will hear from Kip. How is Dad and what is he doing these days? It seems kind of good to get the home newspapers and see what is going on at home. I wish that you could have a picture of me when I have one done. I look like a bull.

Well, Eva, how is the weather and how are you anyway and one of these days you will get a box from me. I am waiting to get paid to get a few more things and then I will send it. Well, I think that I have done well this time and will write again in a few days.

Give my love to all the folks and the best of love to you.

Private 1st Class Raymond W. Maker

9 January

Today I drilled with the gas mask and went for a ride. Weather is cold, and I feel better. Am not getting along with my French very well.

10 January

Today, I worked in a kitchen and the weather is bad. And I still have a little cold.

I had a few French fries. Try some.

11 January

Today is the same old job. My afternoon off. The Army is making life okay.

12 January

Today is very slippery. Worked all day and went to bed at 7pm. Cold about gone. All is well. Fell down about 100 times. People had to tie sandbags on their feet.

13 January

Today it snowed. My afternoon off. Took a bath…first one. Ha. Ha. Am well, thank you.

January 13th 1918
Somewhere in France

My Dear Sister,

I thought that I would write today as I am not doing anything this afternoon. I received another box from Ida and some more papers from you. I am feeling fine and putting on some more fat. I had a nice bath this afternoon and feel fine (in a wash tub) and it made me think of my kid days. We are having a concert at the YMCA this afternoon and movies tonight. How are all the folks and what's the doings at home? Did you get my other letter before this one?

Tell Nucker that I have not seen his letter yet or Kip's yet. I wish that you could be here and see this town and the way we live and compare that to the way that you live. The weather is a little warmer here now and we hope that it keeps up.

Has Dad taken over the stables yet and how does Kip like his new job? Tell Grandma and Gramps that I was asking for them and send them my love. I must cut this letter short as I want to go to the concert and will write again in a day or so. Give my love to all the folks and the best of love to you.

Private 1st Class Raymond W. Maker

14 January

Walked all day and the weather is good. Am feeling fine now. Am going to bed early. Have to get packed for tomorrow.

January 14th 1918
Somewhere in France

My Dear Sister,

As I am not doing anything tonight I thought that I would write you a few lines. I was up to the concert yesterday afternoon and it was good. A girl sang and played the piano and a couple of men sang and played the violin and they had movies at night. Things are going on here just the same as ever and everybody is well. We have had great luck with our outfit; hardly any of the boys have been sick and we have not lost a man yet.

Did you get my cards? Just as soon as I get paid I will send you the box. The reason I have put it off for so long is that I want to get a few more things. Has there been anything done about that trouble with that woman in southern Framingham?

I see quite a few boys from Framingham around here and yesterday Dan was over to see me, and he said that he sent you another letter. I am going over to see Red Collins tomorrow afternoon, if I have time. I have only seen him just once since I have landed. I wrote to Ida yesterday; she sent me two dandy boxes. I have not had a letter from you for about two weeks, but when they come they are all in a bunch. Mullens and I have a great time reading over the Framingham papers and we read everything.

How is Dad and tell him that he never wants to own a farm over in this country because it is all rocks and hills. We had griddle cakes for supper and I helped make about three hundred and believe me it is no small job. Tell Miss Emerson that I was asking for her and when we were learning about France, I never thought that I would be over here fighting the Germans.

I hear that the war will be over soon. I hope so because I want to have on a pair of long pants once more and a white shirt and a collar and a tie, and then I won't know myself. How much are eggs over there? They are a little over a dollar a dozen here and very hard to get. Hayden and I are going to have an oyster stew one of these days. They sell them here and we are going to make one. Well Eva, I think I have done very well this time and will write again in a few days.

Give my love to all the folks and the best of love to you.

Private 1st Class Raymond W. Maker

15 January

Today is payday and it is raining all day. I feel better now.

16 January

Weather is raining, and I went to town. Going to bed early and I'm feeling fine.

17 January

Went to town this afternoon and I had a good time. It is about time to get some letters from home.

18 January

Worked all day, kind of enjoyed it. I'm feeling fine and got a paper from home. Leaving here by eight days.

19 January

Had the day off. Weather much warmer. Had a ride all over this town, but it is very muddy, and I am fine.

20 January

Went to town this afternoon. Weather is fine and I'm great. Went to bed early. All I am doing is getting ready to go to bed early.

January 20th 1918
Somewhere in France

My Dear Sister,

Just a few lines to let you know that I am fine and dandy. I received a couple of papers from you today (December 1st and 2nd), and a couple of cards from Dr. Perry. I am sending a box and there is a statue and one marble tablet that one of the boys wants to have you send to his sister and her address is Mrs. Daniel A. Downey, 92 Sheridan St. Jamaica Plain, MA. He is one of my pals and so I thought that we could send them together. I have not had any mail from you in quite a while, but I have hopes. We are having very good weather here now and it is quite warm and dry. Snow is all gone.

Did you get my last letter and cards? It seems very strange to go down to the main town at night. Everything is dark, no lights can be seen at all, and that is because of the air machines.

How is everything going and how are all the folks? We hear the big guns every now and then. I was down in the town this afternoon and bought some canned hotdogs and we fried them and had some cocoa and they were great. Well Eva, I must close for now as I have got to do some work, but I'll write soon. Love to all,

Private 1st Class Raymond W. Maker

January 20th 1919
Somewhere in France

My Dear Sister,

Well Eva, I am very sorry to say that we are still here. The move has been put off for 5 days. I received a letter from you on the 18th of January. We have all our stuff turned in, but I don't know, it has been like this ever since we have been in France. We receive the last of everything. I see they are having quite a time about the 26th and General Edwards in Congress. They will find out a few things. I found a piece in the paper that is printed in Paris and I am sending it with this letter. I was sorry to hear that you folks have been sick again and I guess that you have fought a war over there, too. I suppose Kip does not like to be part of the service. Wish I was in his place.

I don't know Eva, how long it will be before I get home, but I have good courage. Everything is going fine with me and we are having quite cold weather. Last night I bought some English walnuts and I got 20 for 1 franc. I hope that you are all okay now and keep well for heaven's sake, Eva.

I don't know of much more to write as there is nothing going on and we expect to move sometime this week. I will write again in a couple of days and let you know the real dope. Love to you all.

Your loving brother,

Private 1st Class Raymond W. Maker

21 January

Weather is fine and warm. Went to town this afternoon. Got a couple of papers from home, looking for some letters.

22 January

Weather is fine. Am having a couple of days off. And getting a fine start for…

23 January

Weather raining, but warm. I'm still having a day off. Some of the boys start tomorrow. Am fine.

January 23rd 1918

Somewhere in France

My Dear Sister,

I received two letters today – one from you and one from Red and was very glad to get them because I have not heard from home for quite a while. The weather is very much warmer here now. I am glad to hear that Kip got a good job and is in the Army, but I hope that he will not have to come over here. Has Mr. Charles sent the cigars yet? I was very glad to get a letter from Bessie and I will try and answer it as soon as I time.

I was very much pleased with that little gift and will always try to keep it. I always keep my other case with me. I took out $10,000worth of insurance today and had $5,000 made out to you and $5,000 made out to Kip. It only costs $4-6 a month and I think it is a very good plan.

Have you heard anything about it and when I get back I can still keep it up. I want to. I am feeling fine and have not had any colds to speak of. Tell all the folks that I was asking for them and send my regards to all the folks. I am learning to talk French very well now if I stay here long enough I will be a Frog. I am sorry to hear the Grandma is not feeling very well and tell Mr. Charles that I sure do wish that I could have a half of his bed. I guess that I would not be able to sleep in the sheets. Now with about 6 months of Army life and the Lord only knows how much longer, but I am in good hopes.

Why doesn't Kip write to me? Is he too stuck up with his job? We are very lucky because we have white bread and it is very good. The French people do not have any white bread and no sugar and tobacco. I am very well fixed on tobacco. I am putting two letters in one, so I guess this will do for a while. Give my love to all the folks and the best of love to you.

Private 1st Class Raymond W. Maker

24 January

Weather warm. Some of the boys start today. Had a ride this morning and I go on my way soon.

25 January

Weather fine. More boys left today. I go tomorrow. Went out on a raid for two hours. Move tonight and I am feeling fine.

26 January

Left today and went to the 101st Infantry. Harry will ride over. We leave for the trenches soon. Weather fine and I am good.

27 January

Weather cold. Slept on the bare floor last night. Am fine. This is a fine outfit.

28 January

Today is Sunday. We did not do any work. Got some straw for my bed. Weather cold and I am fine. Bed feels good, believe me.

29 January

Today we started in on our work all morning and hiked all afternoon and evening. Weather fine and I am fine. Got five letters and a box. Great!

January 29th 1918
Somewhere in France

My Dear Sister,

Well, I think that I am very lucky today. I received your box with the cigars and other things, and the gloves – oh boy, just what I wanted and most of all I got five letters and a card from Dr. Perry. Well, Eva, I have left the town I was in and have lost my good friend. I am sorry I cannot tell you where we are or who we are with, but we are with many boys. This town is nowhere near (censored out) but it is up hill and downhill all day. I am not with Mullens now but with a few boys that you know. I am writing this by candle light and it is kind of hard to see.

I am sorry to hear that things are so hard to get, but just think about the people over here. I was surprised to get a letter from Kip and you can tell Dad that I hope to hear from him, too. Never mind sending me a sweater because I have one and it is coming on warm weather now. Tell Dr. Perry that I thank him very much for the cards that he sent to me and some one of these days I will send him a letter. I do not think that you had better send anything by those people in Boston. I do not think much of it.

Let me know if you get my $10 that I am sending to you out of my pay and if at any time that you want to use any of the money do not think about it. Take it. I think I have told you about me taking out a $10,000 life insurance policy for you and Kip and in case that I am disabled I can get it.

Well Eva, I think that I will have to call this about all for now. I hope that you are all well and will be able to get along with the store. These are hard times, and I only wish that I could be there to help you out because I know now what the word "home" means to me. I will close now with the best of love to you and all the folks.

Private 1st Class Raymond W. Maker
PS: What did Gramps think of *Over the Top* – Some book!

30 January

Today we drilled all morning. And it rained until afternoon. I am feeling fine. Weather is fine. Getting ready for the front lines.

31 January

Drilled hard all day. Getting along fine. Weather is too cold. I do not like this place.

FEBRUARY 1918

1 February

Starting another month. Have done fine, so far. Drilled hard all day. Weather a little warmer, am fine, but tired.

February 1st 1918

Somewhere in France

My Dear Sister,

I thought that I would start the month off right by sending you a letter. I received a letter from Grandma this morning and I was very glad to hear from her. We do not expect to stay here very long. I do not like this place anyway. I have not seen Mullens for a week now and do not know when I will see him again. The weather here is a little bit colder now, but only in the morning and in the afternoon, we walk in the mud. We are drilling quite hard these days.

I am wondering if you received my box. There were a few things that they would not let me send so do not send anything to that address that I gave to you. I would like to drop in on you and have what they call a "suave feed." I never want to look another piece of bacon or black coffee in the face again as long as I live. Give me ham and eggs, but I cannot kid you Eva, it is quite a job to find an Army like this one, over here, and I think they do very well.

How is everything going along with you and how are all the folks? Tell Bessie that I was asking for her and thinking of her. I think that I have been very lucky this winter by not even having been sick a day, and believe me Eva, we had to put up with a great many things. I am going to write to Gladys tonight and tell Grandma that I will write to her in a few days.

You do not know Eva; how hard it is to write a long letter and you do not want to feel badly when you do not get one because I always try to do my best. Tell Jap to write to me and remember me to all the Framingham people that I have any use for, but not that slacker J.J.C. if you know who I mean. I had to laugh when I read about the poor boys at …They could not get home for Christmas. They had a right to be here and hear what we think of them.

I have not seen Ed Collins, only once since I have been here. I am a long way from him now, but he is okay, I hear. Well, Eva, I think that I have done very well this time, so I will say that I have the only Sister in the world. Love to you and all the folks.

Private 1st Class Raymond W. Maker
PS: Please tell Dad to write to me.

February 1st 1918
Somewhere in France

Dear Dad,

I suppose that you will be surprised to hear from me. This is a letter to you, but I have the habit of writing to Eva, so I thought you would like to have a letter all by yourself. Eva tells me you are still up to your old tricks, trading horses, but never mind Dad, it is better than playing soldier. How are you feeling these days? I am fine and dandy. I expect to have a furlough for 10 days soon and will take life easy for a few days then. We are drilling quite hard these days. I suppose you are having good sleighing there now. I have not seen any here. I guess the Frogs don't know what they are.

Have you got two stars on the flag now? It must look very nice, the only one in the grave yard. How is Uncle Ed these days? Is he back yet? Tell Mr. Charles that I think of him very often and please thank him very much for the cigars. How is C.C. Esty? Tell him that I was asking about him. Well Dad, I will close now because with the letter I sent to Eva I'm all in for writing. With the best of love and hope to see you soon.

Your loving son,
Private 1st Class Raymond W. Maker

2 February

Today, I went through the gas test. And we had a review by General Edwards. Weather fine. I am tired. Walked ten miles today.

February 2nd 1918

Somewhere in France

My Dear Sister,

I am writing you a few lines tonight because I will not be able to write again for a few weeks, so do not look for a letter for a while. I am sorry that I can't tell you why I cannot write, but I hope that I will be able to get your mail. As I wrote to you last night, it is very hard to write again tonight. We had a great review here today by one of our Generals. I wish that you could have seen it. It would make anybody proud to see a body of men like they were, and I was one of them.

I had to laugh. A fellow was standing next to me when the General came along, and the General said that he "needed to be filled out" and the funny part of it is that the fellow's coat was too long for him, so I guess that the joke was on the General. I am in hopes of meeting Walter Chase sometime. The weather is a little bit warmer here today. I wish that you could see the way the women folks wash their clothes here. They have a wash house and a square of water about ten by ten feet and they kneel in a little box filled with straw and wash the clothes in the water and spank them with a club. And talk about a load that they can carry.

Our lieutenant told us that we would not be able to write for about a month. Do not be worried about me, Eva, because I will be all right and look out for myself. I suppose that you have two stars in the flag now that Kip is in. Tell Bessie that I will write her a letter when we are able to write again and the same to Grandpa. How does Gramps like the book, *Over the Top*? I read it over here, but it makes your hair stand on end. Well, Eva, I will close now and the best of love to you and all the folks and don't worry about me.

Private 1st Class Raymond W. Maker

PS: I forgot to tell you that I broke the pipe that you sent to me.

3 February

Went to my old town. Had a good time. Weather fine, but cold. Am well.

4 February

Some of the boys left today, and I go tomorrow. Weather fine, hate to leave as I am feeling fine.

5 February

Was pulled out at night and had a big hike to the train. Heavy marching orders.

6 February

In boxcars all night and cold. Rode all day and saw some great places. No sleep and I am fine.

7 February

Arrived at S- [Soissons] at 2 am and marched all morning in the rain and we went to a rest place. All places are shot to hell.

8 February

Hiked again and are in a big cave now. I never saw anything like it. Trenches all around. Am fine.

9 February

Today I heard the big boys flying around and saw then land. This place is all destroyed by the Germans.

10 February

Today, I walked around to see the different places destroyed. Weather fine and I am well.

11 February

Today we saw an air-fight. Some sight. We are very near the front lines. Am well. Weather is about the same.

12 February

Today, I saw another air-fight. One plane was shot down. It was great, away up in the clouds. Weather fine. I am well.

13 February

Today, everything was about the same. Am well weather is fine. I think that I need a shave.

14 February

Today, we moved to the front. Not so much of a hike. Moved into a dugout. Am fine. Got a few rats around here.

15 February

Went up near the trench this afternoon and saw an air-fight. Great, but they did not get away. Got up at 3 am.

16 February

Up to the trenches and we got shelled and we had to beat it. Nobody was hurt. Air-fight. Got two letters. Weather cold and I am fine.

17 February

Day off. Bombardment all day long. Saw an airplane shot down…Boche. It is quite cold, and I have a little cold. Washed and shaved. First time in four days.

18 February

Today was about the same. Air raids and a machine brought down. Weather fine and I'm feeling well.

19 February

Things about the same. Weather is warmer, and I am fine. Got shelled this morning. Got a German helmet and some papers.

20 February

Everything is quiet. Got two letters and papers. It is starting to rain tonight. I'm feeling fine.

21 February

Got a box today. Everything is fine, and the weather is warmer. Went up this morning and filled sandbags.

February 21st 1918
Somewhere in France

My Dear Sister,

I did not think that I would be able to write for a while, but here I am. The last few days have been very good for me. Yesterday, I received a letter from you and one from Bessie and a box from Gladys in which was a helmet and today your box #6. Your letter was #16. We have had quite a time the last few days here. I have seen quite a few Boche airplanes brought down and it was great and sometimes Eva, you would think that hell broke loose here, but we are all in no danger.

We were living in a great cave and I don't think that there is one like it in the world and one Sunday we had church in it. The cave was made mostly by the Germans and one of the German's great generals had his headquarters inside of it.

We have been living in dugouts made by the Germans and we had it fixed up just fine. We made a fire place in it and it was very warm, but the rats, they would come up and help us eat our chow. You have seen pictures of apple tress cut down by the Boche, well Eva, you cannot think how they left the towns. They left in a hurry.

I am feeling better than I have ever felt. Please tell Dad that he wants to keep the Hudson at home and don't come here on a wing because they sure shoot at strange machines. I was very much pleased with your letter and with Bessie's and I will write to her soon. I can only write once a week now but will be able to write more in a couple of weeks. I have seen quite a few boys from home here and lots of them from my old Company E.

We had quite a time the other day. We were out working and the first thing we heard was a whizz bang and believe me, Eva, it made my knees shake and they were not a hundred miles away either. You can hear them coming a long way off and when we heard them we don't wait to see if we can see them, believe me, but it is very quiet here at that sometimes. We came through some very fine country and a place where they make champagne. The largest place in the world. Three francs a bottle or 60 cents for the best.

We have not been working very hard but have quite a few hikes and as you know I don't have a horse here. We had flap jacks for supper.

Did you get my allotment that I am sending home through the government and do you understand about my life insurance?

Tell Mr. Charles that I am very thankful for his help and tell everybody that I send them all my regards and tell Mr. Kip that I am sorry that he has to make overtime and don't get paid. I get paid for all the time. I must tell you the way the Boche gets his lines on some places. He comes out in a machine and if he sees anything going on, well about five or six minutes later, "whizz" and all hell breaks out, but they do the same and I guess by what we hear and seldom see, that the Boche gets the most of it, after all.

I may be able to send you a few things now and then. Your letters don't have to be censored. We have seven fellows in our dugout and they are all fine fellows. We play cards every night to pass away the time. Have breakfast at 7 so leaving all jokes aside, we get along well after thinking what we are up against.

Here it is 10 o'clock and I have not opened my box yet, waiting for the other fellows to go to bed. I think that I have done very well with this letter and hope it gets by the O.K., as I think I have not said anything out of the way. So, will close now, with the best of love to you.

Private 1st Class Raymond W. Maker

22 February

Today is a rest day. One of the boys gave a little party…cocoa and jam. Weather fair. Am fine. On guard tonight for gas.

23 February

Worked hard today laying cable. Went on guard for two hours. Had French fried potatoes. Weather fair and I am fine.

24 February

Great feed today. Turkey and all the fixings. Weather is good. Everything is quiet. I'm feeling fine. Shaved and washed up and I got a letter from Gladys.

February 24rd 1918

Somewhere in France

My Dear Eva and Bessie,

I have a chance to write today, so I will write to you both, as I owed Bessie a letter and can only write one. It will have to go for the two of you. Today is Sunday and it being very quiet and before I go any further I must say I am writing this before dinner. We are going to have a great feed this noon and will tell you all about it later. (To Bessie), I was very much surprised to find out that you had to go as far away as Norwell to get tanked up and got a black eye. Eva said it was something like dirt that you got in your eye, but if you were here you would get mud because we do not very often run out of it and sometimes are like the mud men we used to make when kids.

Well, Bessie (or Red as I know you better), I was very glad to get your letters and hope that you will keep up the good work. I hope that you are fine, and I am waiting for the chance when I can eat some more of your great cakes. You hear about all the news that I write so it is about the same day in and out, but I have seen things that will long be remembered and things I wish that you and all the rest could see.

I hope that you will be able to stay with Eva because I know that you are a great help to her and I like a good Red cook myself. I wish that you could see the way we live at this time in a dugout made of sand and which is very hard with 8 bunks in it. We cut a hole (I did) in the side and got some tins and made a stove. Cut a hole in the tins and made a pipe and ran it through and we are very warm. We have hot and cold water to wash and shave. We must shave very often because of our gas masks to make them fit snuggly. Last night I got some bacon fat and some spuds. In other words, "Pomme d'terre" and had some great French fries. Not so bad and we also had chocolate, but we did not have the "du lait."

(To Eva), There is not very much more to write about only to tell you I am feeling very well. Did Dad get my last letter ok? I must go to dinner in a few minutes, so I will tell you some more by and by.

Well, Eva, here I am again but filled up. We had turkey and mashed potatoes and bread and butter with bread pudding and coffee and believe me, it was great and to top it off we all got a little box from the Detroit Newspaper with tobacco and cigarettes. I can hear the big guns often and believe me they sure do make some noise when they cut loose. How are all the folks and remember me to Grandma and Gramps. Why doesn't Hattie write to me? Has Uncle Ed come back from New Hampshire yet?

When you send another box, I would like one of those fruit cakes like you sent before. It was great. We are all having arguments about the different boxes the boys get and who sends them and how good they are and believe me Eva, they have got to go some way to beat a sister like you and the boxes too. I guess that your folks at home know more about the war than we do. It is very hard to get news, but Sherman was right, war is hell. We almost caught a rat last night. I wish that we had Dickie here and he would have some fun.

I am going to take a little walk in a few minutes and settle my dinner down a little. The country is beautiful here that is it was before the Boche beat it out. But about all that anyone can see is hills and trenches and barbed wire now. Well, Eva, I think that I will close now and will send my love to you all and all the folks.

Private 1st Class Raymond W. Maker

25 February

Today we saw a few shells burst over the Boche lines. Worked a while this morning and had the afternoon off. Weather rainy and I am well and fine.

26 February

Moved back into the big cave and we saw a big air battle. Weather fine, but very muddy. I'm feeling fine.

27 February

Today was about the same only very quiet. Rained a little in the morning and at night. I'm feeling fine but have a little cold.

February 27ᵗʰ 1918

Somewhere in France

My Dear Sister,

How do you like this for paper? We have moved again and back to the big cave that I told you about and they have a French and American YMCA here now, and it is a dandy. Yesterday, I saw an air fight and the best part of it was that there were a couple of American air machines in the fight. They are the first ones that I have seen. We are back with our own lieutenant and I am glad for that because he is a white man.

We all expected to have our furlough in about two weeks. I would like to go to London, but don't think that I will be able. We had quite an interesting time while we were up near the front, but there was not much danger. I really hated to leave because we had a dandy little place but it's all in war times they say. There was a lot of mail that came yesterday but I have not had any so far. I seem to want candy all the time, the last couple of months, and I would sure like some fudge, believe me. That chocolate that you sent was très bon…get me. I do not know just how long we will stay here and the sooner we move the better because I don't like this place.

Are you having much cold weather there now? Spring is about starting here now, and I suppose that there will be something doing in the trenches. I hope so because all the boys over here seem to want to go right in and have it over with and get back home. Me for one!

I have seen about enough of France and have given up the idea of trying to talk the French lingo. It gets my goat. Everything is going along very well with me and I hear that I am up for a noncom job. I hope so because I think that I should have a better rating when I see some of these fellows that they gave stripes to in the states – fellows that have never seen a telephone line or ever soldiered before, but I hope good hopes anyway.

Well, Eva, how are things going with you and I hope that you will be able to get along all right with the store and if you want any of the money, it is yours for the taking. I just received a bunch of newspapers from you, but only looked at the pictures so far. How is Grandma and Gramps? Tell them I will write soon and give Bob Bliss my best of luck to him and say that I think that he is starting in "toute de suite" and tell him that I like candy. Give my regards to Mr. Charles and Charlie Esty. Tell Nucker that I did not get his letter yet. I suppose that Dad has received my last letter by this time and also, he has mailed me one. I suppose that he is quite a cook by now. Why doesn't he join the Army as a cook? We had some flap jacks this morning and they were the best that I have had since I left the states. Gee, but I would like you to walk in and sit upon one of the stools now and just sit there but I guess that it won't be very long before we are back. I have not seen Mullens for some time, so I do not know how he is.

I am going to write to Gladys after I write this letter. I suppose she will be sore if I don't write once in a while but there is no love match as I know of. Well, Eva, I will close now and with the best of love and hope that prayers will be answered for a safe return.

Your loving brother,

Private 1st Class Raymond W. Maker

PS: I have started what they call a misplaced eyebrow, and if I have good luck it may have more than eight hairs on it when I get home.

28 February

Today, everything is very quiet, and it is raining. I'm fine, washed and shaved. I think that I've done very well, so far, in keeping this book. And, I hope to have the best of luck in keeping it up, until this war is over, which I think will be soon. Let us all hope so, because our place is at home and not over here in the mud and in fighting, if or for what the Lord only knows. I don't. Just as I got to bed, I thought that all hell had let go, by the way the big guns went off. A barrage on the Germans.

February 28th 1918

Somewhere in France

My Dear Dad,

I thought that as long as I can write one letter a day that you would be glad to get a letter all for yourself and I hear that you keep them in your pocket. You know that in the letters that I send to Eva, that we have been up near the front and that we have seen a few shells burst and have also heard some and believe me, Dad. They sure do make a fellow feel kind of strange, and I guess that when they come very close that there were a few of the boys washing out some of their underclothes, but not me, as yet, but when we heard them coming we never stopped to find out where they landed. We have been living very well the last couple of weeks.

I think that it is hard on you people back home when everything is hard to get, but I don't think that it will last very long because the Boche are about on their last legs coming through the towns. We have seen very many Boche that have been captures and a great many of them were very young, 17-18 years old.

Do you expect to do any racing this summer? If you do, I will drive you in the machine. We expect to have our furloughs in a couple of weeks and I think that I will go to one of the big cities on the waterfront, if I cannot go to London. Has Eva received any more of the State money and does she understand about the insurance [policy] that I made out and has she received any money - $10 from the Government that I am sending home out of my pay? I thought that I might as well send some money home as spend it all here, but at the same time, our money does not last very long because everything is priced so high here and we spend it mostly on things to eat and it is sometimes that we have to wait for our pay for quite a while.

Our last payday was the 15th of January, so you can see $36.60 does not last almost two months with $10 taken out and my insurance policy is $6.60 a month. But, I get along very well, and I have not been sick since I came to France. I guess that mud agrees with me. Has Uncle Ed come back from New Hampshire yet, and, how is he? I see in the papers that they have had quite a time at the Charles River Speedway. I have looked for your picture in the crowd.

How does Kip like the Army life, but I don't wish that he was here. I have been waiting to hear from you, but I suppose you are on the move all the time now, as Eva said you were the first cook and a great man at hearing the fire bell. I think that you had better change your brand. I would like some of Bessie's biscuits now. Well, Dad, I think that I will close now and hope that this letter finds you all in the best of health. Love to you all.

Your loving son,

Private 1st Class Raymond W. Maker

ACTIONS IN LA REINE (BOUCQ) SECTOR – BOIS BRÛLE, SEICHEPREY, XIVRAY, HUMBERT PLANTATION (MARCH 1918)

Between March 18 and 21, 1918, the Division was relieved in the Chemin-des-Dames sector, with the result that good practice was given for in road discipline, billeting, and supply. When in movement, the troops, after a short railroad trip to Brienne-le-Château and Bar-sur-Aube, began a five-day march to the Rimaucourt (Ninth) Training Area, which lay west of Neufchâteau, adjoining the area where the first period of training had been passed.

It was supposed that the Division would have opportunity, on settling down in the new area, to be refitted, to rest, and to perfect its training and discipline. But the military situation required it to return to the line at once. Forty-eight hours after the troops arrived at the rest area, they were taken by motor truck and rail, less the artillery, which marched direct to the so-called "La Reine" or "Boucq" Sector, northwest of Toul, where the Division relieved the 1st Division from March 28 to April 3, 1918.

The line the Division took over from the 1st ran from the vicinity of Apremont, on the left, past Xivray-Marvoisin, Seicheprey, and Bois de Remieres, and as far as the Bois de Jury, on the right, where it joined the line held by the French. Division Headquarters was at Boucq.

The Division's stay in this sector was marked by several serious encounters with the enemy. There were almost nightly skirmishes between patrols or ambush parties, and the harassing fire of the artillery on both sides was very active.

On April 10, 12, and 13, the Germans heavily attacked the lines held by the 104th Infantry in Bois Brûle (near Apremont) and by the French to the left. At first the enemy secured footholds that were not strongly held, and sturdy counterattacks succeeded in driving the enemy out with serious losses. For its gallant conduct on this occasion, the 104th Infantry was cited (April 26, 1918) in a general order of the 32nd Army Corps (French), and had its colors decorated with the Croix de Guerre. The units engaged included 2nd and 3rd Battalions, 104th Infantry; 3rd Battalion, 103rd Infantry; M. G. Company, 104th Infantry; Company C, 103rd M. G. Battalion; and 51st F. A. Brigade.

April 20 and 21, the Germans made a second raid on the Division's lines. This, like the attack at Bois Brûle, appears to have been one of many similar local operations undertaken at this time. To accomplish them successfully, the enemy employed a specially trained and experienced body of elite infantry ("*Sturmtruppen*," or "storm troopers").

The 1st Battalion, 102nd infantry, and the 102nd Machine Gun Battalion, on which the full force of the attack fell, suffered heavily, although Company E, 102nd Infantry, and the 3rd Battalion, 101st Infantry, also endured significant losses. The strength of the attack was such that it looked for a time like the beginning of an important operation. But the enemy force withdrew as our artillery and machine gun fire inflicted heavy losses. If an operation more extensive than a raid to take prisoners was planned, it was abandoned.

On May 27 another raiding party, numbering about 400, attacked the line held by the 1st Battalion, 101st Infantry, at Humbert Plantation, near Flirey, but the enemy was again unable to breach the line and was repulsed with losses. The front held by the Division shifted easterly to include the Bois de Jury and Bois de Hazelle, as far as Flirey. The German attack caught the infantry just as they came into the line, and the artillery (101st F. A.) had barely occupied their new positions.

A third raid was launched on June 16 against the sub-sector held by the 103rd Infantry at the village of Xivray-Marvoisin. Preceded by a heavy bombardment and a dense barrage, a strong German force moved against the village and nearby trenches, but failing to get within our defenses, immediately withdrew, leaving many dead and wounded. Troops engaged were 3rd Battalion, 103rd Infantry; M. G. Company, 103rd Infantry; 103rd M. G. Battalion; and the 51st F. A. Brigade.

As though in retaliation for the decisive check the enemy had suffered, the Germans delivered throughout the day of June 16 exceedingly severe artillery fire on the battery positions and rear areas, as well as up and down the forward parts of the sector. Division Headquarters was forced to change location from Boucq to Trondes. Casualties and material damage were caused in Cornieville, Royaumeix, Bernecourt, Broussey, and Raulecourt, as well as in the already ruined towns of the sector such as Beaumont, Mandres, Ansauville, Rambucourt, and Xivray itself.

The Division undertook two offensive operations at this time. On the night of May 30-31, backed by strong artillery support, 300 volunteers of the 101st Infantry carried out a raid in force against the German positions in Richecourt. A destructive gas projector attack, reputedly the first attack of its kind to be delivered by American troops, fell on enemy lines in the Bois de Sonnard (Saillant du Renard) on June 6.

On June 24-28, the Division was relieved by elements of the 82nd Division and most of the French 154th Division.

During its three months of occupation of the Boucq Sector, relations with the French, both higher command and neighboring units in line, continued the same plane of intimate friendship and mutual esteem that began on the Chemin-des-Dames and continued to the end. The Division, on entering the sector March 28, took over the front of a division, and functioned as such as a unit of the 34th Army Corps (French).

MARCH 1918

1 March

Weather is rotten. Had a quiet day and had a band concert tonight.
I'm feeling fine. Hope that it is quiet tonight.

March 1st 1918
Somewhere in France

My Dear Sister,

Just a few lines as I have time and to let you know that I had a
great big piece of home-made cake yesterday. One of the boys got it from
home. I am waiting for another box as I am broke and have been for quite
a few days. We are in hopes of being paid in 5 or 6 days. Don't forget my
fruitcake. As I have written a few letters this week it is kind of hard to
know just what to write. Do you find any of my letters cut by the censor?
I always try and write so they won't be all cut up. Did you get the box that
I sent?

There were quite a few things that I could not send as they had the
names of the towns on them, but you must have had a little idea where we
were very near at one time by two of the things that I sent. We were all
through the house and were in the old church to live. We were only about
5 miles from that place, but are a great many now, about 300 or more. We
have travelled a great many miles in this country and it all looks about the
same and the towns and cities all seem to be in valleys and the trains look
so strange and very lazy to ride in, and when we get home I will sleep on
the floor.

I guess that it has been very muddy here the last few days and last
night after I got to bed I wrote in my diary that everything was very quiet
and about 5 minutes after, I thought that Hell had let go by the racket that
the guns made, and some of us got up and went up on the hill and we could
see the flashes from the guns very plain. They say that it was American
and Frog batteries saying good night to the Boche. It was a very good night
to some of them all right.

I suppose that it is warmer there now, but the weather here is very
changeable. Some days warm and other days cold and damp. I suppose
that Dad will be glad to get my letter. I sent one to Jap, too. Sleeping in

the lumber yard in Maine helped me quite a bit over here because some of the boards seem soft. Well, Eva, I will close now and write again in a few days, hoping that you are all well and in the best of health.

Love to you and to all the folks.

Private 1st Class Raymond W. Maker

2 March

Snowed all day and we hiked about 11 miles to a cave that is a wonder. Electric lights. One and a half miles from the front lines. I'm fine but tired. Going to bed at 8pm.

3 March

Weather rotten. Stayed in the cave all day. It sure is some cave. We have to have our feed brought to us on rails. I'm feeling very good.

4 March

Everything very quiet. Raining and snowing all day. Feeling fine. Playing cards about all day.

5 March

Today it cleared up. Very quiet this am. Feeling fine. We are very near the frontlines here.

6 March

Today was very interesting with air battles and bombardments. Some noise…The worst yet. Am being well, weather is fine.

7 March

Moved again today, to dugouts. Am on my job at last. Weather is fine and I'm feeling fine.

8 March

Everything about the same. It seems that there are air battles all of the time. And, now, I don't hardly look up at them. Weather is fine. I'm in hopes of having a bath very soon. I need it.

9 March

I got a letter from Gladys today. The weather is about the same only a little warmer. I'm feeling fine, but I'm hungry. Wished that I would get a box from home.

10 March

Everything is about the same. I had to walk over to a canteen and now I'm broke, dead broke. Weather is fine and so am I.

11 March

Last night I had quite a time with a gun on fire. Everything is the same and the weather is fine, and so am I … thank you.

12 March

Same old story about the same things. I have eaten soup so much that I am a soup bone. Weather is fine, me also. Talk about going to a rest camp in a few days.

13 March

Everything the same. Got two letters from home. No. 17. And a box from the Red Cross. And some newspapers. Took a walk and changed my clothes. Weather is fine and me, too.

14 March

The weather is a little cooler. Everything the same. Had quite a walk this morning. Feeling fine, to move soon.

15 March

Everything is fine. Got four letters: Ida, Mable, Mrs. Frost and Gladys. Weather is warmer, and I am doing very well. Had a great walk to the trenches.

16 March

Same old story. Took a walk and got some Boche coins. Weather is fine. A bombardment going on tonight. I am well. We had to "stand to" all night. French bombardment.

17 March

Last night we had a very heavy bombardment and a gas attack. Weather is fine and so am I. Signed the payroll. (Boche gas attack).

18 March

We expect to move to our next camp tomorrow. I have a stiff neck and just had it painted. Weather is fine and so am I, outside of my neck.

19 March

Weather rainy. Started for our new camp at 10pm, and we reached the town at 3:30am. Wet and muddy and cold. Stayed here for about 12 hours. I am well.

20 March

6:15 PM. Rested all day and a hike at 12PM to the train. It was raining all day. We built a fire and dried our clothes. We are on our way to our next camp, at last. Am well, but tired and have a little cold.

21 March

Landed in Bar-Sur-Aube. And went into a nice billet and slept about all day. Weather is fine and I'm well. The place has about 5,000 people in it.

22 March

Walked around the place and it is quite pretty. Met a lot of fellows I know. Weather is fine. A big fight going on up where we were. Feeling fine.

23 March

Looked the town over again today. Weather is great. Met some more boys today. We leave here in a day or so. Am well.

24 March

Hiked 5 miles today, to Lignon du Velay. Weather is fine and I'm a little tired. Am waiting for supper now. Had a poor feed and went to bed early.

25 March

Hiked 10 miles and started around 7 and got to Juzencourt at 11:30 am. Feeling fine. We have about 10 or 15 miles to go to our next camp. Feeling fine. Going to bed at 7:15.

26 March

Started out at 5am and hiked over 15 miles and I am tired and lame. Weather very much colder. The town is Chabannes, and it is a small place. Going to bed at 6:30. Rupe got buried.

27 March

Left at 8am and reached Rancourt, our rest camp, at 10 o'clock. Met Lowell and had a great feed at the MP. Weather warmer and I'm a little tired. Got a letter from home and I answered it.

28 March

Went to Lt. Blen and saw all the boys in the old company. We are going back to the trenches very soon. Weather is fine and so am I, and I have a little cold.

29 March

Got a box and some newspapers. Rained hard all day. Got my Red Cross box and have on some new clothes. And, feeling fine, but still have a cold.

30 March

Rained all day. Got paid, around 40 franc short. Have not had a chance to write home. We leave tomorrow for the trenches. I'm fine.

31 March

Today, at 6am, we started out in trucks, and it rained hard all day. I have about the best bed I have had, yet. And, eggs, oh boy!

APRIL 1918

1 April

Today, we arrived at the trenches. Walked from 4 in the am, until 3:30. It rained hard and the mud is very deep. Am all wet and about all in, but I am game and have a good place to live in.

2 April

Today, I have been on the go. I have a station, but I have not had any sleep. It rained all day as well. This is a bad sector.

3 April

This has been the first real day for quite a while. Everything is fine, and it is kind of still for a change.

3 April

Somewhere in France

My Dear Sister,

I suppose that you are wondering why I have not written before this, but I have been in places where I have not had a chance. I got a box from the town and I have had quite a few letters. I have not had my furlough yet. I was in high hopes of getting it the last of ----, but nothing doing, yet.

It has been raining about every day for the last week, and the mud, Eva, well I cannot begin to tell you how much we like it. Today, is the best day we have had yet. I do not know what to say. I have seen some very hot times during the last few weeks and in a way, I wish that you could hear the noise, but take it from me, it is no joke and when one those shells comes whizzing by it makes one think of many things all at once.

I am in a very nice little place now, and I have a stove and get about all of the coffee and sugar I want and hard bread, so I am not starving. I have read in the newspapers a few stories that some of the boys have written home, but most of them are all bull.

I had some real tomato soup for breakfast (Campbells) and it sure made me think of the many times that I have made it. I had a letter from Ida, one from Mable, and one from Mrs. Davis (Miss Frost), but I have not answered them, Eva, because I have not had a chance. I saw Stanley Fair a few days ago. He said that Ed Collins was fine, but his feet were not doing very well.

You will have to excuse this paper as it is all I have here with me. We are travelling around so much that I only carry just what I can get along with. What do you hear of this big drive they are having? I hope it is the last one. Life is awful lonesome now and sometimes I do feel just a little homesick. But, it won't be long. Eva, I wish that you could have seen the places that we came through when we came back from the trenches. Places, Eva, that were once large towns, all shot down and the apple tress all cut down. It is a shame.

How does Kip like the Army? I hope that he gets paid as often as I do. We got paid last week for the month of December, but it is just as well, as we are where we could not spend it. I saw and talked to two American girls that ran a YMCA in a place I went through and it sure made me feel good to talk to them.

This has been the first winter that I have not had a bad cold and I have felt fine all of the time. Well, Eva, how are things going with you and are times just as hard? What is Dad doing these days and I suppose that Kip will go out with the Hudson. It is almost 9 pm, and I have some water on for coffee. Had another surprise. We had some clam chowder with a little tomato soup mixed in and it was "bon." I could write all night as this is my first letter in a couple of months, but I do not want to overdo it and I will write again in a few days.

Did you send my last box, and did you get the box that I sent to you? I will close now, Eva, with the best of love to you and all the folks.

Your loving brother,

Private 1st Class Raymond W. Maker

4 April

Raining again, but only a little. The same old story. Walked around and wrote home. Am well and happy. Gas attack at 12:30.

5 April

It has been very nice today. Had a look around and now have another man to help me. Gas at about08:30, all well. Am fine, thanks.

6 April

Was under fire this pm. It was not very pleasant. Heavy firing in the am. Now am making some coffee. Had a haircut. I am fine.

7 April

Today, four shells struck our lines and cut all of them. Rainy and fine, but tired. This is a bad place and getting worse.

8 April

Today, rain. Have had little sleep. It is hard today with bombardments and gas. Am well and was out all night.

8 April

My Dear Sister,
Somewhere in France

I have had the luck to find a piece of paper, so I thought that I would write. I want to tell you, Eva, that if you do not get many letters from me now, don't be worried because sometimes we are in places that it is hard to get mail in and out, but I will write every chance that I get as you know.

We are all looking for the war to end now, at any time, but it is hard to tell. You people know more about the war than we do here, and we know of a few things that you don't know, believe me. I will have some stories to tell just like Uncle Andrew used to tell us kids.

Eva, I wish that you would write to Ida and Mable and tell them that I got their letters, and also Mrs. Davis and many thanks for the stockings that she sent to me. The box that I received from the people of Framingham was dandy and the candy was great. I have been very lucky on the tobacco because I always bought it when I had a chance and saved my other, but I have seen times when it was very hard to get, and it was about the best thing to keep up a fellow's nerve once in a while.

Eva, you don't know how much army life changes a person and makes men out of them. We are all toned up being out in all kinds of weather to say nothing of the mud. They say this is sunny France, but I don't see it that way.

What is Dad doing these days and how is Bessie, Mr. Charles and all of the other people? I wish that I could drop in just now. Here it is 8:15 pm, and it is about 3 pm, back there. Just taking a rest after dinner. You were right about what was cut out in that letter. I don't see why they did it. I thought it was alright. Have you heard from Jack Nelson? I met him about 2 weeks ago. I have not seen Mullens for a couple of months. I am on detached service with the 104th Infantry Regiment and it is claimed that they are about the best over here. There are a lot of boys from Concord and around that area and are all fine fellows. We are very well under the fact that things are hard to get, and one knows how hard it is to get things from the States over to here.

Well, Eva, how are you and all of the folks? I suppose that you have two stars on that flag, now that Kip is in the service. I hope he won't have to come over here. If he does he will be away back anyway, and he won't see any service. Well, I must close now, as I don't want to be too hard on the censor and I will write again when I have the time. I have just moved again. I have a fine bomb-proof dugout. Well, Eva, I will say good night and send my love to all.

Your loving brother,

Private 1st Class Raymond W. Maker

PS: Just received a letter from Gladys and she said that Kip was in the hospital. Write me the details.

9 April

Moved to a new place today. It is better. I am very tired. All is very still for a war…

10 April

Moved around…today. Very tired this am, but I am feeling fine.

11 April

Things very still today. Weather is fine.

12 April

Got two letters from home. Gladys and Grandma. I got shelled today. It was fierce. Weather is fine and so am I. But, believe me, a little shaky.

April 12th 1918

Somewhere in France

My Dear Sister,

I received a letter from Gladys a few days ago and she said something about Kip being in the hospital and I have not heard from you for over a month, but one of the boys went down to a place to get some mail and I hope that there is some for me. What is the trouble with Kip and tell me all about it. Things are about the same with me, Eva, only it is very noisy here at times and it gets on one's nerves once in a while, but you could never find a bunch of boys that have courage and are in good hopes, the way that our boys are. We have had very good weather the last two days and that is one thing that helps out a lot.

Did I tell you that I received a letter from Hattie? Why doesn't Dad write to me? Tell him nothing would please me anymore than to hear from him if only a few lines. It is very hard to get mail sent from here, Eva, but we will soon be out where we can write a little more in a few days. Now, what do the papers say about the Massachusetts boys? God, Eva, I wish that you could see the things, just like men of war, and your big brother is one of them, too.

We are supposed to have a service trip now and when we get back to a rest camp (if they have such things) we will get one, too. I wish that you could just have a look at me now.

I suppose that the cold weather is all over now and that must help out a lot. Are there many eateries there now? Did you get the box that I sent? There were a lot of things that I wanted to send, but they would not let me. I wish that you would tell Miss Emerson that I was asking for her and the same to all of my friends and as you know, when I write home, the letter is for all the folks, Grandma and all, because if I wrote to all, the letters would just be the same.

I have not written to Gladys for some time so please tell her I have not forgotten her and the same to Bessie. I have met a few Framingham boys up here. I found Bastine's brother yesterday. I had to laugh because I had a little car that I was hauling some stuff on and I left it at a place and when I came back it was gone.

Well, I walked up the track and I found my car with this fellow and some wood. What I said to him would be cut out by the censor. Well, anyway, I found out it was Homer Bastine. I did not know him, all black and with a brush on his lip. We are all feeding very well, Eva, and I'm saying a lot. We are all expected to be home by Christmas. It will be hard to spend another Christmas over here.

Are you getting my money that I have attached? I am fixed very well for money. I have about 200 francs - $40, but I guess the reason is that there is no place to spend it. Well, I will close for now and please give my love to all the folks and the best of love to you.

Your brother,

Private 1st Class Raymond W. Maker

13 April

Fixed my lines today, that had been blown up. This still gets on my nerves. Weather is fine, and I feel very tired.

14 April

Had a long walk today.

15 April

I will be glad to get a rest.

Somewhere in France

I
A soldier boy lay dying,
On a road "somewhere in France;"
he had tried to get through a barrage

Tho he knew he stood no chance.
A pal knelt down beside him
While the tears ran down his cheek
For this soldier was his lifelong friend
And he longed to hear him speak.

II

When the dying soldier opened
Up his eyes, and look around
And saw his dear old pal
Kneeling side him on the ground
He smiled and said "They got me Jim
Yes, got me with a shell."
"My orders were to take this note
Through water, fire and hell."

III

"Take this message Jim and run it thru
Do not stop for me
It means two hundred lives and more
It's for our company
Fritz made a fake attack this morn
Just at break o' day
If you can only get it through
We'll make those damn Huns pay"

IV

"And when you get around to it
Just write a line or two,
To my mother and my sweetheart Jim
Old pay so good and true;
Tell them I tried to make it
Thru gas, barrage, and shell
That my resting place is heaven
For I went there thru a hell."

V

Then the dying soldier closed his eyes
His pal with tender care,
Gently laid him down
And smoothed his bloody ruffled hair,
And with a sob of anguish
He started down the road,

In his hand he held the message
That was written out in code.

VI

Jim got the message there in time
To quell the Germans' bluff,
He told the story to the boys
How the blood got on his cuff,
The dying words of Bill his pal
A runner dead and gone
And the company paid their last respects
To the brave but silent form.

~Wrote at Apremont by Batt. Runner Blanchard
At the conclusion of a dream – YD Co. F 103. Inf.

16 April

Moved out today and stayed in a barn all night. Rain and mud, but I have not given up. The trip was tough.

17 April

Moved at noon and got to a so-called rest at 7:30. Mud is a fact. Will go right to bed. Am well, but tired and lame.

18 April

Rested up all day, but it is cold and wet and do not expect to stay here very long. Am well, feeling fine.

19 April

I'm still resting but took a walk. Saw some of the guys in A Company. Got a letter from Gladys.

20 April

We were moved up onto the lines today and stayed until 3 am. Am fine and dandy. Weather is good, but a little cold.

21 April

Am a little tired but slept most of the day. Had some good red wine today. Am fine, weather is fair.

22 April

Everything is about the same. Rains all of the time. Am just a little lonesome, but I am well.

23 April

Got two letters today. One from Dad and one from Gladys. Weather is fair, and I am fine.

24 April

Same old story. Rained all day. We are moving soon from here. Feeling fine and dandy. Wish I could hear from my sister.

April 24th 1918
Somewhere in France

My Dear Dad,

I received your letter last night and I was more than glad to get it as I have not heard from you in so long. I heard that Kip has been in the hospital and I received a letter with yours saying about Eva being there, too, and you did not say anything about it and I have not heard from Eva, so I know something must be the matter at home.

I am having a rest now, for a few days. We need it because we have been working kind of hard for the last few days. I am feeling fine and dandy.

Did you hear about the folks at home not being able to send any more boxes, only on a written note for them and not having to be signed by the officers. We are all looking forward for the time to come home because we think that the Boche is about all in.

I suppose that you have read the war news in the papers telling about the Massachusetts boys. Well a lot of that stuff is all lies, but we have heard some noise all right. I am in hope of hearing from Eva soon, now, and hope to find out what the trouble has been with her and Kip.

Is Bessie still there? I hope so because she is so much help to Eva. We are having a lot of rain and it seems that there is nothing but mud wherever we go. I received a nice box sent from the town. I have not had a chance to write before some time and when I do write it is so hard to know what to say. I suppose that you have a machine running by this time and wish you would run over here to see me.

Gee, I would like to see you all right now. Have they fixed up the trouble with that woman in South Framingham, yet? I think that it is about time. Well, Dad, I will close now and will write in a few days.

Best of love to all the folks.

Your Son,

Private 1st Class Raymond W. Maker

25 April

Must rest today. Am feeling fine, thanks.

26 April

Went to tanks today. A big hit with Collis. Got pinned down coming back. Am fair, weather is fair. Parker got me out.

27 April

Went to the market in town and had 12 eggs, Weather is fair and I'm okay, thanks.

28 April

Nothing different. Had a big review today by General Edwards, and a Frog. It rained all day. The Regiment was decorated. Am feeling fine. I wish that I could hear from home.

29 April

Slept about all day. Weather is about the same. I expect to leave here soon and will write home today.

April 29th 1918

Somewhere in France

My Dear Sister,

I have been waiting so long for a letter from you, but I know the reason that you have not written to me and I hope that you and Kip are both well. The Regiment that I am with, the 104 Infantry Battalion, had a Grand Review yesterday, by both an American and French General and a lot of us boys were given the French War Cross and the Regimental Colors were given the Cross of War, so you can see that I am with a good outfit.

I see Red Collins and he is fine, but they had quite a hard time of it. We are taking things kind of soft here for a few days, but it rains about all the time and everything is mud. There is a lot of talk about our (censor) coming, but it is just talk. I have had 3 or 4 letters from Gladys, but have not answered them yet, and one from Dad. Was very glad to hear from him. There is so much that I would like to tell you about us being in the lines, but you know how it is. They came very near getting us one day. Four big shells landed very near us, but they have not got my name on any of them believe me. I hear that they have stopped boxes from coming over here unless they are sent for and the letter ok'd by an officer. I am going to write to Gladys the first chance I get. We have a YMCA here, but stuff is hard to get and there are so many here. I have heard from Mullens and he is ok. We had a little (censored) with some of the boys out of my company but were very lucky (censored) of our company. Now, but I do not see our CO very often. I am with a regiment of infantry.

Well, Eva, I am in the best of health and fat as a pig and this is the truth, I never have felt better but have seen the times when I was very homesick, and, in fact, I am now. Did you get the box that I sent to you? Give my regards to all the folks and tell Nucker that we he had ought to have been with me if he wanted to see barbed wire and trenches and that Collins Co, sure made a hole in the Boche and hung a few of them on the wire. You will have to excuse this paper, Eva, because it is all I can get. Will write in a few days with the best of love to you and all the folks.

Your loving brother,

Private 1st Class Raymond W. Maker

30 April

Took a little walk today and had some eggs. Weather is fine and so am I, but I have not heard from home. Four months now, and I have not slipped up on this book, yet. Not gotten hurt yet, so thankful that I am okay.

MAY 1918

1 May

Today we left Reims and had a big hike. Met Mullen and we stayed together all day. Moved into the lines at Oman. Am fine and the weather is fair.

2 May

We moved up to the lines tonight. Stayed with Mullen all day. Weather is fine. Got a letter from Grandma, about time I heard from home.

3 May

I'm in the front line. But things are still, which I hope will keep up. Am fine, but tired.

4 May

We are very near the Boche and have to be very careful. Am feeling fine. Weather has been very good. The place I am in is all shot to hell.

5 May

All is still, and the weather is fine.

May 6th 1918

Somewhere in France

My Dear Sister,

I have been waiting so long for a letter from you and I am in hope of getting one any day now. I have been with Red Collins for a couple of days and today I was walking down a trench and I walked right into Fat Littlefield, the first time I have seen him since I have been over here. I received a card from Grandma and she had a box to send me, but I will have to write to her for it, not because I want the box, but I owe her a letter. There is a lot of talk about the Division coming home, but I don't know what to believe. I wish that we could. I have seen enough Eva, believe me, and it is no kid's play that we have to put up with – going out and fixing lines under shellfire is no joke, believe me. I have seen a pile of this country while I have been here, but it all looks the same. I do not know if it was like this before the war or not (I mean the places that have not been shelled), but they are all dirty towns. I am going to write to Grandma and to Gladys tonight. I have been feeling fine all the time, so don't worry about me. Did you ever get the box I sent to you?

I was more than glad to receive Dad's letter, but he never said a word about you and Kip being sick – he did not want me to know, I guess. Eva, I want you to do one little thing for me and that is to get a nice little wreath of flowers and put them on Mother's grave for me and just say a little prayer for me and just say that her boy is always thinking of her and trying to live right. I wish that I could be there myself. Eva, and put it there. I hope that you are all ok and everything is going on fine, Is Bessie still with you? I hope so. There is so much to write and say Eva, but being where I am now, I am lucky to be able to write. We are due for a good rest soon because we have been on the go for some time. Well, Sis, I will close now hoping this finds you all in the best of health and love to you all.

Your loving brother,

Private 1st Class Raymond W. Maker

7 May

Three Boche flying machines came over today and we stayed under cover. Weather is fine and so am I. Got two men this am.

8 May

Walked about all night in the rain and dark. And I'm all in in, but well in the am. Leave tomorrow sometime.

9 May

Left the trenches today and had a long hike, so I'm tired. Saw some of the old timers. Am feeling well.

10 May

Went to Boelque and saw the boys. I stayed all night, everything is fine, and I am fine.

11 May

I'm still at Boucq having a good time. Got a box, so back tomorrow.

12 May

Went back to our camp. Raining hard. This is a bum place. Am feeling fine. No news from home at all.

13 May

Got a box from Grandma and it is a dandy. Had a walk and made some money. Weather is fine and so am I.

May 14

Everything is about the same, only no news from home. Am feeling fine, weather is fine. Move back to the lines soon.

15 May

Went to Boucq, today, and had a little time. Stayed all night and I feel fine.

16 May

Back to camp today. Weather is fine and so am I. We expect to leave for the front lines tomorrow.

May 16th 1918

Somewhere in France

My Dear Dad,

Just a few lines to let you know that I am alive and am thinking of everybody. I have not heard from home for over a month and a half and I heard through a fellow that our place has to be sold. Why don't you write and let me know what the trouble is, Dad, because I have been wondering for so long as to what the trouble is. I am fine and dandy and the weather has been very good the last few days for a wonder. We are still waiting for our furlough and we all hope that it is coming soon. I received a dandy box from Grandma and I wish that you would let her know that I received it. I will write to her in a few days.

We have been having some great luck on our trips up to the trenches. I was in a hole once where we could see the Boche very clearly. Now, Dad, I wish that you would let me know all about what is going on and don't be afraid to tell me if anything has happened which I think it has. It is getting warm these days and I am afraid that it won't be very pleasant living here when it gets good and hot. We are going to be paid in a day or so for two months' pay.

Well, Dad, I will write a better letter soon. Love to all,

Your loving son,

Private 1st Class Raymond W. Maker

17 May

Moved up to the lines tonight. Weather has been fine the last few days. And, so have I. No news from home.

18 May

Up once more on the lines. And with the battalion this time. Had a good place to live in. Weather is great, but hot. Am fine.

19 May

We are having fine weather now. Got three letters, but none from home. Am feeling fine.

20 May

Made a custard pudding tonight. Weather is fine. Everything is the same and so am I.

May 20th 1918
Somewhere in France

My Dear Dad,

Just a few lines to let you know that I am ok. I received a letter from Gladys yesterday and she said that you have not heard from me for over 5 weeks. I have written once a week right along. I have not heard from home since I received your letter and I am afraid that there is something wrong at home. I saw a fellow who saw in the paper that you are selling out the store because of sickness. Now, Dad, please write and let me know what the trouble is and don't be afraid to let me know if there is bad news, which I think there is.

Everything is about the same with me. I am feeling fine and dandy and we are having great weather here now. I received a dandy box from Grandma and one from the town a few days ago. I am fixed very well for tobacco and things for some time. Tobacco is about the staff of life over here. I suppose you see in the papers that we have had a few fights with Joe Boche, but it is not as bad as the papers say. The trenches are getting better now that they are drying up. They were sure full of mud and water. We expect to go to a rest camp soon because we have had quite a hard and longtime of it.

I went to a town yesterday and bought some eggs and tonight I made a big dish of custard and believe me, it was the best thing I have eaten since I left home. I should think that Kip would write to me; I heard that he was in the hospital but was all right. I don't know about, Eva. That is what is worrying me. I have a fine place to live in here. It was a house that the French people used to live in. We have good bunks and a fireplace, but I cannot have a fire in the daytime. Is Uncle Ed with you now? Why doesn't Jap write to me? I think that I have said about all I know of and hope that you will write to me very soon.

With love to all, your loving son,

Private 1st Class Raymond W. Maker

21 May

Moving again tonight, about 10 kilometers. Weather is fine and so am I. We leave here very soon.

22 May

Walked over our sector, about seven miles and got all muddy. Weather is fine and so am I, but very tired, but I am game to the last.

23 May

Made a couple of trips today and I am kind of tired. Not much to eat and I had a place to sleep. Weather is fine.

May 23rd 1918

Somewhere in France

My Dear Dad,

Just a few lines to let you know that I am in the best of health and I am feeling fine.

I am still waiting to hear from you folks. Everything is about the same with me and I am on the go about all of the time. I wish that you could see the places that we have to live in at times. They would make the old barn cellar look like a real home. When I come home I will sleep in the barn for a few days.

Did you ever hear of cooties? Well, I have about 1,000 of them and every day I have to take my clothes all off and kill a few. A fellow does not feel just right if he doesn't have a few. You can take it from me, Dad that this trench warfare is no soft snap. It is a good thing for old Joe Boche that he does not fight in the open, but you would be surprised to see how the boys have all to get used to the ways and how good they are at the game and all wanting to put an end to this war.

I have seen some hot times and to tell the truth, Dad, sometimes I think that we are about the best right over here. In fact, I know we are. I think that I told you that the regiment I am attached with (104th) was awarded the Cross of War and there were over 100 of us boys that were given war crosses.

I am still at the telephone game and have it soft at times, until old Joe Boche puts a line out with a shell. How are things going with you these days? Write and tell me all the news and what you are doing. Tell Mr. Charles that I send him my best regards and the same to Charlie Esty. Tell Charlie to send me a few lines, in fact give them all my best regards.

Now, Dad, just a few lines between you and me that may sound a little foolish, but one can never tell, but something may happen to me and I may not come back. That is something that we don't know. We are here to do our duty and that's all.

I have taken out an insurance [policy] for $10,000 - $5,000 for Eva and $5,000 for Kip. That's all I could get, and you know what to do in that case and if I stay here there is one who thanks you and Ma for what you have done for me and it shall never be forgotten. But they will have to go some to get me. I think that I have written about enough this time and will write a more cheerful letter next time. I will write soon.

With the best of love to you and all the folks,

Your loving son,

Private 1ˢᵗ Class Raymond W. Maker

24 May

Had a rest day. Have not had a wash since I've been here. Wrote home, no news from home. Weather is fine.

25 May

Saw one of our machines shot down. And a few shells broke. Weather is fine and so am I. No news from home.

26 May

Saw three Boche flying machines driven back over their lines. Everything is the same. Am not feeling very well. Weather is fine.

27 May

Fixed up some lines that were blown up and got a little gas. Am not feeling very well tonight.

28 May

Was a little shaky today. A few shells landed very near to me. Am feeling fine, today, and the weather is fine.

29 May

The same old story. Heard from home at last. They have all been sick. Weather is fine. So am I.

30 May

Had a little walk. Went to a little town where they put flowers and flags on our boys' graves. Weather is fine.

May 30ᵗʰ 1918
Somewhere in France

My Dear Sister,

Just a few lines today as this is a day that was a hard one for me. I went over to a town and there I saw three Salvation Army girls and two men putting little bunches of wild flowers and an American flag on our boy's graves and then I went to the Salvation Army dugout and heard a little service, and Eva it made a few tears roll down my cheeks when I thought of me being here and wish that I could be home just for the reason to put a few flowers on Mother's grave. I thought that what I have seen today was about the best thing I have ever seen, and the Salvation Army can have all I got from now on. The town that I went to has a place to buy canned stuff and I bought some canned hot dogs and catsup and when I got back I heated up some water with canned heat and had a great feed.

I am sending you a little thing that the censor will let go by because I know of some of the boys who have sent them. It is part of a flare light that lights up no-man's land at night. The light hangs on the strings and comes down very slowly. I was sorry about that box, Eva, because I had two very nice statues of Joan D' Arc that was worth about $20 each and a few other things, but I suppose somebody wanted them. I got them at her birth place. Did I tell you that I was with Red Collins for a couple of days and that I have seen Mullens. I would be more than glad to see Banks and I have wondered when some of the machines fly over, if he was in any of them. Collins said that he had a letter from Miss Emerson. I would like to hear from her and also Charlie Esty. I must write to Grandma. She sent me a dandy box. Did Uncle Ed come down and go to work? Why doesn't Jap write to me? I suppose that he doesn't wake up in time. I had a letter from Mrs. Farnum. She was the one who called up for my address and said she lost her little boy. He was a dandy, too. I used to work with her husband. I think that we have old Joe Boche guessing lately.

I suppose that Dad is running around in the Hudson now, and tell him that he is a good scout at writing a letter and to keep up the good work. Well, Eva, everything is fine with me and I hope it is with you. I am about all in for any more to write, so I will close with the best of love to you and the folks.

Your loving brother,

Private 1st Class Raymond W. Maker

May 30th 1918

Somewhere in France

My Dear Sister,

Well, I am happy at last. I received your nice long letter yesterday and believe me I was glad when I got it. I knew that you and Kip were sick, and I am glad to know that you are all well again. I had to laugh when I read what you said about the underwear. I have seen very near all the boys in Company C, now. They are all detached with different regiments and I think that I told you that I was with the best. The best regiment is the 104th and they have all done fine work.

There is nothing that I want just now, Eva, only to be home and I would give everything that I have, to be there, just for today, the 30th. I don't want you to be thinking of me in the trenches, Eva, but just think of me over here doing my bit along with the rest of the boys. The trenches are not as bad at times and I have seen the times when I wish I was in them, because the shells do not land very near the front lines. They most always land behind. Everything is going on fine and I have been feeling fine all the time. We are expecting to have a furlough soon now, and I have got enough money to have a good time. I have almost 1,000 francs ($200.00), and if we don't have a furlough, then I will send the money to you, but I think that I deserve a good time, Eva, because we have been having quite a hard-longtime of it. I was very glad to hear from Dad, but I know by the way he wrote that there was something wrong.

I am glad to hear that you are sending me a cake and hope that I get it all okay. We get about all the tobacco and candy we want, most of the time. I tell you what I wish that you would send me and that is a bottle of Larkspur Lotion and send it any time. They say it kills the cooties and I am sorry to say that sometimes I have about 1,000. We cannot help getting them because we sleep most every place and in most any kind of old bunks with straw, but a fellow is never at home unless he has a few running around his back.

I hope that it won't be very long before you see us coming down the street with a band playing and believe me we will be the first to leave. The newspapers all talk about the 101st, but I suppose that is because they are from Boston.

Well, Eva, I think that I have written about all I can at this time and will write more after this, as I know everything is all right with you and Kip. Tell Dad I hope he won't take that last letter to heart. Well, Eva, I will close now with the best of love and happiness to you all and best of love to you.

Your loving brother,

Private 1st Class Raymond W. Maker

31 May

At 2:30 this morning, I heard the worst bombardment yet. And they all moved over heads. The weather is fine.

JUNE 1918

1 June

Same old story. I got a couple of letters last night. Move out of here in a day or so. Weather is fine, and so am I.

2 June

We move out at night and have been shelled a lot lately. Am not feeling well. Weather is fine.

3 June

Back in the rest camp. Guess we needed it. Weather is fine. The Division gets relieved very soon.

4 June

Went to Boneau today and had some ham and eggs. Weather is fine, and I am feeling a little better. But I have not made up my sleep yet.

June 4th, 1918

Somewhere in France

My Dear Sister, [On the back of this letter]

I have just made out a money order to you for $50.00 and it is being sent through the YMCA and they will send you a check and the place that it will come from is YMCA 124 E.28th St, New York. So, if you do not hear from them, write to that address.

Love to all,

Private 1st Class Raymond W. Maker

June 4th 1918
My Dear Sister,
Somewhere in France

I am in a much better place to write to you this time. We are out on a rest but no furlough yet, and outside of being a little tired, I am feeling fine. We had very little mud the last time up, so it made it much better. I think that you have done fine on the last two letters you have sent to me. They were so long and cheering. As you know, Eva, it is very hard to write a letter and we don't write them long because we like to give the censor half a chance. I hope that you have received my last letter with the part of a flare in it. I sent it from the lines.

I thought that Dad was lucky that he did not get hurt when the horse ran with him. Please tell Bessie it is about time that I heard from her. I had some feed this noon, went to a farm and bought some ham and eggs and took them to a house and the old Frog said we would have to cook them ourselves because his wife was away. So, I did the job and it was great. We had six slices of ham, three dozen eggs and it cost almost $5.00 (26 francs), can you beat that for the high cost of living. We are going to get paid in a few days and I am going to send you about $50 or $100 because I happen to be lucky enough to have (beau coup) money.

I am sending you a little piece of paper that is a part of a Boche balloon that we brought down. They send them over once in a while with papers telling lies about the allies trying to make them think one or another are not playing the game straight. Don't you worry about me taking too many chances, Eva, because it does not pay in this game and a fellow has to watch his step no matter where he is but, believe me, it does not sound very well to hear one of those shells going over your head, but we can tell fairly well now, which way they are going.

I had a bath yesterday and have new summer underwear, so I feel very good. Did I ever tell you about a fellow I've seen taking a bath in a tin pie plate? The Salvation Army, in the next town, will take orders for pies and doughnuts, and we can get them the next day. I must put in my order tomorrow.

Well, Eva, how are things going with you? I hope that you are all well and give my love to all the folks. I suppose that you understand now that I am only detached with the 104th but I still belong to the old outfit, the 101st. I think the 104th is about the best we have here. Tell Dad that I ran across Captain Dee from Concord. He is in the MPs. Also, my friend Lieutenant Parker is with the MPs also. I am going to try and transfer into the tank corps, if I can. I think there is a better chance for me.

I was glad to hear from Dr. Perry. Eva be sure not to bump into Mrs. Gordon's pine trees with the machine because I want that chance myself when I get home. I would not take a chance with you at the wheel. I would rather go across no-man's-land. I think it would be safer for me. I did not intend to start another page, but I got started and could not stop, Eva, I tip my hat to the Salvation Army; believe me all the boys like them here.

I don't say much about the YMCA. They are not doing what they say they are. I have a couple more letters to write tonight. I think it is about time that I answered Gladys's letter and one to Grandma. Say, Eva, this may sound funny to you, but you tell Dad that if he runs across a good piece of land, at a good sale, to get it for me because when I come home I aim to stay and settle down, if I can find anybody that will have me. I wish that you were my girl. Well, Eva, I think that I have written about enough this time and will write in a few days. With the best of love to you and all the folks,

Your loving brother,
Private 1st Class Raymond W. Maker

5 June

Am making up my rest and I feel so much better. Weather is fine. We are eating rations now.

6 June

Went to Boneau and stayed all day. Saw some boxing at night. Weather is fine and so am I. Rode both ways.

7 June

Same old story today. Went down the front lines and got into a fight. Weather is fine and so am I.

8 June

Wrote home. Everything is the same. Weather is fine and so am I.

June 8th 1918

Somewhere in France

My Dear Sister,

Just a few lines to let you know that I am feeling fine. I sent you a letter a couple of days ago and told you I sent fifty dollars by the YMCA and you will get a check mailed to you from New York. The number of the money order is: 48870 and you should get it in a month. If you don't write to the YMCA at 124th and 28th St., New York and find out about it.

I am writing this the second time, so you will be sure to know about it. I was down at our Signal Battalion HQ the other day and saw some of the boys – Hayden wants to be remembered to you and all the boys you know. I had a good feed and saw some good boxing and a band concert.

Everything is going on fine with me. We are having a little rest now for a few days. I suppose that you are having fine weather there now. We are here, and it seems good to be out of the mud. I have my service strip and when I stop to think I can wear two of them and they look fine. I hope that you have gotten my last four letters as I wanted you to get the things I had in them. They do not amount to much but are good things to keep.

I wrote to Grandma the other night and tell Bessie I am waiting to hear from her. I will send you some more money next month. Did you tell Dad what I said about buying me some land? I bet he laughed. I had a nice apple pie. I think I told you that I was going to have one. It was made by the Salvation Army girls. Well, Eva, I don't know of much more to write and will write in a few days again. Love to all the folks and the best of love to you.

Your loving brother,

Private 1st Class Raymond W. Maker

9 June

Everything is the same. We move back into the trench's tomorrow Weather is fine and so am I.

10 June

Still here. We think we move tomorrow. Weather is fine and so am I. I wrote home.

June 10th
My Dear Sister,

I thought that I would write a few lines to let you know that I am all right and happy. There is only one thing that I don't like and that is it rains here about all of the time. I met Talbot at our camp the other day and he wanted me to tell you that he was asking for you.

It is hard to write a letter here because everything is censored. We cannot tell where we are or anything about what we are doing. I will be glad when I hear from you and tell the folks that I can only write two letters a week, so if I write them to you it is all the same.

You can send me some of the Baker's chocolate if you want to and everything else that you want. They have got a good YMCA here, all kinds of newspapers and things, but cookies are about 5 cookies for a dime and then they are all brown, no white ones.

How are all the folks? We are moving from here in a few days. My love to all.

Your loving brother,

Private 1st Class Raymond W. Maker

11 June

We are here, yet no sign of moving. Weather is fine and so am I, thank you.

12 June

Got two letters from home today. Everyone is fine. We move out tomorrow for a rest. Weather is fine and so am I.

13 June

Left today for Royaumeix. It is a rest camp, at last. Don't know how long we'll stay here. Had a big hike here, am fine, but tired.

14 June

Ran the boards (dugout term) and got relieved at 9 pm. Everything is fine and so am I. Weather, too.

June 14th

Somewhere in France

My Dear Sister,

Just a few lines, as I have a lot of time and not very much to do. We are in a rest camp, moved up last night, so we will try and take life kind of soft. Everything is going fine with me and I am feeling fine. I am going to look up Frank Lowell in the MP's. He is here where I am and when I find him I sure will have a good feed. We are still having some fine weather and it seems good to have it after the hard winter and all of the mud. Eva, you could never understand how it was, but war is war and believe me, Eva, General Sherman was right.

I would like to write to Pete, but I don't know how to address it. Do you know? I sent you a letter a few days ago and also a list of the things I want. I hope that you have received the money that I sent through the YMCA. The number was 48-870. I think that I have told you a couple of times before, but I want to make sure and the address is: YMCA 124 E. 28th Street, New York. I was going to send some more money, but I don't know if I will get a chance to take a little trip to some big place or not.

I guess by the way the newspapers say over here that we are giving it to Joe Boche. I sent you a newspaper that is printed over here for us by mail. It is printed by American soldiers and it is quite a paper, I think. I hope that you get it ok.

I will have more time now to look up some of the old timers in Company C. We have a bunch of new men with us and nearly every state in the Union is represented all the way from California to Florida. We are going to have a ball game in a day or so. I don't know if I know how to play or not, now. I had a good swim the other day and I did not leave my teeth behind because I put them in my pocket.

I do want to tell you that I had the best cup of coffee at the Salvation Army last night and homemade cookies, too. Believe me, Eva, I tip my hat to them and they are mostly all women who run that outfit.

I will close for now and write to you in a few days. My love to you and to all the folks.

Your loving brother,

Private 1st Class Raymond W. Maker

15 June

Met Lowell and Lt. Parker of the MP's. And, stayed with them all day. Good feed.

16 June

The Boche shelled this place and killed a bunch of men. Everybody is moving out. The first time it has been shelled. Am fine, myself.

June 16th 1918

My Dear Sister,

This is the list of things that I wish you would send to me.

A couple of pairs of stockings

A few packs of cigarettes

A fruit cake

A little candy

Raymond W. Maker

June 16th 1918

Somewhere in France

My Dear Sister,

Last night I received two letters from you and I was sure glad to hear from you. I am glad to hear that everybody is all right and I sure am, myself. You wanted to know why it was that I wrote such cheerful letters under the conditions. Well, Eva, it's the way I feel, and we have to be cheerful, but there are times when it is hard and there is the time when it is hard and does not get one anything to be kicking all the time, and most of all is being afraid, but I can't admit that I was never afraid.

You wanted to know if I could keep clean. I have been lucky, so far, but you know, Eva, that we are in the game and we have to put up with the hardships. Yes, I have had a few cooties, but they are not bad. I heard from Harry and it is hard luck, but believe me Eva, they sure did give it to Joe Boche. Collins was there too, but he is all right. I have not seen him since then.

I do the kind of work that you thought I did. I did, and I sure do watch my step believe me. We have not had any furlough yet but are still in hopes. I did not cross out March. It is about time that Jack Collins got wise. You were right about being in the trenches, but we are out now, and I think for a good rest.

I think that Kip would take up the chance. He may make good out of it. I don't think that you had better have anything to do with Mrs. Chase's stuff, because, Eva, I have never seen anything from there, yet, but keep that under your hat. I hope that you have received the fifty dollars I sent to you and if ever you want to use any of the money, why just take it, because if I did not send it home, I would spend it here. I have almost $150 now, but I am waiting for a furlough and if I don't get it I will send more money home.

I am going to write Dad a few lines. Everything is fine with me and we are having great weather. I have been sleeping outside these last few nights. We are in some woods here and you had ought to hear the cuckoos at night. (I mean the birds). I have heard them singing at night in no-man's-land.

I am going to write to Bessie, too. I have not heard from Gladys for some time. How are the pigs? I hope that Billie Barrett gets his nickel if gets this letter. I am on a switchboard now, so I have a good chance to write and nobody to butt in.

I have not seen Mullens for some time, but he is ok and so is Jack Nelson. I heard from all the boys often. Mullens is with the 101st. I see a lot in the paper about them, but that is the way they always had the name, but I am nuts over the 104th Infantry, some outfit. We are moving today, so I will write when we get to our rest camp, if that is where we are going. I will send you a list of the things I want with this letter. I received the lighters you asked about and they are very handy. Well, Eva, I will close now and write again in a few days.

Love to you and all the folks.

Private 1st Class Raymond W. Maker

June 16th 1918
Somewhere in France

Dear Old-timers, Dad and Uncle Ed,
Just a few lines to you both as I would write about the same things to each. I hope that you are both well and in the best of health. I sure am, myself. To Dad – if I remember right this is your Birthday and I will try and make you a little present with a few lines of good cheer. Everything is going fine with me here and I hope it's the same with you. I am sending you a franc note which is about 20 cents in our money. They also have silver ones that look something like our quarter. I suppose you are down to the track most of the time with the fast one – the fastest horse yet. Keep on, Dad, and you will get a world trotter yet. Ha ha!

It is hard to write a couple of letters home at once because it is about the same thing over and over. I am glad that Kip is making good and make him write to me. We are having fine weather here, now, and I think that we have got old Joe Boche on the go. I hope that it will all be over soon because I am just dying to get my hands on the wheel of the Hudson and run her into a bank of the river.

Did Eva get my letter telling you to watch out for a good piece of land and buy it for me because I am going to settle down when I get home. I have seen enough of the world. Well, I must write to Uncle Ed with a few lines and will write you a better letter.

Hello, Uncle Ed. How are things going for you? I hope that you are well, and are you buying any shirts in Marlborough, and are you doing any fishing these days? This war is a little different than the one you were in, I guess, and I have some idea of what you old-timers went through, but I watch my step and believe me I don't take any chances unless I have to. I just broke my pen. I have not heard from Jap, only once since I've been here. I think he is too tired to write at night. I hope that you like your job and I are taking life easy. I hope to see you in a few months as we think the war is about over. I am sending you one of the franc notes, too. I hope to have a furlough soon. Well, I will close now as I have good news and I wrote to Eva. Don't get sore at the way this is addressed.

Love to all,

Private 1st Class Raymond W. Maker

17 June

Went to Toul and had a great time with Reid. Raining all day. Stayed all night. Am feeling fine.

18 June

I'm still in Toul. Having a fine time and staying all night. Leading the life of a King. Am feeling fine.

19 June

Left Toul this am. And came back. The boys are all over the town. Boche shells are too much for me.

20 June

Everything the same: rain and mud. Am taking life easy and feeling fine.

21 June

Same old stuff. Rained today. Met a few fellows and I'm feeling fine.

22 June

Wrote home today. Rain and mud, the same thing. Am feeling fine.

23 June

Same old story. Everything is the same. We are feeling fine. No news about all day. Am fine.

24 June

We are moving out in a few days and getting a real Division release. We are going somewhere near Paris. Weather is fine and so am I.

June 24th 1918

Somewhere in France

My Dear Sister,

I thought that it was about time that I sent you a few lines. We have been moving around quite a lot the last couple of weeks and have not had much of a chance to write. Everything is fine with me and I am feeling fine and dandy. I met Morrow Bradway and Ed Shea the other day and they all wanted to be remembered to you. We have been having a lot of rain the last few days, but the weather is fine again, now. I hope that you received the money that I sent home all right and the other things that I sent to you from the front lines. I have a few cards that I am going to send to you.

I was talking to a couple of American girl operators a while ago and it sure did seem strange. It seems good to be away from the noise of the guns, but we are not far enough yet. The other day they shelled the town we were in and hit us up, but it was the first time the place had been shelled and it was a hard time on the French who lived there. But we have got the Boche on the go now, I guess.

I saw a fight in the air the other day and Joe Boche came down, too. We are feeding fine now and that counts for a lot, believe me. I am going to write to Bessie after I write this letter. I was down to see a boxing match last night and a band concert and it was very good.

I suppose that Dad is running around with the machine. Has Kip gone to Washington yet? If he has, I bet he will have a great time. I am still waiting to hear from Jap, but I suppose he does not get up early. How are all the folks? Remember me to all of them. If you should see Joe Barrett, tell him I may see him in the tanks if I get my transfer. I guess that there is not much of a chance in the Signal Corps for me.

All the boys you know are fine and they all send their regards to you. I am going to try and have my pictures taken in a few days. I don't know if I look different or not, but I sure feel that way.

I would just like to drop in now and see just what the place looks like and have a good feed. I have not heard from Gladys for some time. I guess that she has forgotten I am here. But I should not worry, there is no love between us. I hope that you are all well. I have not heard from Miss Emerson yet. It does not seem as though I have been here for almost a year and in about two or three months I will be wearing my second service stripe. I had to laugh when you said that you and Bessie had been buying baseball tickets and that you were done buying them. Keep it up, Eva, as you may win sometime and when you do you will make up for what you have spent on them. I am getting near the end of my rope for news. There is no news here anyway, only the same old thing, day after day. I will close now, with the best of love to you and all the folks.

Your loving brother,

Private 1st Class Raymond W. Maker

June 24th 1918
Somewhere in France

My Dear Bessie,

I thought that I would write you a couple of lines as I have a lot of time and nothing to do. I suppose that Eva reads the letters I write here to you and it is kind of hard to write a couple of letters because they are about the same. I am taking life kind of easy the last couple of weeks and I am running around looking for the boys I know and looking at different towns, if they can be called towns.

The country here is quite pretty now and about all we can see are grapes growing everywhere. They are very strong for their wine and the wine is quite strong, too. I told Eva that I was going to try and have my pictures taken. If I do, you can have one. I hope that you are not working too hard these days. Are you reading the love letters in the newspaper? I suppose that you could write a nice one by this time (why don't you try it?). I wish I was back home, and I would take you for a ride in the machine and would not hit the river because I have driven quite a lot since then.

Well Red, how are things going with you these days and do you ever think of me away over the sea with no one to love me. I think it is kind of tough myself and if I only had someone to write to me, you know the way I mean, I would feel a lot better. Eva's letters are great, but they are only a sister's letters and a fellow wants more than that in this country. I don't know how I happen to write just what I did but I am feeling blue and have been for some time and you could cheer a fellow up a lot if you wanted to. Well, Bessie, I don't know of much more to write about this time. But if you will write to me I will be able to write more the next time. Please excuse this writing as this pen only works well some of the time.

Give my love to all the folks and some for yourself.

Private 1st Class Raymond W. Maker

25 June

We leave tonight, and I am glad we started at 8:30. And, we'll get to Rully at 12:15, and I am a little tired. Weather is fine and me too.

26 June

This is a good place. And very near Toul. Went into the church and all around. Grape vines are everywhere. Weather is fine and me too. Chick party, ho, ho, ha!

June 26ᵗʰ 1918

Somewhere in France

My Dear Sister,

Just a few lines to let you know that I am okay, and I hope that you all are, too. We are taking life easy the last few days and I'm feeling fine. We had quite a time – the Boche flew over at night and dropped a few bombs. Buy they did not hit anybody, but they sure made noise when the bombs went off. The town we are in is a very old one and very pretty and the big walls are all covered with grape vines. This is a great grape country. They have a lot of caves and there are all kinds of statues in them. They are very old. I hope that you and Bessie received my last letters. It seems good to have a little rest, but we have to drill a couple of hours each day just to keep trim.

The people here are nuts over our white bread and they send the kids out at meal times to get all that they can. We are the first Americans in this place and I guess they think we are nuts by the way we run around and yell. Three American nurses came up the hill where we are, and I guess we all went mad. I hardly knew how to talk to them. It has been so long since I have had a chance to talk to girls like that. I don't think I will have a chance to have my pictures taken here.

Did you get the money yet? I have met a lot of the boys from home in the (censored) artillery the other day. I guess that the Italians are doing some fighting now. I hope that you folks are all well and remember me to all. Everything is going fine with me.   Did Joe Barrett go into the tanks yet? Gary Holbrook, the Chief of Police's son is near here in aviation. I am going to try and see him. I think it is him because a fellow was there, and he asked for me. I have not seen Mullens for some time, but he is all okay, and so are all the boys. They have a good YMCA here, but they have nothing in it for me as does the Salvation Army. It has them all beat. They were going to have a dance here, but it did not go through. Can you picture us dancing with our hob-nailed shoes on?

I hear that we will be home by the 25ᵗʰ of November, but I have heard that stuff too many times. I would write to Bessie, but it would be the same kind of letter and I wrote to her and I am waiting to see if she has any love for me and then I can write to her, I guess. I always did like

Bessie. What is Dad doing these days? I hope that he is well, and Uncle Ed is, too. I have not heard from Kip yet. I should think that he would write to me. Well Eva, I must close for now and I will write again in a few days. Love to all the folks and the best of love to you.

Your loving brother,

Private 1st Class Raymond W. Maker

27 June

Today, three American nurses came up the street and all the boys went nuts. Weather is fine and so am I, thanks.

28 June

The Boche came over last night on a raid. Nobody hurt here. We drove East and then West today. Up on the big hill. Played a little ball and had good eats. Weather is fine and so am I. I hope that the Boche won't come tonight.

29 June

We leave here at 2 pm and hiked to Fariq and got on a flat car and am here. I am riding all night. Weather is fine and so am I. I felt a little sore.

30 June

Rode all day and got very near Paris. Got off at 3:30 and had a very long hike, about 20 kilometers. And, I am all in… foot sore. Got to our town at 2:30 am. I have done very well so far, keeping this book. Am well…weather is fine.

THE DIVISION REST AREA
(JULY 1918)

Upon relief from the line (July 25-26, 1918) the Division (less artillery, which rejoined some days later) marched to a place in reserve with headquarters at Merv-sur-Marne. There was some opportunity for recuperation, but training for open warfare, with target practice, was promptly resumed. From August 13 to 18, the Division moved by rail to the Châtillon Training Area, with headquarters at Mussy-sur-Seine. Here, replacements arrived, along with new clothing, and service animals.

Active training continued until August 25, when the troops began moving again, by rail, to the vicinity of Bar-le-Duc, as a unit in the 5th Army Corps.

ACTIONS DURING THE AISNE-MARNE (CHÂTEAU-THIERRY) OFFENSIVE

(JULY 15 - AUGUST 6, 1918)

Upon its relief from the Boucq Sector, the Division was transported by *decauville* (tramway) and marched to the area around Toul. Two days later it proceeded by rail to the vicinity of Meaux, with Division Headquarters at Nanteuilles-Meaux. On July 5 it moved into support positions near Montreuil-aux-Lions, and between July 5 and 8 it relieved the 2nd Division in the line just to the northwest of Château-Thierry.

The great German drive southward between Compiègne and Rheims had reached the Marne, for the first time since 1914. A renewal of the attack was to be expected and was intended to start not later than July 15, just before the great counteroffensive planned by Marshal Foch was to begin. The Division resumed active duty, taking over the hotly contested and hard-won line from Vaux to the vicinity of Bussiares. It formed part of the 1st Corps (U. S.), commanded by Major General Hunter Liggett, together with the 167th French Division and the 2nd Division (afterwards the 4th) in support. On the Division's right was the 39th French Division. For the first time, an American corps entered the line to attack as a unit. And in the lead of the corps, was the 26th Division.

In this so-called "Pas Fini" Sector, the Division suffered as it awaited the attack. With no system of trenches or shelters, the men were starkly exposed to enemy machine gun and artillery fire. The woods and villages on the line (Vaux, Bouresches, Lucy le Bocage) were drenched with gas. The vigilant and aggressive enemy allowed no respite in his attentions. On July 12 and 13, the Germans made a vigorous thrust against the 26th's positions in Vaux, held by the 101st Infantry, which beat back the blow as fiercely as it was dealt.

On July 18 the Division attacked as part of the general operation to reduce the Château-Thierry salient, and thereby relieve the threat to Paris. The 103rd and 104th Infantries took the lead. The whole operation was a very difficult maneuver, for the Division's right flank (101st Infantry) could not advance until the general line to the left had been brought abreast of its positions near Vaux. Furthermore, no other element of the Division could attack until the elements further to the left had advanced sufficiently to straighten the general line. The Division's axis of attack required two changes of direction to be made. The closest liaisons were required of every unit down to companies.

The attack of July 18 advanced the line of the 52nd Brigade successfully. The villages of Belleu, Torcy, and Givry were liberated in the advance. Hill 193, behind Givry, was twice won, but had to be abandoned because the French supporting troops had not been able to make rapid enough progress to secure the position. Heavy opposition was encountered, especially at Bouresches railway station and Bouresches Wood, with the enemy employing many machine guns and well-placed artillery fire.

On the afternoon of July 20, the Division's right flank (the 51st Infantry Brigade) moved forward, clearing the eastern part of the

Bouresches Wood and other pieces of woodland where enemy machine guns and snipers found ideal positions. By noon on July 21, the Division reached the Château-Thierry-Soissons road, where it halted briefly before resuming its advance toward the Épieds-Trugny position and its more distant objective, the Jaulgonne-Fère-en-Tardenois road. Later that day the advance guard (102nd Infantry) developed the enemy positions at Trugny and Épieds. An attack on the morning of July 22 made some progress but could not be sustained.

On July 23, following thorough artillery preparation, the Division attacked again, with the right flank endeavoring to clear Trugny Wood, while the left flank drove on Épieds and the woods behind it. Despite stubborn opposition and severe losses, the troops went forward steadily all through the next day. The attack was to have resumed on July 25, but the frontline elements of the Division were relieved.

Even a summary history of the work of the Division in the Aisne-Marne offensive would be incomplete without reference to the high commendation it won from the French Army Commander (General Desgouttes). His only criticism was that the American troops were too impetuous, that in attack "they went ahead too fast." The efficient work of the military police and of the services of supply and evacuation, through a week of continuous attack and advance, was highly praised, as was the audacious dash of the motorized 101st Machine Gun Battalion, which preceded the final forward movement of the infantry toward the Jaulgonne-Fère-en-Tardenois road in the same manner as independent cavalry.

JULY 1918

1 July

I think that I have done fine so far. And, I have been very lucky. We are about to go into some hard fighting now. I will try to do my bit, as best that I can. Slept about all day. Am all in, feet are sore. We move out of here tomorrow for near the front.

2 July

Found an old bucket and a well and I had a bath. Had a bath and washed my clothes. We move out after supper. Am feeling much better. Weather is fine and me too.

3 July

Did not move. Went over to see William Foley. He is in B Company, 59th Battalion. Got back and the gang had moved. A day that will not be forgotten.

4 July

Walked all night, 10 kilometers. And I am all in. I go into the front lines tonight. Got shelled going in. Walked until 2 am. Am well, but very tired.

5 July

Well, here I am in a very hot place. Shells landing all day and no good dugouts.

But, I will make it, if the rest do. Am feeling fine, but I am tired.

6 July

Today is the worst day I have had yet. They shelled us all day and the fellows around me are getting hurt. But, I guess that God is with me and looking out for me. Am tired and all in.

7 July

Today, is Sunday, and it is a little better, but during the night there was heavy shelling. Feeling a little better. Weather is fine.

8 July

Today has been another hard day. No feeds and shells all day. But all of us are brave and can stand it. Am feeling as well as can be expected.

9 July

Today has past very well. A few shells and a bunch last night. Am here for five more days. Hope to have good luck. Am well so far, as I know, but I am nervous.

10 July

We pull out tonight, thank God! Worked all last night under fire. Haveland and Covelaci were hurt bad, but luck was with me. Am about all in.

11 July

Stayed in the woods all day. And we moved in autotrucks about 8 miles. Am tired.

July 11th 1918

Somewhere in France

My Dear Sister,

I know that it has been sometime since I have written to you, but it could not be helped. Eva, I have moved around so much and been in places where I could not write. I am just back from a trip that never shall be forgotten, and I want to try and tell you about it, but we went through hell all night and God was with me and believe me, Eva, I did pray more than once.

I am feeling fine, but I am tired, and my nerves are not very good. I hope to get some mail now that we are out. It has been sometime since I have heard from home (June 12th) and I am still keeping my diary and wish that you could read it. I have some Boche buttons and other things that I will send to you later. We had a line run through a piece of woods and there was a German's leg stuck out and we had to take a couple of turns around it to keep the wire in place. Talbot was here and a couple of weeks ago I went nine kilometers to see William Foley – I was never so glad to see anybody. He just came over, and if you want to write to him his address is B Company, 59th Infantry USA AEF. He said he saw you a little while ago before leaving and wants to be remembered to you all. I have not heard from Mullens, but I guess that he is ok. I have been in the outskirts of Paris for a short time and I have seen the big tower and the strange double decked cars.

When I stop to think I have been here for almost a year now and will soon be wearing my second service stripe. I would like to have a couple of mince pies now. Did you send me the stuff that you were going to? I sent a letter with the note in it. I wonder if you get all of my letters. Sometimes I write a lot and other times I don't have a chance, but don't worry Eva, when you don't hear from me at times. I am writing this letter on the top of my mess kit – all that I have left of it, so I must get my eyes on another one.

Things go very funny around here at times. They had an air raid in one of the towns I was in and when the bombs went off they sure did make some noise, believe me. Sherman was right when he said that war was hell. But he never saw this one, so I don't know what he would say. I hope that you folks are all well and give my regards to everybody.

Is Kip still at home? I hope so, because it would make it better for Dad. I suppose that you are having good weather and hope that you are trying to tale life easy. I try to, but life is what one makes of it over here and I will try and write again in a few days and I will write to Bessie, too.

How are things going on at the store and how is everything? I have not had my pictures taken yet but am still in hopes. I am waiting to get some eats now and wash up and shave. I have not washed in eight days - can you beat it? Water was very hard to get where we were, just one canteen of water a day and it had to be carried over five miles. That's war all right. Well, Eva, I will ring off for now and as I said, write again soon. With the best of love to you and all the folks.

Your loving brother,

Private 1st Class Raymond W. Maker

12 July

Moved over the town and some of the boys were given war crosses by General Pershing. Met Frosty and was some surprise to me. Am still very tired. We move back tonight.

13 July

Stayed in the woods all day and it rained all day. I have had 5 letters and it makes me feel much better. I rested up a little, but I have got two sore legs.

July 13th 1918

Somewhere in France

My Dear Sister,

I received five letters the day before yesterday and I feel much better, but I have had some surprises; the 12th of July we went to a town to be decorated by a big general and I was walking by a big place with a pal of mine and I heard someone yell to me. I looked up and saw Ed Hay in the window and he came down and we talked for a while and I let him, and he called me back and said that my cousin Frostie was here. Well, by God, I was so surprised, but I could not see her until after five o'clock. I went back and met Frostie and had some talk with her. She was not allowed to talk with buck privates, but she did not worry. I am going to try and see her again before I leave here.

We have been having a lot of rain here the last couple of days. I saw William Morrow again and a lot of the boys. I received a letter from you, one from Bessie and Kip, one from Ted, two from Gladys and one from some friend of Kip's a Miss Rogers, but I do not know her. Frostie was looking fine and dandy, but I guess she likes the country just like I do (par bon).

We have had quite a hard time on the last trip to the trenches, but the boys all stood up very brave and there were some very brave deeds done, but us fellows never get any credit for what we do. They say it is in the line of duty and believe me, Eva, if I do say so myself, I have done some very hard jobs, but it is war, Eva, and they have to be done and it sure does take "war men" as you say, to do it.

I don't take any chances and I am careful, you can bet on that because I figure that I am coming home safe and sound at that. I am glad to hear that you folks are all okay and please tell Bessie I will answer her letter just as soon as I can. We have been feeding fine for the last few days and it seems good after only having one cold meal a day and we had to get that in the dark. I hear that Russia is coming back again. That will help out a lot and the Italians have given the Austrians a good time. We are all looking for the war to end very soon now, and I hope and pray I can eat my Christmas dinner at home. I am writing this letter on my gas mask and there are a bunch of our machines flying overhead. Once in a while I hear a shell, but outside of that it is a very peaceful country.

Kip says he wants to be here, but you tell him I would love to have him with me, but nothing doing, Eva. Make him stay there as long as he can. He has a good job. We call it a shell-proof job, twelve more days and I have been a regular soldier for a year. The time sure does fly by.

You said you were going to send me some pictures. I hope you have not forgotten them. We tried to have ours taken, but did not get a chance, but we will have a rest before long, I hope, and then we will all feel better. We have been in this dugout for some time. Eva, and I don't know of much more to write about. If you don't hear from me for a long time don't be worried because it is hard to write and get letters out at certain times like we have.

Give my love to the folks and the very best of love to you.

Your loving brother,

Private 1st Class Raymond W. Maker

14 July

Moved out at 10:30. The night of the 13th received two letters, walked about an hour into more woods. Stayed all night and it rained. No sleep. This is a hell of a war. Am well.

15 July

Am still in the woods. Have had two fine feeds today. Am fine and well.

July 15th 1918
My Dear Sister,
Somewhere in France

Just a few lines to let you know that I am all ok and feeling fine. I have not seen Frostie since I wrote last and I don't know when I will have another chance to see her. We have moved away from where I met her about an hour before I started this letter. I saw a balloon shot down and some of the burnt pieces came over near me and I have some. I would send it, but it would all break up. I will try and write Bessie a few lines. I received a couple of more letters several days ago with one from you and one from Ida. She said that Kip looked like candy to her. If he were over here, he would not keep his clothes looking very fine. I wonder what he would do if he had cooties? I strip down a couple of times a day and find a million or more, but we are used to them by this time, and if a fellow has not got a few he is not a soldier.

I heard that the Buck fellow that worked in the wardrobe got killed – shot right in his dugout. You remember Lund, the fellow who was in the tent and had a flat nose, he was with Buck, poor fellow, he got it too. One can never tell, Eva, what will happen, but we all watch out steps and we are careful as we can be, and if we get bumped off I suppose that it is God's will and for a good cause.

I hope that the war will be over soon, as we all have had enough. I saw Fred Hogden the other day and I had to laugh when you wrote what he had said in the paper. I know well where that town was. We have been there many times. There was quite a fight there and your nibs was there too. It was where Harry was taken. Hogden has it soft, driving around, and gets stuff by in his letters where I can't. To hear some of those guys talk, you people would think they had seen service, but they hardly hear the big guns go off. That's what gets us. Those kinds of guys writing home and telling all kinds of stories, who were never in a trench, but have jobs where they can get stuff by in their letters.

Yes. Eva, we get tobacco for our issue now and it comes in very handy, believe me, and it comes about when we are all out. Kip said Dad was away with some horses and that he was going to Maine this summer. Ida says that she is going down this summer, too. I wish that I could be somewhere near the water for a little while. I think that I have done very well in writing to you the last week or so and I hope that you got the fifty dollars I sent to you. I was going to send more, but I did not get, and I am still waiting for a furlough. It is getting quite dark here now and I must hurry up and put this to an end because we cannot have lights here. I hope that this letter finds you all right and all in the best of health. I cannot write to Bessie now because I can hardly see here now. Tell Uncle Ed to write me a few lines and also Col Esty. Well, Eva, I will say good night with the best of love to you and all the folks.

Your loving brother,
Private 1st Class Raymond W. Maker

16 July

We are still in the woods. Stood to all night and I had a bath today, so I feel better. Have been eating fine and am feeling fine. Very hot today. We blew up a brook with a bomb to get a little bath.

July 16th 1918
My Dear Bessie,
Somewhere in France

Just a few lines to let you know that I think of you and also that I received your letter ok and I am very glad that you can find the time to write to me. I wonder if you received my last letter. I hope that you will excuse this paper, but this is all I have, and it is better than nothing. A pal of mine addressed Eva's letter so I suppose she will wonder who it is from. He had a pen. I was telling Eva that I wished that I was near some water and so today we found a little brook and it was almost one inch deep and we took a grenade and fired it off in the brook and so made a nice little place to wash in, so I had a bath. We have been feeding fine since we came out of the trenches and we had doughnuts twice yesterday and biscuits for supper tonight, but believe me Bessie, we sure did earn it because we were only feeding once a day for six days and the food was all cold there because they had to carry it about five miles.

Oh, Bessie, it was a hard time and they shelled all the time with what we call whizz-bangs, and by God what a noise they make, but this is war and I wish that you could see the courage that all the boys had and stood up the way they did. I had a chance to get a lot of Boche stuff, but I don't want any things that have to do with the war. The only thing I want to bring home is my mess kit and I have about all of the towns covered on it that I have been in.

Well, Bessie, how is the world using you these days and you said that you hoped that you would be there when I get home and I sure hope that you will, and I am glad that Eva has you to help her out. I am looking for this war to "fini tout de suite." The Boche have started another drive and I guess that this will be their last. They will never drive Uncle Sam's boys, I can tell you that. We are not built to be driven by anybody, but we can drive them. I have been over here but have been very tired at times. The Red Cross gave us some smokes and chocolates today, but we never get anything free from the YMCA. The Salvation Army are the people that I tip my hat to over here and every place after this and they don't brag about what they do. Well, Bessie, I will close for now and hope to hear from you soon. Give my love to all the folks and love to you, too.

Private 1st Class Raymond W. Maker

17 July

Rained about all day, we are in a very hard place. Right where the Boche are making their drive. Am well and happy but would like to be home.

18 July

Our boys went over the top this morning. We hiked all night and we moved again tonight. I pray that God may be with me during what we have before us to do. Am well, but tired, but am in good courage.

19 July

Hiked all night and slept about all day. I don't know what is ahead of us tonight. Have made up some sleep so I feel better.

20 July

Am all in. Got gassed this morning. And so, I hiked back and here I am at our old battalion, waiting to go to the hospital. Smithy was with me and we came very near seeing the end, I guess.

21 July

Stayed at the battalion all night and moved to two hospitals. Rode all night in a truck and here I am in a hospital car and on my way someplace.

22 July

Rode all day and most of all night. It was a hard trip; my lungs are quite sore. But, I guess I will pull through all right. This is a fine hospital train, with 435 men on it.

23 July

Well, here I am at a base hospital. I got here at 7am. American nurses, the town is Contrexeville. And I am in a big hotel someplace and not very well. Got a box from the Red Cross.

24 July

Here I am in bed, and it seems strange not to hear any big guns.

25 July

Am still in bed and getting along fine. Am on half feed and having a hard time trying to sleep. Am getting fine care. Weather is fine outside, and I'm dying to get outside.

26 July

Am still in bed and I'm feeling kind of bummed. Lungs are very sore, but I'm getting along fine and getting the best of care. Hope to be out in a few days and back to my company. Raining most of the day. The boys are still driving them back,

July 26th 1918

My Dear Sister,

I suppose that you have been and are quite worried about me since the big fight has been pulled off and our boys were in it, but I am safe,

Eva, but I am in a base hospital. I got a little gas, have been quite sick and had a few burns and I am getting along fine and hope to be back with my company before long. I am getting the best of care here and by American nurses, can you beat it.

Well, Eva, I don't know what to write about or what I can say, but we sure did give old Joe Boche Hell (excuse my English). It was most all open country that we were in and we all had an idea that there was a fight coming off soon and one night we were hiked up to the line and in the morning the boys went over to make a call on the Boche and are still calling. Words cannot tell what happened because everything seemed strange and the dead and the wounded were lying all around, and shells were whizzing overhead.

Well, Eva, the next night I was about all in and we had a station near a dugout and a fellow by the name of Smith (my pal) and myself crawled into the dugout and had a sleep. Well, we had not been asleep very long when someone yelled, "Gas, Gas!" And I guess that they yelled too late because by the time we got our masks on we started to throw up and then everything went black for us. We came to a little while later and were sent to the hospital and then on to Base Hospital 31, and here I am. I could not ask for any better care and things to eat.

This noon we had squash pie and to night chicken. I am getting along fine, but I guess that I need a good rest. I have been here for five days now and the first day the Red Cross came and gave me a bag with cards, tobacco, a toothbrush and paste and quite a few different things that are very useful.

Now, Eva, I don't want you to fret about me because I sure am all right. I don't know if I've done right in telling you about this, but it's over with. We sure have got Joe Boche on the go and I am very sorry that I was not able to be with the boys in driving them. They are an awful bunch of cowards. When we get near them, they would yell "*Kamerad" and run away, but it was mostly "pas fini, Kamerad" with our boys.

There was some mail that came in the day I left, and I hope that there was some for me. Did you get the money I sent you, yet? Well, Eva, I must close for now as I cannot make this a newspaper and I will write in a day or so. Hope you are all well and happy. Love to all the folks and the best of love to you.

Private 1st Class Raymond W. Maker
*(Comrade)

July 26ᵗʰ 1918
My Dear Bessie,

As I have written a letter to Eva, and told her all about what happened to me, there is no need of telling you, but believe me Bessie, I sure have seen things that would sure make your blood run cold. I never thought that I could stand such things, but I think a fellow is not in his right mind when he goes through such things as we went through. There were Germans shooting at us from trees with machine guns and from behind rocks, but the only thing we thought of was going ahead and killing them. I am in a base hospital, as I wrote Eva, and am getting the best of care. There are American nurses here who sure do make life worth living after all. It seems very strange to sleep in a bed with white sheets and eating like we did at home.

I hope that I will be back with my company soon and help the boys along with their good work. Well, Bessie, how are things going at home? I wrote to you and Eva just a couple of days before we started our drive, but I don't know if the letters were lost or not. I guess it won't be long now before we will be home and then Bessie you want to look out for I sure have got someone to love me and help me make up for all of the hard days I have had over here. I wish that you could see me here, now resting in a nice little bed with a nice bath robe and pajamas. The place we are in was a large hotel and there are about three beds to a room and with electric lights. I lost about everything I had but, I have the little book you gave me and the kit that Eva gave me. I have the case she gave me, and I always carry it in my pocket next to my heart.

It seems strange to be away from the sound of guns and shells exploding, and it seems like living in a strange land. I have no idea just how long I will stay here but a little rest won't hurt me much. Well, Bessie, I don't know of much more to write about as I will write again in a few days. Tell Kip I wrote to him, but I don't know if he will get the letter or not as it went into the lines by a fellow that was going to mail it for me. I think I will close for now and I hope that this letter finds you folks all well. Give my love to all the folks and tell them all to write. Best of love from,

Private 1st Class Raymond W. Maker
PS: Tell Uncle Ed that the Battle of Bull Run was nothing like the one we were in.

DULCE ET DECORUM EST (1)

Bent double, like old beggars under sacks,
Knock-kneed, coughing like hags, we cursed through sludge,
Till on the haunting flares (2) we turned our backs
And towards our distant rest (3) began to trudge.
Men marched asleep. Many had lost their boots
But limped on, blood-shod. All went lame; all blind;
Drunk with fatigue; deaf even to the hoots (4)
Of tired, outstripped (5) Five-Nines (6) that dropped behind.
Gas! (7) Gas! Quick, boys! – An ecstasy of fumbling,
Fitting the clumsy helmets (8) just in time;
But someone still was yelling out and stumbling,
And flound'ring like a man in fire or lime (9) . . .
Dim, through the misty panes (10) and thick green light,
As under a green sea, I saw him drowning.
In all my dreams, before my helpless sight,
He plunges at me, guttering, (11) choking, drowning.
If in some smothering dreams you too could pace
Behind the wagon that we flung him in,
And watch the white eyes writhing in his face,
His hanging face, like a devil's sick of sin;
If you could hear, at every jolt, the blood
Come gargling from the froth-corrupted lungs,
Obscene as cancer, bitter as the cud (12)
Of vile, incurable sores on innocent tongues,
My friend, you would not tell with such high zest (13)
To children ardent (14) for some desperate glory,
The old Lie; Dulce et Decorum est
Pro patria mori. (15)

Wilfred Owen
Thought to have been written between
8 October 1917 and March 1918[vi]

27 July

I'm still in bed and it rained again all day. I guess that the damp weather makes me feel poor. Had a sweet pie for dinner.

July 27th 1918
My Dear Kip,
Somewhere in France

Just a few lines to let you know that I received your letter and I answered it about two weeks ago, but don't know if you will get the letter or not as everything was all mixed up for a few days. Well, Kip, we sure had some time, but I was not able to do so very much as I got a few smells of some gas and that put the KO onto me, but I saw all I wanted to. The fellow that was with me and myself laid in a large shell hole for about 30 hours running a telephone station, and then we got out and we went into the woods and found a dugout, and being about all in, we fell right to sleep and then the Boche started shooting over gas. We did not hear the shells and a fellow came running in with his mask on and yelled, "Gas, Gas." Well, Kip, we put on our masks but a little too late because it had gotten us before, while we were asleep. And if that fellow had not yelled when he did, I would not be writing to you now, I guess. So, here I am, in a base hospital getting the best care that can be given and I am feeling as good as can be expected and hope to be out soon.

Believe me, Kip, our boys did some work when they went over the top and you don't know what a feeling a fellow has waiting for the word to go over. The Germans would shoot as long as they were safe and when our boys got close they would yell, "Kamerad," but there was a pile of them that would never yell again. They are very dirty fighters and we don't take any chances with them. They are safer dead than alive. Well, they are on the run and I guess before they get through they will want to talk peace and I hope it will come soon.

Well, Kip, how are things going with you and are you working hard? You want to help Eva out as much as you can because you know how hard it is for her to keep the place going and I want you to take good care of yourself. I'd like to have you with me, but you are better off over there so don't get foolish. You are in the service and won't be in any draft so stay where you are. Well, Kip, I must close for now and write to me soon. Did Eva get the money I sent to her? Please give my love to all the folks and tell them not to worry about me as there is nothing to be afraid of. So best of luck and regards.

Your brother,

Private 1st Class Raymond W. Maker

28 July

Well, another day passes and I'm feeling bad. Lungs are very sore, and I cannot sleep. I'm still in bed. Rained about all day. Wrote home and read about all day. My burns are about all healed up.

July 28th 1918
My Dear Sister,
Somewhere in France

Just a few lines to let you know that I am getting along very well. I am still in bed but hope to be out soon. I hope that you got the letters I sent to you and Bessie and Kip. I suppose that you are working hard and that you are having hot weather. I suppose that Dad is away racing horses and having a good time. Gee, Eva, I would like to be home just now. I suppose that the home papers are full of news of the big fight. As the days go by, now, it does not seem that I have been here almost a year and I hope that when the year is up that we will be on our way home. I should write to Grandma, but it is so hard to write more than one letter home because they would be the same and when I write they are for you all, but you always come first for me. Well, here it is, another day and it is quite hard to lay in bed with fine warm weather like we are having outside today. I have not run across any nurses from home. All the nurses are from out Chicago way that are here.

I think I wrote to you that I met Frostie over here and hope that I will be able to see her again. I have not heard from Mullens or Collins or any of the boys from home yet, so I don't know how they came out of it. I had quite a bunch of things I picked up that I got from live and dead Germans, but I lost about everything except a little case and kit that you gave to me. Did you get part of the flare light and the other things I have sent to you?

I have been able to pass the time away reading about all the time and I have been lucky because I have money and can send out and get candy and other things. I am feeding fine and we have peas and corn quite often and dandy white bread and cake. It seems something like being on a vacation. I suppose that you folks are reading all of the war news.

Gee, Eva, but it was some fight. I have been in a few sham battles in my old days, but it had them all beat, and I guess now that the Germans don't think we are fooling. We sure gave it to them. Well, Eva, I don't think of much more to write about at this time, but I will write again in a few days.

Please tell all of the folks to write and give all of them my regards and best love from your loving brother,

Private 1st Class Raymond W. Maker

29 July

Am feeling much better today. A bunch of wounded came here today. Weather is fine, have been here a week now and expect to get my clothes soon and get out.

30 July

They have me still in a bed and the time is going by very slowly. Am feeling better and would like to get out. Am weak when I stand up.

31 July

Was outside today for the first time, but only to get a bath. They are keeping me in bed yet never saw such grat baths as they have here.

July 31ˢᵗ 1918
My Dear Sister,
Somewhere in France

As I am lying here having nothing to do, I thought I would write a few lines to you. I suppose that by the time you get this you will have received my other letters telling you how I happened to be here. But don't fret Eva, I am feeling very much better and I am able to walk around some, but I have not gotten my clothes yet.

This is a very nice place, in fact the best I have seen in France, yet. It was a summer place with large hotels and many springs where people come to get cured by the water. I guess that it cures all right. A couple of glasses beats all CC (cough and cold) pills I have ever had. The town itself is not so very large, but very clean and the best part of it is that I am so far away from the front lines that I don't even hear a gun. We are very well looked out for here by the Red Cross. They come around about every day giving to us. I suppose Dad is away having a good time and I hope he does.

And for you, Eva, I hope that you be able to have a vacation. I guess that you will need it all right. Did Jack Collins ever enlist and there are a few more around town that had ought to be over here. But when we get back, believe me, we will tell them slackers a thing or two and will make life kind of hard for them like it has been for us. It sure does make a fellow feel sore to think of them having all the good times and when they do have to join they go to work in some shipyard or something. Has Uncle Ed gone on any fishing trips this summer? I would like to go one with him. Tell him to write to me. I am going to write to Grandma today.

I would like to have Gramps over here and hear what he would have to say when he heard a big shell break near him. But, the boys all say that this is the only war and we have got to take care of it. I never got the pictures that you were going to send to me. I am glad that my transfer did not go through for the tanks now because we sure did turn out to be a lot of help and I was out all night during the hard shelling and there were two of our boys on the other end of the lines and a shell came in and smashed them up quite bad.

God must have been with me for I got the lines fixed up and not a hair hurt and then they say it was only in the line of duty (which is true), but War Crosses have been given for things much less than what we have to do sometimes.

Well, Eva, I will close now and hope that this letter finds you are all well. Love to you and all the folks.

Your loving brother,

Private 1st Class Raymond W. Maker

AUGUST 1918

The month of July will never be forgotten by me and I will have some great tales to tell, if I'm lucky enough to get home, which I hope I will. I have done fine, so far, in keeping this book up.

1 August

Well, here I start another month, am still in bed and I feel very good today. I wish that I could see some of the boys. Hope to be out of here soon.

2 August

Rained all day and I feel rotten. Am in bed and the time goes by very slowly. Roosevelt was in this place. I have written quite a few letters while here. Have been here almost two weeks.

August 2nd 1918
My Dear Sister,
Somewhere in France

As I have nothing to do, I thought that I would write you a few lines. I am feeling fairly well and just a few minutes ago the doctor came in and looked me over and said that I could have my clothes back tomorrow, so that makes me feel much better. We get all new clothes. It has been raining about all day and I just came back from having a fine bath. I wish that you could see this place, Eva, and the baths that are known the world over and they say that many rich Americans have been here. I don't know if and when I leave here if I go right to my company or not, but I would like to have a little rest and I guess that our Division sure has done enough work to get one, but I guess the only way to beat the Germans is to keep them on the go, and believe me Eva, they sure have.

I suppose that there are great headlines in the papers since we started in to fight and Joe Boche will never forget we know how to fight and when it comes to open warfare, well Eva, that's our own game, but it sure is hell out there with all the shells flying around and machine guns shooting, but somehow a fellow doesn't mind it so much. It's after everything is all over, when some great deeds done there and Eva, if a fellow is lucky enough to get home he will have some great stories to tell. I wish that it was over, and we were on our way back, but I am afraid that there is still hard work to do. But, it won't be long now, and here's hoping that I will be back to buy you a new Easter hat. I have had a good chance to make up for all the letters I have not answered, but I think that I do very well in writing to you and I hope you get them all. I try and write about every chance I get because you are about the only one to write any way.

I don't know, but I think that I have fallen a little bit in love with Bessie since I have been over here. I always did like her, and don't you know Eva, it is hard to be away over here without anyone to really love me. But, believe me, Eva, I'll make up for all of this lost time someway when I get home. Well, to change the subject there are three of us in a room here and one of the other two is a draft guy, and maybe I don't rub it in to him. He has only been over here since May and then I jump on him and tell him a few things and to make matters worse his folks are German people. So, you can see how it is. We still continue to feel very well and have the same good care. I am going to write a few lines to Bessie tonight, so I will ring off now. So, give my love to all the folks and the best of love to you.

Your loving brother,

Private 1st Class Raymond W. Maker

August 2nd 1918

Somewhere in France

My Dear Bessie,

I have just sent a letter to Eva and I have about 24 hours a day to do nothing else but to write and read. I suppose that Eva reads my letters to you, so I will try and not write anything that I write to her. This makes the second letter to you since I have been in the hospital and I hope that you get them all right. Well, Bessie, how is the world using you and are you still reading the love letters in the Boston Post? I was sorry you had to read them when I was home, but you know you had the Swede up there on the farm, so I thought that I had better lay off. I think that you told me he was drafted. Tough luck.

We had some mail come to our company the day I came here so I was out of luck in getting mine if there was any for me. It has been raining here about all day, but it is in for a good rain now. Well, here it is another day. Last night the doctor was in to see me and said that I could have my clothes today, so I expect to leave very soon and to be back with my company again. I suppose that things are going on in about the same old way at home and that you folks are hard at work there. They say that there is a fine YMCA here, but I have not had a chance to see it yet, and also a movie place. It seems very different living here and when I think of dugouts and trenches I wonder how a fellow gets along, but to tell the truth, I feel more at home in the lines than I do here, having been away from nice things for so long.

A fellow almost forgets how to act and when we get home we will all be like a bunch of wild men and will have trainers to tame us down so there is a good job open for somebody. I started this at 8 o'clock this morning so you see I was up bright and early. Tell Jap when he come out to the house, to take a few minutes of his time and write me a letter and please tell Kip not to forget me. He wrote me one letter and it took him a long time to get started. Does Hattie still work around there? Well, Bessie, I don't know of much more to write about at this time, but I won't forget you. Give my regards to all the folks and tell Uncle Ed and Mr. Charles and the Honorable CC Esty that I will have some great stories to tell them sometime. Ewell, Bessie, I will close now and don't forget to write to me. So, best regards Red, old top.

Private 1st Class Raymond W. Maker
PS: Is my Dad at home?

3 August

Weather has been fine today, and I expected to get my clothes. As the doctor said that I could go out but have not seen them yet. I am feeling well, but not so good. Wrote to Bessie.

4 August

Today is Sunday. I wrote home and played cards about all day. Rain and damp. No clothes yet and am feeling fine. I'm in a hurry to get back to my company, and also for the war to end.

August 4th 1918
Somewhere in France

My Dear Sister,
Today, being Sunday, I thought that I would keep up the good work writing to you. I was supposed to get my new clothes yesterday but have not seen them yet. I was just thinking are you getting the ten dollars I was having sent to you very month from Washington? You never said anything about it. If I remember I made out the papers last December and it has to start the first of January. I suppose it has not been time for your answer, if you got the fifty dollars I sent to you by the YMCA and if you have not received it, yet I will tell you once more to be sure the numbers of the check and the address to write to if you did not get it. The number was 48,870 and the address is YMCA 124E. 28th St, New York.

I expect to get a few letters when I get back to my company. I am feeling fine and I will be glad when I get out because you know I never did like to stay inside very long at one time. I have been here for two weeks now and when I came here I was looking at that lucky piece that you sent to me Eva, and I guess that it is a lucky piece all right, if it could speak it could tell some very strange stories. I may be able to have my pictures taken here. I hear there is a place and I hope so.

I wrote to Bessie yesterday and I hope you get the letters all okay. I will write to Dad tomorrow and if he is not home, send him some of the others he would be very glad to see them or are you a little miser with them as you said you prize them very much. I don't know who thinks the most of our letters you or I, and believe me Eva, I am glad to say that I have a sister like you and one that has been like a Mother to me since our dear Mother died. God, Eva, if she could only be there to see me come home, but I know that she watches over me and has a guiding hand for me over here.

It is raining very hard here just now. The weather is about the same as ours back home with all the showers, but no thunder and lightning. I thought the world was coming to an end a couple of weeks ago. I have not heard from or seen Frostie since I saw her. I forgot to give her my address and I don't know hers. I hope you folks are all well and having a good time. I am waiting for supper now and I am just a little bit starved. Well, Eva, three pages seem to be my limit, but I will write again soon. I will close now with love to all the folks and the best of love to you.

Your loving brother,

Private 1st Class Raymond W. Maker

August 4th 1918
Somewhere in France

(If Dad is not at home please send this to him).

My Dear Dad,
Just a few lines to let you know that I am still alive, and I am feeling fine. I said still alive because I have seen a few times that I thought that my days were about over, but I guess that I fooled them alright. I did get a little gas and I was quite sick for a little while. After I got to the hospital with the good care and nice beds to sleep in, I was not very long in getting well. I have been in the hospital for two weeks now, and I hope to have my clothes soon because I am well enough to go back and help the boys keep on their great work in driving the Germans back. It sure has been some fight so far and I think the Germans will never forget us Americans and they know now that we were not kidding them along.

Kip wrote me and said that you were away somewhere with your horses and so I wish you good luck and be careful Dad. You are getting to be an old timer and look out you don't get hurt. If you wanted a fast ride you ought to be here when some of the German shells come over and I guess that you would make a record trying to run away from them. They sound like a train of cars coming along, but they have not yet got my name on any of them, take it from me.

I have had fine care while here and it seems strange to have American nurses taking care of us fellows over here. I suppose that if you are away racing you don't hear much of me. This is the first time that I really had a good chance to write for some time and I have written to home about every day. There is no need of telling you about this fine place as I tell Eva and she can read what I write to you.

Well, dad, I suppose you still have the Hudson or some kind of car that I can run into Mrs. Gordon's hedge with because I sure am going to have a blow out when I get home. I have great hopes in being home in a few months now; things are starting to look very good, but we still have a hard job ahead of us. Well, Dad, I will close now and hope that you can find a few minutes to write to me as you can write a good letter if you start it because you know you wrote me one. Love to all the folks.

Your loving son,

Private 1st Class Raymond W. Maker

PS: I am sending you a piece out of a paper we get over here that tells a little story of the Salvation Army that I tip my hat to.

5 August

I had a fine bath this afternoon, and I had a chance to see a little of this town. I have not gotten my clothes yet but will get them tomorrow. Am feeling fair. Weather has been damp today.

August 5th 1918

Somewhere in France

Dear Uncle Ed, Mr. Charles and the Honorable C. C. Etsy,

I thought that I would write to you three old card sharks and let you know that I think of you all and miss having a little game. If you are still playing, watch out for Mr. E. H. because he sometimes thinks he has more than he really has. Well, I hope that this letter finds you all in the very best of health. I am feeling fine, but I am in the hospital yet, but expect to be out most any day now. I could not forget you folks. I suppose that you see by the papers what we have done and are doing, and I guess it was not very much like the war you were in Uncle Ed, and I guess that the Makers have a good name as fighters now. I have been expecting to get my clothes any time but have not seen them yet.

This is the best place I have been in since I have been here and when I stop to think I left the States a year ago next month, so I will be wearing two service stripes next month and it makes a fellow feel a little proud to wear them when there are troops coming all the time. It's a wonder that you three can't find the time to write me a few lines. I would be very glad to hear from you yourselves, so get to it. I suppose Charlie is still after his coffee and that Uncle Ed is after his coffee too. I don't know what you are after, Mr. Charles, unless it's some fine-looking nurse.

I have just come back from having a bath and I had a chance this time to see some of the old town and it is some place. I am going to cut a piece out of a newspaper we have over here, and I know that the picture is true because I see the same things myself. It was some fight, believe me, but I was unlucky and did not see all of it, but I saw enough. I suppose you are all taking life easy these days and I hope that this letter finds you folks all well. Give my regards to Mr. Joyce and the folks around there. I think that I will close now, and I hope that I hear from some one of you soon.

Best regards,

Private 1st Class Raymond W. Maker

6 August

Got my clothes today and walked around a little and found Mosley. Could not walk very much because my lungs are still quite sore.

August 6th 1918

Somewhere in France

My Dear Sister,

Just a few lines to let you know that I am about ok and the best of all is that I got my new clothes this a.m. I cut out some pieces out of the Stars and Stripes newspaper that you may like to look at, so I will send them to you with this letter. They are all true. I sent you one of the papers once and I wondered if you received it. It is a newspaper printed over here by our fellows and for us. I am going for a little walk after dinner and look the place over and I will be able to tell you more about it.

I wrote to Uncle Ed yesterday and I have written about every day to some of you folks and I hope that you get the letters all right. I wish you could see me now; I have a pair of English pants. They are about like what we wear in civilian life, long legs and I like them just fine.

It is starting to rain. I suppose it will rain all afternoon now that I can get out. Just my luck. I expect to be back with my company soon, now. I hope so, anyway. Captain Hobbs was very good to me. He came over and paid me before I left for here and the money sure came in handy. It will be a couple of months before I get paid again so I will have to go light. I only draw 114 francs a month – that's about $20, and it does not last very long over here with everything so high and the Frogs do love to soak it up. You see, I pay $6.60 a month for my life insurance and the $10 that I send to you just about gets me along although there are fellows that do not have half that much to spend. But, you know me Eva, and I might as well have a good time while I can here because nobody knows just how long one is lucky enough to stay on this nice green earth. That's the way I look at it.

Well, Eva, I don't know of much more to write about at this time, but I will write again soon. Give my love to all the folks and the best of love to you.

Your loving brother,

Private 1st Class Raymond W. Maker

7 August

Went to a show today in a real theatre and had a good time. And, I'm all in tonight. Feel quite sick. Weather is fine.

August 7th 1918

Somewhere in France

My Dear Sister,

Well, I have my clothes and I have been out for a little walk around the place and there must be ten hotels here and a very large spring that has a large glass dome over it and a large square with fine buildings all around it. It is very pretty. There are not many French people here as the Government is using the buildings as hospitals. I met a few fellows I know here and one from my own company. I expect to leave most any time now, but I am in no great hurry, but I do want to get back to my company and get my mail.

Well, here it is, another day. Yesterday afternoon I went to a real theatre and the YMCA put on a little show and the funny part was a fellow was singing a song and another fellow was playing the piano, when a French man came on stage and stopped the show for a minute and found out what he wanted. Well, maybe we all didn't yell, but what he wanted was to tune up the piano. So, the YMCA man said, "fat chance" and let the show continue. Can you beat it! That's the way with the Frogs – always butting into something.

I am not feeling quite as well as I have been. I guess the damp weather has a lot to do with it, but I am up and around. We can go outside from 1-5 and sometimes from 6-9. I had some postal cards, but I cannot send them to you. I was told that there is a band concert on for this afternoon, so I must take that in the theatre. The theatre is about the size of a grand ballroom and is very handsome. It is the first one I've been in over here. They have movies there, too, so I will have to see them all. These things are all done by the Red Cross.

I was wondering if you have received my letters all in a bunch? If you do, will you get a bunch all right, because I have written home about every day since I have been here. Yesterday, I bought a pound tin of chocolates and they were great. We can only buy them once a week. That's enough or I would be broke I guess.

Well, Eva, it is getting very near dinner time, so I must close if I want to eat and we get cake for dinner, so I cannot miss that. Love to all the folks and the best of love to you.

Your loving brother,

Private 1st Class Raymond W. Maker

8 August

Stayed in bed about all day. I'm not feeling very well. Got three letters from home. Rained about all day. Wrote home and I hope to be better tomorrow.

August 8th 1918
Somewhere in France

My Dear Sister,

I was out this afternoon watching a French concert. I say watching because I could not understand it to listen to and to my great surprise when I came home, there on my bed were three letters; yours of the 26th of June one from Gladys and one from Mrs. Farnum and you can believe me Eva, I was sure glad to get them. You see they sent them from my company and I think it was Captain Hobbs doings. You wanted to know about the flare light. Mr. Charles was right. They are shot out of a pistol and are something like a shotgun shell and they go up in the air and over the barb-wire and they sure do make some light and they last for over a minute. There are some kinds of flares that they drop from out of airplanes. I had to laugh when I read about Jap. Tell him to wait until the war is over. He can get a Ford cheap. They have so many here they will sell after the war.

I am glad to hear that Uncle Ed is still normal. I have heard from Dr. Perry and must write to him. I am sorry about Jack Collins. I have not seen Ed Collins for some time. If you see Charlie Foley again you ask him, if they take more chances in the Merchant Marines than we do, then why didn't he get into the Army? He would never take much of a chance. Mr. Charles says he wants to see me, well the same to him and many of them. I am going to try and send you the cards I told you about with this letter. I am very much caught up for news writing so much so, that I have nothing else to do. I had a couple of cups of nice chocolate at the YMCA this afternoon. I am going to play a game of checkers now. I am a regular guy at that game now and will write by and by. Well, here I am again, and it is the next morning and raining very hard. I had a couple of doughnuts for breakfast and I guess that I am getting to be some nice eater. I never ate them at home.

I am glad to hear that Dad is having a good time at the track and I hope that he has good luck with his fast horses. I suppose that Kip and Ben think they are about the works around there all dressed up in their summer OD's. Well more power to them. I do hope that Kip won't have to come over here, but still, I would like to have him with me in a way. I was wondering if they will draft Jap. If they do, you tell him that he should tell them that he drives a truck and can get a good job as he is a good man on a truck. Well, Eva, I don't know of much more to write about at this time, but I won't forget you and I will write again soon. Love to all the folks and the best of love to you.

Your loving brother,

Private 1st Class Raymond W. Maker

9 August

I am better today. Went out in the afternoon and I'm going to be in early tonight. Wrote to Gladys.

10 August

Went to a movie show this afternoon. It was very good. I'm feeling about the same, but still have pains in my chest. Wrote a couple of letters. Weather is not very good.

11 August

Today I had quite an examination. And I don't know how much longer I will stay here. But I should worry now as I am beginning to like it here. Weather is fine, and I had a walk.

12 August

Today, I walked around and I'm very tired. I still seem to have the pains in my chest. I guess that I got a good dose of gas and maybe it will be some time before I get over it.

August 12th 1918
Somewhere in France

My Dear Sister,

Just a few lines to let you know that I am getting along fine. I am still at the hospital and go out every afternoon. Yesterday, I was out and going by a nice house and there was a lady and her husband sitting out front and I stopped and talked with them and got along fine with my French. They asked me to come around again and I think I will.

I went to the movies this afternoon. They were fine. It is getting kind of tiresome staying here as I don't know anybody very well, but I don't think I am quite ready to leave as I have bad pains once in a while. But they sure look out for a fellow here and try to make him happy. I suppose Kip will have a birthday by the time you receive this letter and please tell him I wish him the best of luck. That's all I can do, and also please tell him not to get too many on a string as it takes a lot to buy Christmas things for them. I am about all in for news as I have written so many letters while here. I hope you will get all the letters I have sent to you. I hope you were not worried about me when we made our big drive.

I have not heard from Mullens or any of the boys, so I don't know how they came out. I suppose the next letter I get I will know if you received the money I have sent to you. I hope that Mrs. Farnum came out to see you. I wrote to her yesterday. I suppose that Jap has that auto by this time and is taking his lady love out to ride.

Well, Eva, here it is the 14th and I have not gotten this letter written yet. I have been out looking the country over every afternoon and it is a very handsome place. There is a band concert tonight here and I hope that I will be able to go out and hear it. I washed the floor in my rooms this morning and I keep it very clean (we have to anyway), and it helps to pass away the dull hours that go by so slowly sometimes. I don't know how much time I have spent trying to write this letter. I was thinking of home about all day, today. I hope that everybody is well, and I hope you are trying to enjoy yourself as much as you can. Did Bessie get my letters? I suppose that Dad is down Maine by this time and is having a good time. Well, Eva, I will close this up now as it is pretty near supper time and I will write again soon. Tell Dr, Perry that some time I will write to him. Love to all the folks and the best of love and happiness to you.

Your loving brother,

Private 1st Class Raymond W. Maker

13 August

I went to the movies this afternoon and they were great. They have band concerts tomorrow, so I will have to take it in. Feeling about the same. Met a fine little French girl, but I cannot ling-o with her.

14 August

Today, I walked around, and I will try to take in the concert tonight. Am feeling about the same. I want to get back with the boys once more, but I think it will be some time before I can.

15 August

Had an x-ray taken today. And, I went to the band concert tonight. It was rotten. Wrote home and I'm feeling very well tonight.

16 August

Everything is going on about the same. Went up and stayed with Mosley for a while in the afternoon. I'm feeling much better than I have been feeling. Wish they would let me out of here and go back to my company.

17 August

Went to the movies this afternoon and I received five letters yesterday and I answered them all.

18 August

Walked around this am and went to a band concert this afternoon. Am feeling bum today. Have a little touch of home sickness and I guess the weather is fine.

August 18th 1918
Somewhere in France

My Dear Sister,

Well, here it is Sunday again and I thought that I would be back with my company by this time, but I am still here. I sent you another Star and Stripes yesterday and I hope that you get it all right. I have written to Dr. Perry and Nucker and to Ben Littlefield and I guess about everybody since I have been here. I think that I will go to church today. It will seem kind of hard to leave my nice white bed and go back to the old life again but to tell you the truth Eva, I can sleep better in an old dugout or on the ground than I can here.

I had a couple of nice letters from Gladys. I got five in all. I can picture you with your book and maps trying to find out where I am. I am still waiting to find out if you received that fifty dollars that I sent to you, but I suppose that it is not time yet to hear from you. I sent it on the 6th of June. I suppose that Dad is down Maine by this time.

Do you go up to Concord very much now? When you go up again please give my regards and tell them I was asking for them and also tell Jap it is about time that he sent me a few lines, or does it take all of his spare time over near the spring. I hope that you will be able to read this all right as I have the habit of writing small again. I suppose that Jack Collins finds it kind of hard to be a soldier but tough luck. He had his chance but was too wise he thought.

You see I did not make any mistakes, but you should never have stopped me from going to Mexico because I would have had a good job by now. But, never mind Eva, I am not kicking. I hope that it won't be long before you find a good girl to help you and you tell Kip for me that he wants to take hold and help because if he doesn't he might be sorry.

Say, Eva, you remember the picture I used to have of you in your nurses' suit, well send me that picture in a letter if you can find it. I have a picture that us three had taken. Do you remember that time? I suppose Kip is a good-looking soldier or he thinks that he is.

Well, Eva, it is about time now that I can wear two service stripes on my right arm. Well, I am going for a little walk and I will be back later. Well, here I am. I did not go to church because by the time I got out I guess the service was about over.

They had a good band concert this afternoon and a ball game, but I did not go to the game because it was up on a hill and I did not feel much like walking up there. I was laying down in the park while the concert was on and gee, Eva, the music made me home sick and I am not over it yet. I went by a store and there were some dates, so I thought I would get a few. I did all right. Nine of them for ten cents.

Everything is very high here and I guess it is because everything is so swell. I will be glad when I leave here but somehow, they don't seem to be in a hurry to get rid of me. I have written you so many letters Eva that it is hard to think about what to write about, but I will do the best that I can.

I gave a fellow a couple of letters to mail the night before we went over the top. One was for Kip and one was for you, and I just learned that they were not mailed because the poor fellow is here with those bad wounds. He lost everything, and I am glad that you will never get them because I kind of felt that I was not coming back from there, but I fooled them. They have not got my name on any of their shells yet.

Well, Eva, it is about supper time and I think I have written enough for today, so I will close now. Wishing you all the best of luck and happiness. Best of love to you.

Your loving brother,

Private 1st Class Raymond Whitney Maker

19 August

Went out on a hike, but I did not pass the examination, so I'll have to stay longer. Went to the movies last night. Weather is fine.

20 August

Walked around the town and had some eggs and French fries, and it was great. I washed the dishes for the lady and had quite a time. Had to sneak into the hospital, no pass. Going on a hike tomorrow. Hope I get past the doctor.

21 August

Went on a hike and got past the doctor okay. And, now, I hope to leave here soon. Weather is fine and so am I, in a way.

August 21st 1918

My Dear Sister,

Somewhere in France

Just a few lines to let you know that I am getting along just fine. I have been out on two hikes and today I was passed as OK, so I guess that means I am all fixed up and can go back to my company. It seems as if I have been away from the boys for months. I got a dandy coat this morning. Somebody had it made over here and it did not fit, so I got it and when I get my two service stripes, and a wound stripe, and my service ribbons on, I will be fixed up and look OK. I was over to the movies the other night and there was a three-reel movie of Charlie Chaplin. Well, I laughed until I made myself sore. I hope that you got the papers that I sent to you and I will try and send you some more. I had a fine piece of squash pie for supper and last night I was going by an inn where they serve meals and I said to the fellow I was with, let's get some eggs and French fries. So, we went, and we had to wait so long that I went into the kitchen and tried to hurry them up and before I knew it I was up to the sink washing dishes. Well, Eva, I thought that I have washed a few at home, but last night took the cake. Well, I got my eggs and French fries in about an hour and I had to peel the potatoes at that, and she would not take only half of what they charge other people and I thought that was tough luck. I have done more reading and writing since I have been here, so don't worry Eva, if you don't hear from me as often as you have been.

Don't worry, because I will write every time I have a good chance and something to write about. I think that I have written about everything under the sun to you and will have to start all over again soon. Is Mrs.

Emerson still in town teaching school? I never heard from her. I would like to. If you only knew Eva, how much we all want mail. I hope that you have a girl to help you by this time and that you are finding the time to have a few minutes to yourself. One-year next month and I will have been here a year. Believe me, the time sure does fly sometimes, but I can't say that it has while I have been in the hospital. I am quite tired, so I will write some more in the morning. Well, it is after breakfast and I have my room all cleaned up and the hall all washed. I think that I will leave here tomorrow as the doctor said this morning that I was OK, and I am glad to get out.

My watch has just gone on the bum for the first time and I will have to wait now until I run across a place to get it fixed. There are none here. Well, Eva, I think I will close now, and I will write later. Love to all the folks and the best of love to you.

Your loving brother, Private 1ˢᵗ Class Raymond W. Maker

22 August

Went over another examination today, and I think that I will be able to leave here tomorrow. Saw movies this afternoon and a band concert tonight.

23 August

Well, I pulled out at last at 5:30 this morning, and I'm on my way. I don't know where I am going. Very tiresome riding all day. Got into Is-sur-Tille (Bourgogne) about 12 pm and I am very tired.

24 August

After running around, I got a place to sleep. I will beat it out today. This is a class rest camp for casualties. It is raining very hard here now. I pull out for God knows where at 10 pm. Chatillon-sur-Seine.

25 August

We rode all day and got into Chatillon at six pm. And, I'm all in…very tired. Go to my outfit tomorrow.

26 August

Well, here I am. Back with my old company once more, thank the Lord. I'm going to stay here for a while. The weather is fine here.

27 August

Have to get up early here, that is the only fault here. I'm feeling good, but I have no money. Weather is fine.

28 August

We move out of here in a day or so, and I don't know for where I go with this outfit. Weather is fine and me too.

29 August

Stayed around all day and the weather is fine, and I'm feeling good, too. Am taking life soft. We leave here tomorrow for the front lines.

30 August

We pull out of here at 3 PM. But, nobody knows for where. I am on a flat car with a Boche machine gun. Weather is fine.

31 August

Got to a place at 1 am, and I'm staying here with the baggage. Rain and I am tired. Stayed here all day.

SEPTEMBER 1918

A year ago, this month we left, and we came here like Norman Prince, dying to get France, and now, I'm dying to get home, I've seen a lot of active service and have been very lucky. This little book is about the only treasure that I own, and I hope that I will be able to get it home with me, if I ever get there.

-Raymond W. Maker

1 September

I am still with the baggage, but we leave tonight, and it rained all day. We are near the Verdun front lines.

2 September

Got into town at 10:00 pm, and I'm all in. Rain and slept on a hard floor. We expect to pull out of here tonight.

3 September

We are still here, and I guess that we will have to stay here for a few days more. Am feeling fine.

4 September

We are still here and very near the Verdun front lines. We start and drill tomorrow. And then we may be shelled. Am fine.

5 September

We are ready to move nearer the front. I guess that some are coming off the lines soon. Rained today and feeling fine.

6 September

We move out of here by train tonight. And, thank the Lord that I don't have to walk. Am fine, I got to our new place around 1 o'clock.

7 September

This town is about all shelled to hell. And we have to be very careful. Am feeling fairly well.

8 September

Last night the band came out to play and they stopped it two miles from the front lines. I guess they wanted to give the Boche a little concert.

9 September

I have a new job…mail clerk and I have been working quite hard for the last couple of days. It rained about all day. Am damp, and don't feel very well.

10 September

About the same old story. Rained about all day. Our boys are going over the top in a couple of days. Am feeling fine.

11 September

Rained again today. It is very muddy. I have been on the job with the mail and I must write home soon.

12 September

Last night about 12 o'clock, the bombardment started, and our boys went over the top. And they are going. Yet, they got 8,000 prisoners the first day. And more are coming in all of the time.

THE ST. MIHIEL OFFENSIVE
(SEPTEMBER 12-15, 1918)

As fast as they detrained near Bar-le-Duc, the Division's troops were marched north. The greatest efforts were made to keep their movement secret. By day the troops stayed under cover, and circulation was reduced to a minimum.

Concentrated first near Sommedieue, the Division moved almost at once to the so-called Rupt Sector, where, on September 5 it relieved the 2nd French Dismounted Cavalry Division. The line it took over extended from Les Éparges, on the left, through the Bois des Éparges, Mouilly, across the Ravin de France, and thence in a generally southwestern direction to Vaux-les-Palameix. Until September 12, the sector remained quiet. On that date, however, the great attack on the St. Mihiel salient by the 1st American Army, which had been long in preparation, finally began. At 1am, the artillery opened a heavy preliminary bombardment of seven hours. At 8am most of the infantry advanced, following a rolling barrage. The 102nd Infantry was held out in reserve with the 101st Machine Gun Battalion. The advancing troops made rapid progress, despite the enemy resistance.

The principal defense of the Germans was machine guns, well placed in concrete pillboxes. Artillery was sparse. All objectives were reached by the evening of September 12. The French, on the Division's right flank, had been equally successful. The enemy retired rapidly and appeared to withdraw toward St. Maurice-sous-les-Côtes, on the edge of the Woëvre plain. Since the Division's mission, like that of the French, was to drive the enemy off the high ground of the Côtes de Woëvre, the French division commander proposed that the Americans should act jointly and move on St. Maurice. This plan was on the point of execution when word came from headquarters that every effort must be made to reach Hattonchâtel and Vigneulles to effect a junction with the American advance from the south.

Just a half hour later, the Division's reserve troops were on the march, the machine gunners carrying their guns and ammunition by hand. The 102nd Machine Gun Battalion and 101st Infantry followed shortly thereafter. Pressing forward at top speed along the Grande Tranchée de Calonne, and through woods not yet completely cleared of the enemy, the 102nd Infantry entered Vigneulles at 2:30am on September 13. Detachments sent toward Heudicourt and Creue contacted the left flank of the 1st Division a few hours later. The 101st Infantry occupied Hattonchâtel. On the left, the 52nd Infantry Brigade cleared the high ground from Thillot-sous-les-Côtes to St. Rémy, and, following the retreating enemy with energy, established outposts far out in the Woëvre plain at Wadonville and Saulx, with patrols going even further.

The success of the St. Mihiel operation was complete. At comparatively slight cost, the Division accomplished the mission required of it to the letter, with all elements outdoing each other in zeal. Hardly less noteworthy than the night march to Vigneulles was the work of the engineers in making the wrecked roads passable for the field artillery, which was able to follow almost on the heels of the advancing infantry. A great store of artillery and engineer material was captured, as well as many prisoners.

13 September

Today, I went up to where they started the drive and in the Boche trenches they were all knocked to hell. A bunch of Boche came in tonight and one band was playing. It was great.

14 September

Today, we moved to another place. We are still on the drive and the place we are in is good and Bill and I have a fine place to sleep.

15 September

Well, today Bill and I and a couple of more pals went for a walk and it was some walk, 20 Kilometers. I received two letters today. I was very near Verdun.

16 September

It has been raining about all day. There is nothing to do, but to sleep and eat. And the eats are no good.

17 September

I went up to the front and brought back a few things. It has been a good day, today, and I feel kind of good.

18 September

Rained about all day, today. And it is the same old story. We got paid today and I got 42 francs. I wrote home tonight.

19 September

I have a fine place to sleep in, with electric lights and a fair bed. Wrote to Gladys.

September 19th 1918

Somewhere in France

My Dear Sister,

I thought it was about time that I wrote a few lines. I received two letters from you and one from Gladys a couple of days ago and I was very glad to hear from you. I am still with our company and I am having a fine time. Not much to do, only look after the mail and that is quite a job at times because I have to send it to all the fellows in the hospitals and to other places.

I am glad that Dad is home again and that everything is going on well and that Kip is still there. It has been so long since I have written with a pen and I cannot write the same. I will send you some things that I got in our last drive and believe me Eva, it was some drive and there were not half as many hurt as the other one I was in and I wish you could have seen the Boche that we got -8,000 prisoners in one day. They would not stand and fight and they all ran to us with their hands in the air and we got a large bunch of their stuff; trains and touring cars and trucks, oh everything and the funny part was that we got a lot of beer and it sure came in handy for the boys because water is not known on a drive.

I am feeling fine and dandy and I think that it won't be long now before we are home. I see Mullens quite often now and he is fine, and he looks well. I have a fine place to sleep in a little dugout and I have an electric light and my pal Bill Reardon and I are the only ones that live in it, outside of a few large rats and I think a skunk makes his home around near there sometimes by the smell of him.

We expect to have a furlough before long now and I am going to try to go to New Chateau, where we were last winter. I am still trying to have my pictures taken and I hope to have them soon. Everything is going on fine with me and I hope that you are all well. I have not heard or seen Frostie since I met her. We are not so very far away from Verdun and to hear the guns sometimes, well Eva, you would think it was a great thunderstorm.

I don't think that I ever told you about our trade mark. Everything in the Division is marked with it. It is the Yankee Division, the YD, and the Boche call us the Yankee Devils. I suppose Dad has a couple or more horses to race again. How is Jap getting along with his machine and tell all the folks that I am well and waiting to hear from them. I only had one letter from Hattie and that was up in Soissons last winter. That's where they are fighting hard now.

I have sure seen some of this country and believe me a few trenches, too, and it seems just like being at home to be back with my company, and to see the boys, but most of them are all out with the regiments, about 250 of them. All the boys you know are well and want to be remembered to you. I have not heard from Charlie Esty yet, but I had a letter from Joe Barette. The fellow I was with when we got gassed is still in the hospital. I guess he got it bad. I had to laugh when you said I should sleep in my gas mask. I guess you have no idea how nice they feel on a fellow. But, I sure have been lucky since I have been here, and I guess that little lucky piece that you sent to me is worth my life. Well, Eva, I don't know of much more to write about at this time and I will write a little more after this as I know how it is to wait for letters. Give my love to all the folks and the best of love to you.

Your loving brother,

Private 1st Class Raymond W. Maker

20 September

Went for a ride, about 20 kilometers. And saw a pile of things, airplanes going up, it was great. Played cards all night.

21 September

One year ago, and we left from the good old USA, and I have pit in a very hard year, and also a very lucky one for me. Have seen some very hard nights, but it is all in war. Rained today, and I am just hanging around. Most of the boys are back from the hospitals.

22 September

It is about the same old story. Everything is still, and it rains about all of the time. Am feeling fine and dandy.

23 September

Today, we got a stove. And I put it in our place and we have electric lights. And we have some place here. French fried potatoes at night.

24 September

Went to Recourt today and had a feed of eggs. And Bill got chased by an old Frog woman. It was sometime that we had.

25 September

Hung around all day, and not doing much of anything. Expect to go for a ride tomorrow. Am feeling fine. Weather is good.

THE MEUSE-ARGONNE OFFENSIVE (SEPTEMBER 26 TO NOVEMBER 11, 1918)

The Division remained in the line for some time after St. Mihiel apart from some minor adjustments. The position at Côtes de Woëvre was organized for defense against a possible counterattack. The Division passed under the command of the 2nd Colonial Army Corps (French), headquartered at Troyon-sur-Meuse.

The Division took many prisoners in raids. Enemy artillery fire, both gas and high explosive, inflicted considerable losses, while weather conditions and lack of shelter made the occupation of the sector very difficult. When the situation warranted, elements that could be spared were withdrawn to positions in rear, where better living conditions were available. It was at this time that the Division adopted its official insignia -- a blue Yankee Division monogram on a diamond of khaki color worn on the left sleeve.

On September 26, the Division carried out a heavy raid against the German positions at Marcheville and Riaville, as a diversion from the American First Army's general attack on the Meuse-Argonne front. Similar raids were executed by the other divisions at the same time. The 26th Division's operation, undertaken under cover of dense fog by a battalion each of the 102nd and 103rd Infantries, was strongly supported by machine gun detachments and the divisional artillery in the face of heavy enemy resistance. The 103rd Infantry entered the enemy lines in perfect order, while for the meritorious conduct of the troops of the 102nd Infantry, its regimental colors, and its 1st Battalion were decorated with the Croix de Guerre by Marshal Pétain in person on January 14, 1919.

Withdrawn from this sector, the Division passed into reserve, concentrated in and around the old battlefield at Verdun. On October 14, the 104th Infantry was transferred to the reserve of the French 17th Army Corps and relieved elements of the French 18th Division. In this role, on October 16 it took part in an attack on the Bois d'Haumont, supported by tanks. The following day, the Division Headquarters was moved from Verdun to the advanced command post near Bras, and the 18th Division's relief was complete. Its occupation of this sector (Neptune) continued through the armistice and until November 14. While the larger part of the American First Army, in conjunction with the French Fourth Army, was operating in the Argonne Forest, the 17th Corps (which included the 33rd, 29th, 79th, and 26th American Divisions, as well as three French divisions) was charged with protecting the army's right flank and extending easterly and northeasterly by clearing the enemy from his positions on the Côtes de Meuse above Verdun.

Holding this line, which guarded a main line of communications, was vitally important to the Germans. The successive reduction and occupation of strong points in the general position proved a difficult task. Conditions were hard on both sides. Influenza was spreading, the rain was almost continuous, and shelter was insufficient. The enemy occupied positions of great natural strength and was backed by powerful artillery. What estimate the enemy placed on the importance of the Verdun front may be judged from the following captured German document:

Vth Army Staff
Ia No. 10619 Secret

ARMY HQ.,
Oct. 1, 1918

According to information in our possession, the enemy is about to attack the 5th Army east of the Meuse and try to push toward Longuyon. The object of this attack is to cut the Longuyon-Sedan line, the most important artery of the Army of the West. Moreover, the enemy's intention is to render it impossible for us to exploit the Briey basin, on which depends in large part our steel production. Thus, the heaviest part of the task will once more fall on the 5th Army during the combats in the coming weeks, and the safety of the Fatherland will be in its hands. It is on the unconquerable resistance of the Verdun front that depends the fate of a great part of the west front, perhaps even of our nation. The Fatherland must rest assured that every commander and every man realizes the greatness of his mission and that he will do his duty to the very end. If we do this, the enemy's attack will, as heretofore, break against our firm will to hold.

THE COMMANDER IN CHIEF
VON DER MARWITZ
GENERAL OF CAVALRY AND ADJUTANT

To ensure that the Verdun front would hold, the Germans concentrated their best remaining troops. And that as many German divisions as possible should be pinned there, and thus diverted from the defense of the Argonne line, was the purpose of the higher command.

From October 23 to 27, 1918, the Division attacked. For the possession of Bois de Belleu, the 101st Infantry struggled desperately. To win a foothold on Hill 360 beyond the Bois d'Ormont, the 102nd Infantry gave its best, just as the Division's neighbors on the left (the 29th, 33rd, and later the 79th Divisions) had fought for every meter of ground between the American line and the river Meuse. The units' rapidly waning strength in effectives became critical, and no replacements, either of officers or men, were forthcoming at the time. On October 24, Major General Edwards was relieved and replaced by Brigadier General Frank E. Bamford. From October 14 to 25, Colonel H. I. Bearss (of the 102nd Infantry) temporarily replaced the indisposed Brigadier General G. H. Shelton's as commander of the 51st Infantry Brigade. On October 25 Colonel E. L. Logan of the 101st Infantry was replaced by Colonel H. P. Hobbs.

Following the attacks of October 23 to 27, the next few days passed without any action save patrolling to take prisoners. The divisional artillery, however, took heavy retaliation every day on the German battery positions and assembly points. But following the reported commencement of an enemy withdrawal on November 7, the Division, with its general axis of advance changed from east to southeast, executed a second attack on a wide front, toward the Jumelles d'Orne beyond the C Chaumont-Flabas line.

The attack continued daily up to and including the armistice, which took effect at 11am on November 11. The Division's battalions, reduced to mere skeletons of their full strength, pushed forward slowly but steadily in the face of heavy opposition, the enemy yielding only very gradually. At the hour of the armistice, the line extended southward from Ville-devant-Chaumont, past Cap de Bon Esperance and St. André Farm, to the vicinity of the Ouvrage de Bezonvaux, where the cessation of hostilities brought the active operations of the Division to a conclusion. The Division's stay in the Verdun sector was longer than that of any other (twenty-five full days) except for that of its neighbor, the 26th French Division. Its gained ground amounted to a depth of 5.5 kilometers, every millimeter of which was secured by the hardest fighting against the greatest difficulties.

On November 14 the Division was relieved in the Neptune Sector by the 6th Division and proceeded by march to the Eighth Training Area, where it established headquarters at Montigny-le-Roi on November 23. There it followed an extensive program of training -- drill, ceremonies, terrain exercises, and maneuvers. The troops were refitted, and many replacements arrived from hospitals and depots, restoring it to full strength. On the occasion President Woodrow Wilson's visit on December 24-25, 1918, the guard of honor was furnished by the 2nd Battalion, 102nd Infantry, with the band of the Engineers. The Division was represented at the Presidential Review at Humes by a provisional battalion of infantry, and detachments from the 102nd Machine Gun Battalion, 101st Engineers, and 101st Field Signal Battalion. President Wilson ate Christmas dinner with the commanding general and officers of Division Headquarters, and officers who had received American or French decorations.

On March 14, 1919, orders arrived for the Division's embarkation for home -- almost exactly eighteen months from the date its first units arrived in France.

26 September

Had a long ride today and I am tired. Tonight, there are heavy guns firing all night long. Some noise and I am feeling well. No news from home.

27 September

I went to a show that we had, very near the front lines and it was great. A Regimental band, and it was as good as I have seen in the US. I am well, and the weather is fine.

September 27th 1918
Somewhere in France

My Dear Sister,

I am writing this little letter in my dugout under two electric lights and a fire going in my stove and on my stove is a pan and, in the pan, there is some water getting hot to have some dropped eggs and they say that there is a war on. Oh, and I have the bread all toasted, and I have some potatoes all cut up and some bacon fat already for French fries. Can you beat it, and Bill and myself are the only ones that are in the place outside of our mascots which we have; a butterfly that has lived here with us and last but not least is a fine little skunk.

Well, Eva, the first round is over, eggs and potatoes, and I have more potatoes on the fire. I never tasted anything better. Everything is going fine with me. Since I have the mailman job, I have not had a letter from you or Gladys, but I live in hope. Last night I went to a show given by the boys in our Division and it sure was great. I have seen a lot worse than that one in the States.

Well, Eva, we put one of our lieutenants to rest, this after he got struck in neck with a piece of shell. We have been very lucky so far in this war. I have had only one letter from you since I left the hospital. We have a Chaplain for our company now and he is all OK.

I guess that it won't be very long before we start for home now as things have changed a lot in the last few months. Can you think of us being in towns that the Germans were in just a little while ago and using their railroads and things and one town that they had for four years and our boys were the first to get there OK.

Eva, if you could only see their trenches after the barrage. A fly could not have lived in them and they call it all war. I never thought I would have the heart to see such things but the sooner I forget them the better. Captain Hobbs was asking me how you were the other day and he wants to be remembered to you all. He is quite a Captain and Happy (Al Hopkinson) you know who drove for Wright, is a Master Sergeant of B Company.

I see Dr. Morrow and Braddway quite often now as I am in the same towns with them. The Germans flew over last night and let a few bombs go, but they landed in a field. I don't know of much more to write at this time, but I will write again soon. Give my love to all the folks and the best of love to you.

Your loving brother,
Private 1st Class Raymond W. Maker

28 September

I am a day ahead here, somewhere. I went to another show that was a show of real actors who played in New York. Three girls and two fellows. It made me homesick. We have quite a supply of wine, still in our home, now. Still feeling fine

29 September

We had chicken tonight and I fried it and French potatoes, and it sure was great.

September 29th 1918
Somewhere in France

My Dear Sister,
Well, this has been a tough drive. Here I am again with a nice fine chicken cooking on the stove and I am going to fry it after it is done and have some French-fried potatoes. I had received a letter from Kip today, but I did not see any of yours yet. But, I suppose that I will get them all at

once. The weather has been nice the last few days and I hope it will keep up because we are sure driving Joe Boche back to the Rhine all right.

I paid 14 francs for the hen that I got and that's almost $3.00, but I shouldn't worry when I can eat like that. There is a house next door to our dugout and the cellar is full of potatoes and they won't sell us any, so I have a long piece of wire and I stick it through the little window and so you see we have all the potatoes we want.

I was very glad to hear from Kip and I will write to him. How is Dad and what is he doing these days and is Uncle Ed still there? Did they ever get my letter, Mr. Charles and CC Esty? I did get a Framingham newspaper and there was a picture page that was very nice.

Everything is going on fine with me and I am feeling fine and dandy. I don't think I have felt any better. I just wish you could see the place that I'm in. I will try and tell you about it. The village is small and has not been shelled, so very much and in the back of the barn under a roof is our dugout and just room for two with a bunk on each side. We stole the stove and have a table and I put in the lights and they come on at 7pm, and last about all night. It's the best I have been in outside of the hospital since I have been here. There are not many French here, only two or three, but quite a few Frog soldiers.

I hope that Kip won't have to come over here. He may think it's fun, but I guess I ought to know by this time and I have seen enough. But, he will have a bomb-proof job if he does come, at some post I guess. I have not heard from Banks and Bill Nucker. I have never heard from him and tell Dad that in his spare time to please write me a few lines. In fact, the same to all at home. I have a chance to be a noncommissioned officer, but I think I will stick to the mail job for a while and will stand more of a chance of getting home. Mullens is okay and so are all the other fellows you know.

I don't know how long it takes to cook our chicken, but I am letting it cook for an hour and I am going to fry it in bacon fat and make a stew out of the broth. Can you beat it! Last night they had another show at the YMCA. They were all high stars from New York and they were great – a movie star and two who had played at the Follies and a couple of fellows. It made me homesick, but I am over it now. There is a very heavy bombardment going on and the gun flashes light up the sky greatly. But the noise, Eva, you can't have any idea that it's like and they call this War.

I hope that everything is all ok at home and that everybody is well. I had a letter from Grandma and she said they had a farm. What will Dad do with the house they lived in? I hope he doesn't sell it. Well, Eva, I don't know of much more to write about at this time, but I will write again soon. Give my love to everyone.

Private 1ˢᵗ Class Raymond W. Maker

30 September

This morning we had six dropped eggs and fried onions. And I guess that we are leading the life of a King. While this is the last month of the year over here, and it has been some year. We were lucky. That is all I can say.

OCTOBER 1918

1 October

Bill and I have a new way to dig potatoes. We have a wire and spear them in a cellar. Can you beat it!

October 1ˢᵗ 1918
Somewhere in France

My Dear Sister,

Well, Eva, I received your letter today and one from Gladys and I was sure glad to get them. I am glad that you all are all right and well because I am myself and I am getting quite fat again. I received a letter from Mrs. Farnum and I think she will be out to see you. She is very nice. Gladys was in the hospital about the same time that I was. I had to laugh about Jap and his car and I am glad that he is on the water wagon. I do hope that everything is going all right at home and I think that it won't be long before we are home now because we sure saw them on the run in all sectors.

I cannot just tell you where I am, but we have just driven them out of a place that they had held for four years, so read the papers kiddo. Read the papers and you'll see what the Yanks are doing. I will have to write on both sides of the paper as it is getting quite short. I think that I told you about seeing a show with real American actors in it.

Well, I saw it again, and a Mrs. Mayo, a playwright, was the head of it along with a couple of movie stars. It was fine, and it did make me homesick. Well, Eva, we wear our second service stripe tomorrow. Over here a year and me with my wound stripe and there are only a few in the outfit that can wear them, and I prize it too, believe me, because I sure did suffer for it.

But, now that's all over, Eva. I thought that I was done for and when they came to get me, the things that I had in my shirt pocket were mother's picture and the lucky piece you sent to me. And I know why I was spared. You don't have to worry about me Eva, because I have seen too many of the boys that wished that they had. Well, Eva, I got the order for you and if you note, I did not say how much I wanted. In a way it's up to you.

I have been feeding fine. I cook about all of our meals and I will never look a pig in the face again because it's bacon all the time and most of the time Tinned Willie. Do you know him?

I will send you another paper and I will see if I can have them sent to you every week and I will send you a German helmet soon. I have a pile of them but did not know that they could be sent home. I have had a lot of German stuff and I had to throw them away and up to Chateau-Thierry I lost about everything.

Well, Eva, I don't know of much more to write about, but I will sure write again soon. So, give my love to all the folks and love to you. Tell Dad I will write to him. Your loving brother,

Private 1st Class Raymond W. Maker

2 October

Well, today, we had some dropped eggs and French-fried potatoes. This is a hard drive. Got two letters today, so I am happy. Am well and fine.

3 October

Well, tonight, we had a little party. And Bill and I had some time. Flap jacks and French fries and wine. Oh, boy, some time.

4 October

A year ago, we landed in France. We had more French-fried potatoes, and I guess we are not staying here. Weather is fair and I'm feeling fine and getting fat every day.

5 October

Another feed tonight and the Boche came over and the search lights were great. Everything is okay and me, too. Weather is fine.

6 October

Went to ride on a truck today and we had a little party at night. One case of beer. Am fine and the weather is kind of cold and damp. And we move out of here soon.

7 October

We move tomorrow, don't know where to. Rained all day, and I hate to leave here. Am well and the weather is bum.

8 October

Moved today, and here we are at last at Verdun. And it is some place. Tunnels everywhere. All forts. The town is all shelled to pieces.

9 October

Went around today and I'm looking the place over. It is some place. Put on the stove on our new place. Weather is fine and me, too.

10 October

I put in lights today. And I walked around some more. Saw several air battles. Weather is fine and me, too.

11 October

Everything is about the same, and there is talk of peace. But, I don't take much stock in it, yet.

October 11th 1918

Somewhere in France

My Dear Sister,

Just a few lines to let you know that I am well, and I hope that you all are the same. I have left my nice little place that I was in and now I am in a place that has about the greatest history in this war and after I leave here I will tell you all about it. We are living in tunnels and they are wonderful and there are about 8 miles of them and everything is in them and I have been lost several timed so far. I have some things I will send you when I leave here. I think I will lay up for the winter after this drive. I have a dandy German machine gun belt that I will try and send it, too. I am still on the mail job and I will try and keep it because I have had enough of the trench life for a while. Almost seven months without a rest.

Jack Nelson is here with me too, now, and I see the old boys quite often. I wish that you could see this place, Eva. It has a large place, but the houses are all knocked to pieces and only the church steeples are about all you can see above the ground. I have some glass out of one of the stain glass windows and a piece of the alter. I put lights in the place where we are, and I brought the stove we had with us, but we do miss our potatoes.

Well, Eva, everything is going on fine with me and I guess that it will be over very soon, now, as we sure have driven the Germans back on all fronts and have taken many prisoners into our camp. And, I guess that Austria is about done. The weather is not very good the last couple of weeks. It rains about all the time and it is cold.

Al Hopkinson kids me about the time you told him about that the boarder and he said you ought to see me now. Did you forget to send me the pictures? I had a fellow take a few pictures of me, but it is hard to get them fixed up because we never get into a large town where there are people that are not fighting.

I got another letter from Kip and I will have to write to him. I am just waiting to get Dad's letter. They have some very large guns here and when they go off they shake the place, believe me. Well, Eva, I don't know of much more to write about at this time. I am sending you a newspaper with this letter. Well, I will ring off for now and will write again soon. My love to you and all the folk.

You loving brother,

Private 1ˢᵗ Class Raymond W. Maker

October 12

Rained all day, am still leading the life of Riley. Am well. Good war news tonight.

October 12ᵗʰ 1918
Somewhere in France

My Dear Kip,

Just a few lines to let you know that I am well and that I received your last letter all ok. I hope that you are all well. I am in a place now that I have been waiting to see ever since I have been here. The town was a large place once, but it is all shot up now, but I wish that you could see the tunnels. It would make Boston look sick and they are all lit up and have a church, theatre and bakery and everything else all around the forts. It is a place the Germans have been trying to get ever since the war started and they had the bloodiest battle here, ever fought, so you may have an idea as to where I am. I guess it won't be very long before the war is over now. I hope so, because I am sick of it; over here so long and everything is so hard to get, and the prices are so high. So, stay where you are, Kip, if you can because I have not received Dad's letter yet, but I have a little one for him with yours.

I just got a slip for you to send me a box. I don't know what you can send me, as the box is so small, but chocolates are about the best or fruit cake, and please be sure and do it up good and strong. I had a machine gun belt to send home, but they would not let me send it. Things look very well for peace here now, but we are still hitting them and hard, too. We are not taking any chances until we have them across the Rhine River. I wish, in a way, you could be here with me to see the great things I have seen, but these were things I never want to see again. But it's all in war and thank God that it's not all the time or we would all go nuts.

Well, Kip, I hope to be home soon now, and when I do we will have some time, just think of me over here for a year and going over the top three times and I am still able to write and I feel better than I ever did, but there was once that I thought I would never see it through. I was lying in a shell hole one time for four hours before I could get out. Machine guns were shooting every time I moved, and I had to wait until dark to sneak out and nothing to eat for three days.

I will write again in a few days because we expect to leave here and then I can tell you all about where I am. Last night they dropped a few 14" shells over here and they made a little larger noise than a .22 rifle, believe me. Well, love to all the folks and write soon.

Love and good luck.

Your brother,

Private 1st Class Raymond W. Maker

13 October

Great news today and I hope it's true. Am well and it rained here all day. No news from home.

14 October

Got a few newspapers and read them all. Rained about all day. Made some money tonight. Some of the boys leave tomorrow. Am doing well.

15 October

Got two letters from home and, best of all, one from Dad. Everything is well, and the weather is bum.

16 October

Well, I had a bath and I have winter underwear and an over coat. Rained all day and I have a bad cold, but I will pull out.

October 16th 1918

Somewhere in France

My Dear Dad,

I received your very welcomed letter yesterday and believe me I sure was glad to get it. I don't know of much to write about because everything is about the same and I am well, but the last few days I have had a bad cold, but I am better now. The weather has been bum and it rains about all of the time. Yesterday, I went down to a church that is, or was, one of the greatest in the world and under it were some shower baths, so I had my first shower since I was in the hospital and I feel like a new man now, after I have gotten rid of about a million cooties.

I guess that it won't be very long before the war is over. This place I am in was very hard hit and everything is all under the ground and they have some great tunnels. I had a letter from Charles Esty yesterday and one from Eva. It is so hard to write when we are in a sector so long because after you write a couple of times, everything is the same. I have a dog with me now and he is quite a pet. We are still fighting, and I guess our Division will be until the war is over, but believe me Dad we have some Division, too.

I was having a bath yesterday when Frank Sibley, the Boston Globe Reporter, came in and we had quite a talk and one thing led to another and he asked me if I knew Frostie, and we at once got really friendly. He thinks that the war will be over soon. Everything is going on just fine with me and I still am on the mail job. I have it quite soft. There are days that I don't have anything to do but sleep.

I hope that you have noticed that I have never sent home for money that I can remember, but I have been quite lucky. You see we have to have a little game now and then and I have not been paid for four months now and I have almost ten hundred francs. That is almost over one hundred and eight dollars in our money. How's that and saying nothing of what the boys owe me. But, I suppose you won't think much of it, but believe me, Dad, if you were here over a year and had to put up with what we have and never knew when you may get bumped off, you would do the same thing.

I am writing this near my stove that I have carried with me. I have been very lucky to get this job. I had a chance for a non-commissioned officer's job, but I had to go back to the front lines. But I have done my bit and paid for it, too. So, I am going to stay here at the Battalion, if I can and be sure of coming home because the war is too near to an end to get it now.

Well, dad, I will close now and hope to see you all very soon. Best of love to all.

Your loving son,

Private 1st Class Raymond W. Maker

17 October

Everything about the same. Some of the boys leave tomorrow for the front lines. Big time coming off soon. Am well.

October 17th 1918

Somewhere in France

My Dear Sister,

Just a few lines to let you know that I alive, but have had a little cold, but it is about all better. Al Hopkinson is sitting on the bed side next to me and telling me about some of his hard luck stories about a Master Sergeant, but we will let it go at that. Jack Nelson wrote to you yesterday and the card he sent was of the new church near Bois de Belleau. I wrote to Dad yesterday and believe me, I sure was glad to get his letter. I owe Kip a letter and I will write to him tonight.

I am still on my post office job and I am sending you a newspaper with this letter. You know Hoppie? He used to work for Wright. I guess that we will all be home soon, now, Eva, because things look very well. We are still keeping up our drive and we won't stop because that is what beat the Italians, when the Germans told them that they would make peace. We won't trust them yet.

There was a big Boche Air Machine that came over just now and maybe there were some shots taken at him, as shells were flying along with machine gun fire. He got away, as far as I know, as it is quite hard to hit them in the air with anti-aircraft guns. But, C'est la guerre, as the Frogs say. It means "That is war." It's a great saying with us when we buy anything, and we kick on the price then we all say it.

I don't know if I ever told you about the fried bread we have. They make a batter and they fry it in bacon fat and it is great. Try it and canned Willie is done the same way, too. Fine dishes in the army.

Well, I got Charles's letter and I was very glad to hear from him. Tell Mr. Charles and Uncle Ed that it's their turn now. I don't expect to hear from Jap. Well, Eva, I don't know of much more to write about, but I will write again soon. Best of love to all.

Your loving brother,
Private 1ˢᵗ Class Raymond W. Maker

18 October

Bill left today. Rained about all day. Am well and am not doing much of anything.

19 October

Well, some boys left today, and some came in. They go out tomorrow. My cold is better, and I am well.

20 October

Our boys started the drive and it is hard going. Am well and the weather is fine.

October 20ᵗʰ 1918
Somewhere in France

My Dear Kip,

I received your letter today and one from Nucker at the same time and I was very glad to get yours. I am pleased that you are writing a little more than you have been because you don't know how much better it makes a fellow feel to get mail from home. I don't believe that this war will last too much longer. We are in a very hard sector this time and I don't know if the Boche will fight or not. I have written to Nucker and I have a letter from Gladys to answer tonight. I wrote to Eva and Dad a couple of nights ago. I hear that there is a lot of that Spanish sickness going on over in the States now. I wonder if it came from here. I am sending home another newspaper. I think that they are great. If you can find a Saturday Evening Post dated July 27th, and look on page 3, it's the first story, and read it you will know all about where we are and all about this place.

We have been having some bum weather and the mud, well it is some mud. I have had quite a bad cold, but I am all over it now, thanks, and I have got be very careful because I don't want to get sick after getting that dose of gas that I got. Eva said that I should wear my gas mask when I go to sleep, but if only she knew how much we like them she would quickly change her mind. This would be a good war only for the gas and we get it here about all of the time. Last night they sent over some large shells and one of them hit our place and knocked the corner off the place and it made some noise. I suppose that you look about the candy in your new suit but wait until I get home and I will show you how to be a soldier. What would you do if you had to sleep in shell holes, all covered in mud, and sleeping on old bed sacks, all lousy and go for days without hardly anything to eat. Oh Boy, you don't know that you are well off and to say nothing of the constant shelling. Stick to your job, Kip, old-timer.

The war is about over, anyway, and in another place, you would be sick looking at the sights. I have got some nice medals, but I don't want to take a chance and send them home because they are too nice to get lost in the mail. Everything is going fine with me and I hope that everybody is well at home. I don't know of much more to write about, but I do hope that you will keep up your good work in writing to me. I will ring off for now as I have one more letter to write. So, love to all the folks and take good care of yourself.

Your brother,
Private 1st Class Raymond W. Maker

21 October

We are about ready to drive on the Boche. It is still raining. Mullen got hurt and so did quite a few of the boys.

22 October

Our boys started the drive and it is hard going. Am well and the weather is fine.

23 October

The drive is still on. Quite a few of our boys in our company are hurt. Am well and weather is fine.

24 October

Last night I heard General Edwards talk and he leaves the Division. Am well. The drive is still on.

25 October

Played cards and made a few francs. Weather is bum. Am well, and Bill came back. Mullens got hurt the day before yesterday.

26 October

Had a bath today and I feel fine. Weather is raining and cold. Wrote home and I'm well.

October 26th 1918
Somewhere in France

My Dear Sister,

I thought that it was about time that I wrote a few lines to let you know that I am alive and well and also that I received a couple of letters from you; one yesterday and one the day before. Well, Eva, we have been at it very hard and we are in the hardest of the fighting now and thank God that I am not in the middle of it and when I stop to think of what my pals are going through it makes me feel as if I was a coward.

Eva, they sure have been through hell and that's no lie – mud and shell holes to lay about in for two weeks and the shells and gas that the Boche send over is awful. Mullens got hit in two places, but I don't think he is very bad. Don't tell his mother, and we had three in our own company get bumped off the last week. I guess that the Boche won't let us go very far, but we sure pay them for all they do to us, by about five to one. I don't know if I will have to go up to the lines or not, but I would be very glad in a way to help out in any way because I know how and what they are up to.

But, we'll break through. We get a little ground every day but pay for what we do get.

I met Dr. Glass today and had quite a talk with him. He wanted to be remembered to you and all the folks and he told me where Frostie was and I am going to write to her and when I hear from her I will send you her address. I had another dandy bath today and my cold is about all better now.

I don't like to talk much about the war, Eva, and I know you must be very restless about me, but don't worry because I look out for myself. Of course, I have to take a chance. I am in a war and we all surely can't get through it all ok, but leave it to me, I have a four-leaf clover and I will put it in this letter. I got it here. We expect to have a Division release very soon and I hope that we will have a rest then. We have not had one yet. I don't think I will send the clover. It might break my good luck.

I owe a letter to Kip, but it is so hard to write and when we are at the front anyway. I will try and write to you again tomorrow as I am tired, and it is kind of cold. So, I will hit my feather bed. I stole it from a house that the people moved out of and brought it with me. What do you know about that?

Well, Eva, give my love to all the folks and the best of love to you.

Your loving brother,

Private 1st Class Raymond W. Maker

27 October

Played cards and hung around all day. They shelled very hard here, today. Wrote home and I'm well.

28 October

About the same old story. No relief yet. And the boys are all in. I'm fine and dandy. Weather is fair.

29 October

Had a great trip to??? And stayed all night in the YMCA. Leave tomorrow to go back to the same place.

30 October

Got back about 7:30 and it is quite cold and raining. Am fine. Played cards all night. Paid today. Am well.

31 October

Had another ride today and had some wine. First in some time. Have done fine with this book. Am well. Weather is fine.

NOVEMBER 1918

1 November

I have a new pen, so I will try and write this book over when I have some time. Am well and things are about the same. Played cards all night.

2 November

Rained about all day and I wrote home. Played cards at night. Am well. Got a letter from Gladys today.

3 November

Today is Sunday and I received a letter from Bessie. Played cards at night and made over 500 francs. Weather is fine, and I have a little cold.

November 3rd 1918

Somewhere in France

My Dear Sister,

I am trying to write on this type-writing machine, so you will have to excuse all of my mistakes. I wrote a letter a couple of days ago, but I gave it up as a bad job. First of all, I am very well and happy and I hope that you all are too. I had a great trip a couple of days ago. I went to a large town about 25 miles from here. We left here at noon and stayed a while at the YMCA all night and got back here at noon the next day. We took some fellows down to take a train for a school they are going to. I sent you a German helmet and a piece of a machine gun belt and a few pieces of glass that I got out of the window of a large church that was all shelled.

Our boys have had it very hard in this sector and I guess that we have lost more men here than in all of the other sectors put together, but as the days go by it brings us nearer to a close. I suppose that you folks are starting to have some cold weather there now. We are here, but I would rather that then all of the rain and the mud that we have had the last couple of months. I must tell you about the YD that we are wearing in our Division. We are wearing them on our left shoulder and they look like the one I made at the top of this page. I see in paper that the Turks have given in and Austria want to very badly.   I hope so because I want to eat my Christmas dinner at home. What do you say about that? I think that I have done very well so far at this letter, don't you? My arm and my fingers are getting a little bit tired now, but I guess that I can stick it out all right.

It has started to rain here again, and the mail has just come in, so I will have to lay off for a little while. I heard a truck and thought it was the mail, but it was not the mail truck, so I will try and write some more. I heard that our Division was going back to the States soon. Now I think it will be tough luck if we do.

We have a fine place to sleep in here and the eats are quite good now, so we have no chance for a kick while we are having it the way we are. But, believe me, Eva, it sure is hard and very hard up on the lines and I have often wondered if you folks at home really knew what the boys over here are going through.

I think that I am getting all of your mail ok now. Did you get my letter with the money order in it? I hope so. I suppose that you all went to the Brocton Fair, but I bet that there was not the crowd that they had a couple of years ago. But I bet that I will see it next year if they have it.

I think this will be my last letter on this typing machine and in fact I am done now. I have a new pen, and this is the first time that I have used it. It sure is much faster for me to write with a pen than with the type-writer.

I had a letter from Gladys a few days ago and she said that she would have to have her tonsils taken out. I suppose that Dad is still looking for an auction somewhere and that Uncle Ed and Mr. Charles are hard at work. Eva, I think that I will close for this time, but I will write again, soon.

Love to you all,

Private 1ˢᵗ Class Raymond W. Maker

4 November

Walked around and got to the YMCA. We expect to have a big drive very soon. Have a bad cold and expect to go over the top with a bit of luck.

November 4ᵗʰ 1918
Somewhere in France

My Dear Sister,

Just a few lines as I have written a couple of letters to you in the last couple of days and I am sending you a money order for a few dollars that I don't want to carry around with me and as it is getting near Christmas it might come in handy to you. I wish that you would buy a few things for all the folks for me and send Gladys something and Bessie if she is there. I received a letter from her last night and I will try and write tonight. We are going to have some big doings in a day or so and we will be in it so don't worry Eva, if you don't hear from me for a little while because I will be where I may not be able to write.

Everything is going on fine with me. I have a little cold, but it is not too bad. I saw a German come over today and he brought down one of our balloons. It was a great job, but I don't think he got away. I guess he got his. I wish that you could have seen it, He dove right down out of the sky and opened up with his machine guns and set the balloon on fire. I think that this will be our last fight. I hope so. I think that Austria has given in.

Well, Eva, I said don't worry about me because I sure will take care of myself and come through all OK. If I don't leave here in a day or so, I will send home some more money as I think I will need it when I get home because I will have to have new clothes and all of those things. I hope that you folks are all right and have not had any of the sickness that is so bad there.

Our boys have been very lucky here so far very few cases of sickness compared with all of it there. I hope that Dad is all OK and that

Uncle Ed is still at his job. I wish in a way that he could see this war. It is
so different from the one he was in I guess. Please ask him if he ever went
along the road and all of a sudden, a German machine gun opened up from
the skies and a Boche flew right down on you. That's what I call war and
when they dropped bombs, by God, Eva, one never knows what it is over,
here.

Well, Eva, I will say night and trust to God that I will have good
luck and that I will see you all very soon. Best of my love to you and Dad
and Kip and Uncle Ed and Mr. Charles and all the other folks. I hope you
won't worry over this letter Eva, but you know one can never tell what
will happen in this war. Well, I will close for now, so the best of love.

Your loving brother, Private 1st Class Raymond W. Maker

November 4th, 1918
Somewhere in France

My Dear Bessie,
I was very glad to receive your letter yesterday and I thought that
you had forgotten all about me, but I see that you have not. I wonder if you
are back with Eva again, or just back from a little trip. I am feeling very
well, and I hope that you are yourself. We are in about the worst sector
that we have been in yet, and we have gained ground, but Bessie we have
paid very dearly for what we get. But now we have them on the run again
and I guess this about the end of it all. I hope so, because the Turks are
out, and I think that Austria is out now, too, and I am sure that the Germans
could not lick us alone, never mind the rest of our allies.

I am in one of the most noted parts of France and I wish that you
could see the place. The town was a quite a large place and it has a very
large church in it, but the place looks about like Salem after the fire, but
only worse, all knocked down to the ground in pieces. They say that there
are about 12 miles of tunnels here and I guess there is. I have been lost
about a dozen times, so far and they are some tunnels, believe me. Some
have electric lights and steam heat and are very well drained, but on the
other hand the trenches are the worst and all mud and water, and they are

not very deep, and it was at one time only about 50 yards between the two lines and we could see the Germans and pick them off great.

I sent Eva a few things, but I will send you a German helmet when I get a chance. I have a great job here now taking care of the mail for our company and some days I don't do anything but sleep all day long. I saw a Boche get one of our balloons yesterday and it was a great job that he did. The balloon was up quite high and the fellow inside jumped out (they come down on parachutes like they do at the fairs.) And then the balloon caught on fire, but we have another one up early this morning that doesn't bother us very much, but I guess that they got the Boche all right. We are getting a pile of their flying machines. Well, Bessie, I don't know of much more to write about at this time, but I hope to see you all very soon. So, give my love to all the folks and love to you.

Private 1st Class Raymond W. Maker

5 November

Yesterday afternoon I saw one of our balloons getting hit down by a Boche flying machine. Weather is fine, and things are very quiet here now.

November 5th, 1918
Somewhere in France

My Dear Kip,

I thought that it was about time that I answered your letter, but I have been putting it off so many times, so here I am. I am well and dandy and hope you are at home, but I have not heard from home for quite a little while. Things look very well for peace now, and with the Turks and Austria about on the way out and believe me Kip we sure have been giving the Boche some hell the last couple of months, but we sure have paid for it. I guess that Mullens got wounded in two places in his back, but I have not heard from him since he went to the hospital, but I guess that he is coming along all OK. We have had 3 men killed in our company at this sector and quite a few hurt and they go and come from the hospitals all of the time and it keeps me quite on the go, trying to keep their mail straight.

I have a bombproof job here, but believe me, Kip, I have been through enough to earn it. I don't know if I will go back with a line company or not, but if I do I have a chance for a noncommissioned position, but it is too near the end of the war to take any chances. Things are going fine with me and we are eating just fine.

I sent home a few things and there was a machine gun belt and you can make a belt out of it. I have one with a buckle on it. Well, Kip, this is a couple of days later and I guess that we have a job ahead of us in a day or so. I sent home some money yesterday and told Eva to help herself with what she wanted. I think that this will be our last drive and that we will all be home very soon. I had a letter from Bessie a day ago and I wonder if she is back helping Eva and if Eva is sick. Well, Kip, I will close for now and wish you the best of luck. Love to all the folks.

Your loving brother,
Private 1st Class Raymond W. Maker

November 5th 1918
Somewhere in France
My Dear Sister,
Just a few lines to you as I am not doing anything, and I am all washed up and shaved, but to tell you the truth, I don't know what to write about. First of all, I am well and dandy and I hope that you all are at home. I have not left here as I expected to, yet, but may move almost at any minute. What do you know about Austria and I guess it won't be long before Germany does the same because all of the allies will be on her heels and us Yanks have got them going some, believe me. You can bet that I am proud to be a Yank and a regular one at that. I have hopes of eating my Christmas dinner at home, but at the same time it takes some time to move a Division and I suppose that they will try and keep us here about as long as they can because our Division gets about all the dirt and hard luck. We have so far been in five different fronts and have had fights, and three drives and no rest, and other outfits have had furloughs, so that's what I call hard luck if there is any. But, I will pay up for it believe me, when I

get home and I guess that I will have a couple of months of good rest and good times before I go back to work. No more Army for me.

I know I have always been strong for it, but I never want to wear the clothes any more FINI (no more). I have not heard from Mullens yet, but I guess that he is OK because he was not hurt so bad that he would die. We have lost quite a few boys in our company since we have been over here, but we have been quite lucky on the other hand. I was quite surprised to hear from Bessie, thought that she was married or something.

I hope you get the things I sent home and also the money, and don't be afraid to use it because I would only spend it if I had it here. I think that I have done quite well in saving money over here and in fact I have saved more than I would if I was at home. What sayest thou? Well, Eva, I must fill up my paper and have a smoke and hear the line of talk that is being spoken throughout here. I will write more later.

Your loving brother,

Private 1st Class Raymond W. Maker

6 November

They started to shell us today. Nobody was hurt. It rained about all day and I am about over my cold. Wrote home and sent home $100 for Christmas things for all.

7 November

We are still waiting to go up front and I guess that we will go up very soon. Am well and fine. Rained about all day.

8 November

Today I had and saw quite a time. The Japanese Royal Family were here, and one of them came up to me and asked me if I was an American soldier. We expect to go up tonight.

9 November

We went up at 2 am, this morning. And I ran wire and went over the top at about 8 am, and I got caught in a German artillery barrage. I was lucky, a small shell fragment got to my leg, only a few others hurt and killed. Am all in, tonight. Such mud. Leg wound not serious.

10 November

Stayed back today, thank the Lord, and went to church tonight. Weather is fine. Boche came over and got one of our fellows. Fine after a good sleep and feed.

November 10th 1918
Somewhere in France

My Dear Sister,

You can see that this letter is written a few days later than the one on the other side (November 5th). I was out to the front and I am back again now. We had quite a time up there in the mud and on the hills. I never saw such fighting before and yesterday morning we were right after a battalion that was getting in formation to go over the top and we were up on a hill just a little away from the Boche lines and then the Boche put over a barrage on us and it was some barrage, believe me.

They killed a few, but the fellows I was with got out lucky. I wish you could have seen the way we ran for the shell holes. We ran wire right behind the infantry and we had quite a job. I wish you could have seen the place, Eva. It sure was worth seeing, but as I said, the mud was terrible, and it rained all day long to make matters worse.

Well, I guess the war is about over and I heard that it will be over at 4PM, but I don't know. But, I hope to see you all very soon. I am quite tired, and I am going to wash up and shave and then hit my old feather bed for a while, so I will write again in a few days. Best of love to all.

Your loving brother,

Private 1st Class Raymond W. Maker

11 November

Today is one of the happiest days of my life. The War is off, thank God. And all the boys have gone about half mad with joy. Bands are playing all day and at night all kinds of flares in the sky. The best part of it all is that our Division was in the front lines and we were at Verdun, the greatest place in history.

12 November

We expect to leave here soon, now. Met Bus Ochard today and went for a ride. Am well and it is quite cold here now.

13 November

The Sixth Division is moving in and I think we move out tomorrow. Am well and it is quite cold here now.

14 November

Went up to the front line and buried one of our fellows (Walls) who was killed the day before the fight ended. Move today about 25 kilometers and it is quite cold here. Am well.

15 November

Well, today is my Birthday. (Issencourt) and we are in hopes to get home very soon. Had some wine to celebrate my Birthday and I'm feeling fine.

16 November

(Pierrielette) Stayed in place all day and we move out tomorrow. The weather is very cold, and we are on our way home, thank God.

17 November

(Nancois Le Petit) Got into this town about 10:30 and it is very cold and no place to sleep. Got by okay and I am well. Move out tomorrow for Veachateau.

18 November

Moved to Bouvee-sur-Barboure and stayed all night. Moved out in the morning and I am a little tired. But, I feel fine. Weather is fine.

19 November

We stayed in a town by the name of Bonnet, but it was too cold to walk around, so we hit the hay. It is quite cold, but I am well.

20 November

We slept outdoors all and it sure was cold. We have some hike, but we will hit our place tomorrow. The name of it is Odival.

21 November

Moved into our camp around 1 pm, and it is a fair place and I'm about all in. We have had quite a hike from Verdun, but I'm still with them.

22 November

Went to a great town next to us. It is the largest place we have been in yet. The weather is still cold, and it gets colder all of the time. The large town is Nugent.

23 November

Today was kind of bad and cold. Went to Nugent and had a feed of pork chops. Am well, but I need a bath.

24 November

Today is Sunday and not much doing. We are all restricted to camp. Hard luck. Have not had much of a chance to write home, but I'm doing well. Put on new clothes this afternoon.

25 November

Worked hard all day with the mail. Rain and cold all day. Got a couple of letters from Gladys. No news from home. Am well.

November 25th 1918

Somewhere in France

My Dear Dad,

I thought that it was about time that I sent you a few lines, but it's the truth, it is the first chance that I have had for some time because I have been on the road for nine days. We walked all the way from Verdun to where we are now, in a place called Odival and we are taking life kind of soft, but believe me Dad, we sure need it after Verdun. Of all the places I ever was in, that sure was hell from the start to the end and thank God it's over. We have been on the go since last February 5th, when we went to Soissons.

I understand that we will be home very soon now, and I hope so. I think we are getting ready to move now. I will never forget Verdun as long as I live. The very last day I buried one of our lads in my company and it sure was hard. He was killed the day before it ended, and the Germans had not left their lines and they were only a few yards away watching, so you may know how I felt.

I have not heard from home in some time and I am wondering if you are sick or something. We are eating fine and yesterday we had oatmeal and this morning something like cream of wheat. I think, Dad, that I have been very lucky over here and I sure have been through enough. I guess that I can sit down with Uncle Ed and talk war with him and make him open his eyes.

They say that we are to be home by Christmas, but I don't know. We can tell of the places we are in now and the places we have been in, but as for myself I want to forget them for a while.

I am feeling fine. I have had a little cold, but I am all OK now. I wonder if Eva got the one hundred dollars I sent home. I had a letter from Mullens and he is getting along fine. He had a couple of holes in his back. He may be home before me, as I will come home with my company.

I don't know of much more to write about at this time, but I just wanted you to know that I am OK. I will write more in day or so. Love to you and all of the folks and I hope to see you by Christmas.

Your loving son,

Private 1st Class Raymond W. Maker

26 November

Everything is about the same. It rained about all day and there is lots of mud. Am well, no news from home.

27 November

Went to Nugent and met Lowell. He is in the 5th Army and we had quite a time and some time coming down the hill. Mud.

28 November

Today is Thanksgiving and there is lots to be thankful for. We had a good feed of pork and pie. It rained all day and we were to have a football game.

29 November

It rained all day and I worked hard. Have a little cold. Went to Nugent and had a good feed of pork chops and fried potatoes. Am doing fine.

30 November

Had a bum inspection, today, the first time the sun has been out for some time. I went and had a bath and got some clean underwear and a new pair of pants. We are hopes of going home next month, but I don't know what to think. I saw Brandway and some of the other boys and I'm feeling very well tonight.

DECEMBER 1918

One more month to go and I have had some time this past month. Have had some trip over to France, but I don't know what it will cost me, but why should I worry.

Raymond W. Maker

1 December

Everything is fine, and the weather is fine, but it is muddy, and I'm going on my furlough and can hardly wait. I'm fine.

December 1st 1918
Somewhere in France

My Dear Sister,

I am writing you a few lines and I am wondering if there is anything the trouble at home with you. It has been some time since I have heard from you, so I wrote a few lines to Dad. Everything is fine with me and we are having it much better in a way, but we had so much rain and mud, Eva, it has been very bad. We are in a town called Odival and it is a few minutes away from a town called Nugent, and if you look on the map you will find it near Chaumont. We don't expect to stay here very long, and all the talk is that we will be home soon, or in the army of occupation, so I don't know what to think about it, but I know that we are safe from the shells and believe me that is something that sure helps. We sure have had a hard time while we were here. We have been on five fronts and have had fights in all of them, and the last one, Verdun, that was surely hell.

I wrote and told you that I was going up to the front lines and I sure did. I went over the top with the 101st Infantry and we sure got into a fine German barrage, believe me, but there were only a few of us were hit and killed, but I will not talk about that stuff now. We have been on the road for nine days and have been here for about a week. It is a rotten place, but we go to Nugent and have feeds, but we sure pay for them.

I hear that we are to be home by Christmas, enough said. I am still in the mail job and it is quite hard now because all of the boys are back in the company and we have about 170 now. We had 185 when we left Neuf-Chateau, last winter. We have lost quite a few boys killed in our company and thank God it's all over. You must have felt great when you got the news that it was over of course. Peace is not signed yet, but it's about the same. We have them tied so that they won't be able to fight. The town we stayed in last winter was Noncourt and then I went to Soissons and all around up there. Then we went to the Toul front for about two months, and that's where the Germans got Harvey as a POW. Then we went to Chateau-Thierry and the I went to the hospital and got back to my company just in time to hit her up again and that was in Saint Mihiel, and then we wound up at Verdun, and Eva, we never retreated one inch in all of the fights we had. We have had fifteen battles and have received sixteen citations and if there is any division outside of the 26th, the old Yankee Division, I want to know where they keep it! We tried to have a good time, as the 26th had a good dinner of roast pork, but it was nothing like last year, but I will soon make up for all the lost things. Well, Eva, I will close because I am going to have a bath. Best of love to all and a very Merry Christmas.

Your loving brother,

Private 1st Class Raymond W. Maker

December 1ˢᵗ 1918

La Bourboule, France

My Dear Folks,

Here it is another day but raining. It seems that it rains about all of the time in the country, but thank the Lord there is not the mud here. Well, I got up for breakfast this morning and we had eggs and hot chocolate and then I went and had a bath. Some bath, I'll say. The hot and cold water comes right down from out of the mountains in large pipes and the water is so hot that you have to put cold water in it. I have heard of these things before, but I have never seen it until now and it makes me feel fine. I am going to take a bath every morning while I'm here. There is not much to this place except the hotels and most of them are closed up now.

There are two divisions here, ours and the 35ᵗʰ, and there are quite a few fights because when they get together they try and tell us what the war was and when it comes to that there is not a division in France that can tell war to the old 26ᵗʰ. We were the first American division to take over a front for ourselves and the first to have a fight and never had a furlough until now and we did the best work at Verdun and when I say Verdun, I mean Hell because it sure was and the Frogs say you never saw war until you hit Verdun and there are many that hit Verdun that will stay there.

We don't get any credit here because we are nothing but "National Guard," but by God we showed General Pershing's regulars up and we took our objective two days before Pershing ever got started and that was up in the St. Mihiel sector and that was never in the papers. And they gave the regulars credit for getting the 8,000 Germans that we got. Oh, there will be some great stories to tell when we get home. I never have had a chance to have our old 26ᵗʰ talked about the way the Marines (another big joke) were, and the regulars. They talk about the Marines at Chateau-Thierry. Well, I was in the 1ˢᵗ Battalion of the 104ᵗʰ Infantry on the 5ᵗʰ of July when we relieved the 5ᵗʰ Marines at the Belleau Wood and they told us that they held the Germans there, but they were afraid that we could not, because we were not guards.

Well, I put in 7 days of hell there and we were shelled day and night and many poor fellows I saw got killed there in the woods and then we were relieved for 5 days and we went and were decorated for the second time by the French. That's where I met Frostie and then we went back and on the 18th of July is the day that we could not hold the Germans. So, we drove them 17 kilometers the first day and in all 22 miles, and that's about 32 kilometers and we are only National Guard! General Pershing told us last winter at Neuf-Chateau that we were nothing but school boys, but what's the use? Some people are thick and hate to admit the truth. Well, I did not intend to make a speech, but it makes me mad to hear those bastards try and tell what they had done.

I sent home some more postcards today, but I have a few for tomorrow. I am going to take a trip tomorrow and will get some cards from that place, Mt. Dore. They have the largest YMCA in France there, so they say. Well, I think that I have done very well and will try and write tomorrow. So, the best of love to all the folks and hope to hear from you soon.

Merry Christmas and Happy New Year to all.

Private 1st Class Raymond W. Maker

2 December

Things are about the same. Weather is fine and me, too. No news from home yet. But, I'm in good hopes. I wish it was Wednesday, so that I could leave here.

3 December

Got up at 3 am to start on my furlough and got to the station and stayed there all day. I went to supply and stayed there all night.

4 December

Am still waiting. No train yet, but we are feeling fine. We hear all kinds of news, but it is all off, but I hope not.

5 December

Well we are here, yet I guess that we will leave tomorrow. We are head over heels in mud, but I am feeling fine.

6 December

We are on our way, started at 3:30, in 3rd class cars. Rode all night and it is quite cold, but I don't mind that as long as I am on my way.

7 December

Am still on the train and we have seen some great country. Big mountains. I guess I will have to change my mind about France

8 December

Well here we are. Got here at 8 pm and got to our hotel. Oh boy, some place. And feed of chicken and a great bed. And I will have some sleep. Mountains are around us and they sure are fine.

9 December

Have spent a very fine day here and things are fine. Wrote home and it rained here a little. I hope that it stays as good weather while we are here. Am fine and dandy thank you.

December 9th
My Dear Kip,

I have written three letters today, so far, and so I will try and write you a few lines to find out the real truth of what the trouble is at home. I have not heard from any of you for over six weeks and with all the sickness that has been going on over there I am afraid that there is something wrong. So, Kip, tell me the truth because I don't like to be wondering and thinking that there is something wrong.

I wrote to you all and told you where I am and all that was of any interest so far, but I will try and write you a good letter.

I think that I have received all of your letters (three) and I hope that are still at camp and are having a good time. I am fine and dandy and I sure do feel fine to be out of the trenches, and to tell you the truth, Kip, I sure thought two days before the war ended that I had seen my last day.

I don't like to write about it to Eva and dad, but it is all over now. I went over the top with the 101st laying wire and they laid down a barrage on us and I went into a shell hole and a shell landed a few feet away and broke, killing two fellows who were trying to get into the hole with me and covering me with dirt and mud. That is one of the few of them believe me, I said my prayers and then a fellow in my company almost to the side of me after we started again, got picked in the guts with machine gun bullets. Well, I guess that I am lucky that's all. The fellow who was with me when we got gassed is now at home. He got it worse than I did, and I guess that if I tried really hard I could have gone home too. But I came to play the game and I played it to my best. I did not get cold feet, but after I left the hospital I went back to my company and I even ran away from the replacement camp without any of the people there knowing, to make sure that I got back with my old company.

Oh, I could tell you many tales, but I will tell you when I get home. I have seen some awful things in the war and at the same time I have seen some wonderful things in France. I am in what they call the French Alps and they sure are wonderful. I have yet to see what they call the great French dames, I have not seen one yet that I would want to fall in love with yet, so I am watching my step and I am taking good care of myself and I think that is what makes me feel so good and why I have been so lucky.

I never did expect to see home many times, but now I expect to be home very soon. I don't know just how long it will be. I don't want my third service stripe in this country, but I am very near to it now. It does not seem as though I have been here so long and have been at war, but it's all in life. Well, Kip, I will close now and wish you all a very Merry Christmas and Happy New Year. And be sure to write to me.

Your loving brother,

Private 1st Class Raymond W. Maker

December 9th
My Dear Folks,
La Bourboule, France

Well, here I am on my furlough at least and believe me I am in some place. It took us two days to get here and it looked at first that we were out of luck because we waited three days before the train left and thought that they had called the furlough off, but here I am as I said before.

We rode in third class cars and sometimes in box cars. There are about 1200 out of our Division here and there are a bunch of the 35th Division here as well. To start with, we arrived here at 6:30 at night and we had to wait until we had our passes all stamped and our hotels all picked out and then it was about 9 pm. Well, they took us to a hotel called the Splendid and it sure is some place. I have a room with a fellow by the name of Marden who worked at Jackson's farm. We have two dandy beds and a feather bed and hot and cold water right in the room.

We are all of the second floor and last night when we got washed up, they gave us supper and it was fine chicken soup and bread and bear. (I can hear Dad saying something now). Well, I hit the hay about 11 pm, and I think that I sure did sleep and this morning when I awoke I stretched out my arms and wondered if it were all a dream. I did not get up for breakfast. I had a fine dinner and here I am at the YMCA which I must say is the best ever. It is a very large place and was the second Monte Carlo. And they say that I sure will spend money here. They have reading and writing rooms and a theatre and a band going on about all of the time and all kinds of things to eat.

We have not been paid for two months now and we have our pay books here with us and we hope to be paid tomorrow, I have quite a few francs coming to me. Well the country is very beautiful here – We are in a large valley and there are great mountains all around. I have seen such a wonderful sight before. I have not taken any walks as yet, but I will tomorrow and will write and tell you all about them.

They have hikes here every day and the YMCA are in charge of them. They say that they are quite nice. Well I am here for seven days and I don't see any reason why I won't have a great time. The only thing, I am going by myself because I have not got much use for the bunch that are with me. In my company there are 80 of us and most of them are all from the south and replacement draftees. I expect to have my pictures taken here and will send you some.

I am feeling fine, but I don't know what the matter at home is because I have not heard from any of you for over six weeks. I don't know what to think but I trust that you are all well and happy. I am writing a letter to Gladys and I have sent home some cards and I will send some every day that I am here.

I wish that you folks could see this place. The town is not so very large, but it is a fine place. The government pays 8 francs a day for each of us. That is about $1.50, and we are being treated very well so far. Well, I think that I will close now, and I will promise to try and write to you every day. So, I wish you all a very Merry Christmas and a happy New Year and I am in great hopes of being home by the 1st of January.

Love to all and I hope you are all fine and dandy.

Private 1st Class Raymond W. Maker

10 December

Well, everything is about the same. Weather is bum. Rained about all day. Wrote to home and had a great bath with hot water. It comes right from the mountain.

11 December

Walked around the town and the weather is about the same. Good times at the YMCA and that is all. I am fine.

12 December

Went to Mantdore today, some walk. And some great mountains. Stayed all night and I am feeling fine.

13 December

Well, here I am back again after quite a trip around the country. I am a little tired, but that doesn't worry me.

14 December

Went on to another town today. We may leave tomorrow, but I don't care. I'm sick of this place. I got paid, so I feel much better.

15 December

Well, we leave tomorrow, and it rained all day. So, I'm in a hotel. I will be glad to get back to our company.

16 December

Could not get my gun, so I would not go away without it. I leave tonight at 8 pm, and it rained all day. I missed the train and I will have to make it back along in the morning. I am fine. I am writing this on the train.

17 December

Stayed in Clearmont all night. And, it is some place, here, the best I have seen yet. I leave tomorrow. I had my ride in an electric car here. It is some place.

18 December

Pulled out of Clearmont and headed for Nevers, and here I am in a place called Roanne. Stayed here all night, No American are here. Some place. Met a fine Jane here and walked around and got a room. But I never saw the town. 15 francs for the room. Oh boy.

19 December

Well, here I am in the best place yet, Leon. And, I stayed here all night. It rained all of the time. But, I'm having one fine time. I am well, but tired.

20 December

Am still on our touring job, and I'm getting tired of it. Have had a great time so far. We pull out of here at 06:30 for Marseilles, but got hung up here, and could not get into the city. We pull out at 5:35 for Avignon. I am very tired, but this is the life for me.

21 December

Got to Avignon at noon. And we pulled out for Paris at 2:30. This is a very large place and quite large with a very old church and a large fort. I am on a train now and back again at Sayor, and getting off at Dijon, I guess, but nothing but 1st and 2nd class for me.

22 December

Pulled out of Dijon at 3:30 and got to Langers at 8 pm. And we pulled out of there at 4:35 am for Foulian and got here at 6:30 and I leave for Nugent at 10:30, so I'll be back very soon with my company.

23 December

Here I am, back with the company once more. Got here at 4 pm. Nothing was said to me, so I guess I got away with it okay. It rained all day.

24 December

It rained all day and I'm back at my old job. This is all mud, just the same as before, and I guess it will be a bum Christmas tomorrow.

December 24th

My Dear Sister,

Odival, France

At last I have received the long-awaited letter or letters rather. I just got back to the company yesterday after having one great time. I did not come back with the boys when they left Bourboule where we were on our furlough, but I waited until the next day with a couple of other fellows and started to see France, and we sure did.

The only trouble was that the money did not last. Well, if you look on a map of France, we got to Clairmont and it was there that I had my first ride on an electric car. We went from there to Nevers, and from there to Mon Moulins and then to the great spring of Vichy and on to Roanne. From there we rode to Lyon and from there to Marseille and on to Avignon and then we were caught by the MPs and sent back. Well, then we went to Dijon and finally back to our company.

We were gone for 8 days and I certainly thought that I was in for an AWOL charge, but I had them ok because I had my pass stamped at all of the places we visited. So, I have seen France and by 1st and 2nd Class rail and it never cost a cent to ride on the cars.

I did not know how badly sick you were, but I am glad that you are better, and Kip too, and all of the folks. I was not injured in the shoulder or even rifle shot, but I did get hit in the leg with a piece of shell, but it was really nothing. I was in three or four terrible barrages and I laid wire over the top but did not know that I was cited for it. But, God knows that I sure did earn it.

I don't know how long it will be before we are home. There are all kinds of stories going around. The President will be at our camp here tomorrow (the 25th) but it will be a poor one for us. No turkey or anything and all the mud. Oh, it sure is hell here and cold places to sleep in, but we have put up with much worse. But there is no need of it now. I did not get nay pictures taken at La Bourboule because they were all bum.

They say that we will be home by the beginning of January, but I don't know, Eva, just what to think. Oh, but won't I be glad to get home again and get the good old clothes on once more. Jack Nelson got your letter and I am glad you finally got the money that I sent to you because if I had it I would have spent it by now.

I had a bunch of letters waiting her for me when I got back so I have a job now to answer then all. I am glad that Dad has the machine but if he wants to sell it tell him not to let me stop him. I think that I will stop my allotments as it runs out at the end of the month and they have had so much trouble with them.

Well, Eva, I will say good bye for this time and I will write in a few days. Wishing you a very Merry Christmas and New Year.

Your loving brother,

Private 1ˢᵗ Class Raymond W. Maker

25 December

Today is the worst day I have spent in France. Wilson came by, but he didn't stop. A bum dinner and I have been sick all day in the rain and snow.

26 December

I have felt sick all day and I'm supposed to be in bed. I feel a little better, but I am lamed up. I hope to be well soon and at home.

December 26ᵗʰ
My Dear Sister,

I wrote you a letter a day before yesterday, so I will tell you how I spent my Christmas. To begin with, the weather was bum, and we were cleaning up all around because President Wilson was to stop in here. We had to lay all of our stuff out on our bunks and at 11:15 we had to get outside and stand in a field on the side of a road with mud all over our shoes and wait almost four hours for Wilson to come and he came by at 2:45 and never stopped.

We had a bum dinner. Nothing but roast beef and potatoes and coffee. We did have some candy. I was half sick all day and today I feel more like myself. You spoke about Dr. Owen getting a promotion in the lines, but I don't think he ever saw a trench line in his life.

I am back at my job again and the last few days I was never so sick in all of my life in the Army. We drill all day in the cold but thank the Lord I don't have to drill all of the time. I have no idea when we get home, but it can't come too soon for me. We have just received a new bunch of replacements and most of them are non-coms and never saw the lines. Yesterday, one of these guys tried to make me do something and just told him to go to hell. I won't take any orders from those guys.

I hope that you are all feeling well and that you had a very happy Christmas. Did you hear what General Edwards said about our Signal Battalion and our Division? I don't know if Mullens is on his way home or not. I heard that they were sending the worst of the wounded home and he sure should have the chance. He went out and id a job when some of those southerners and westerners got cold feet and beat it. Oh, Eva, I have some great things to tell you about guys staying in dugouts and getting all of the credit while other fellows were out fixing the lines.

I suppose that you have snow there now and that it is quite cold. It snowed a little here today, but it's all gone now. I am glad that you received the money ok and I hope that you could use it.

Hobbs is here in the office, but I don't know, he does not seem to have much use for me for some reason. I am going to send home part of a 75 shell that I was making, and I will fix it when I get home.

Well, Eva, I don't know of much more to write about at this time, but I will write again soon. My love to you and to all the folks.

Your loving brother,

Private 1st Class Raymond W. Maker

27 December

Went up to Nugent with Jack Nelson and hung around all day. And, I'm all in just a little cold.

28 December

I am feeling better today and so I'm working in the office and working at my old job. It has rained all day, and I went to bed early. I will be glad when we get out of the mud here.

29 December

It is the same old story. No one knows when we are going to move. Went to Nugent with Jack and Bill and we had a feed of eggs and potatoes.

30 December

It rained all day and we did nothing today. I took a walk and did some work for a few francs. Met Bill and Jack and I am doing well.

December 30th
My Dear Sister,

Just a few lines to let you know that I am alive in mud here and that I am feeling fine. I don't know if you have seen in the papers anything about the 26th Division being all the talk when Wilson went through.

They are starting some more furloughs, so it looks as though we will be here for some time yet. I hear that we will be on our way home by the 17th of January, but I don't know what to think. It has rained here about every day since I came back and I wish in a way that I had stayed away a few more days but as bad as it was I had a fine trip and I will send you a map of the trip I had and believe me, Eva, I saw France for a while, but the money did not last.

I got my box today, but I have not opened it yet. I am saving it for tonight. We had a little time with some Frog kids and gave them dolls and toys and movies.

I am back on my old job here and I don't have much to do. I don't get up for breakfast until it's all over and I don't have to drill with all the nuts, so I suppose I can't kick, but Eva, I am getting so sick of this man's Army.

Smith, the fellow that got gassed with me is home and I think that I could have been with him, but I have seen it all and I am alive, so that is something to me to be able to say. Well, someday, I will be home and when I do I guess that I won't eat or sleep for a week anyway.

What is Dad doing these days and how are all the folks? Gee, but I would like to be there right now, but as I have said before, all we can do is wait and we are good waiters. The boys are all coming back from hospitals now, so that looks as though we are on our way.

Well, Eva, I don't know of much more to write about at this time, but I will write again soon.

My love to you and to all the folks.

Your loving brother,

Raymond W. Maker

31 December

Well, I'll close out the book for this year and have done a fine job, I think. A big day tomorrow. I wish I had another book. Good bye and good luck old year,

December 31st

My Dear Sister,

Well, just a few lines today because tomorrow I will start a new year, so I want to write one more letter this year. For a wonder, the sun is out today, and it is just a little bit cold. I had a great feed last night. One of my old pals came back from the hospital and he had a couple of chickens with him, so we took them to a house and had them all fixed up fine and we had French fries to go with them.

Things are going on fine with me here and I hear that we are to leave here by the 15th of January, but I don't know for where, but there is only one place that I want to go to and that's on a dock and onto a boat. But we don't know what to believe.

I am going to try and see Ed Collins. He is near me here, but I have not seen him yet. I saw him when he was moving out of Verdun. We are going to try and have a little party to night up in Nugent, but our funds are quite low. We hope to be paid in a few days.

I sent home a 75-millimeter shell that I was making in Verdun, but I did not have the things I needed to put on it that I wanted, so I will fix it when I get home. It was one of the last shells fired by the 101st Artillery, so I prize it a little.

Well, Eva, I don't know of too much more to write about at this time, but I will write a few lines tomorrow,

Love to you and to all the folks.

Your loving brother,

Private 1st Class Raymond W. Maker

JANUARY 1919

January 2nd 1919
My Dear Sister,

Well, I will start the New Year right and will write a few lines. I have not made any new pages because I don't think that I have done anything the last year to cut out. I had a day off yesterday and went up to Nugent and Hayden gave me some steak and bread and a couple of my pals went up to and the old Frog lady gave us a fine feed and it was very cheap, in fact it had to be; my allotment ran out last month and I don't think that I will have it made over again or not because they have had so much trouble with them.

It still rains here about all the time and Eva it sure makes one like this life now. I got a letter from Kip a day ago and he said you got the helmet ok. Was there a key in the helmet? If there was don't lose it because I stoled it out of the north gate at Verdun and it is worth something.

The talk about moving is about the same, but I think that we will move soon from here because the French are coming in here for the winter. I hope so.

Hayden is acting mess sergeant now and I hope he gets the job. I think I told you that Hobbs was going to make me a corporal, but there is a division order out now that we have to get all of our noncoms from a replacement camp and we got about 108 a few days ago. They never saw the lines, some of them, and that's the kind of company we have now. About all replacements are drafted, but they don't have anything to say to me. I winged one a few days ago and a sergeant at that. So, they keep off from me. There are about 25 of our old company of over 300 now. Can you beat it!

Well, Eva, how is everything going on with you these days and I hope that you are all well and happy. I hope that you all had a good Christmas and the war being over must have made it great for the people at home.

But to tell you the truth, Eva, I have been in better places in the lines and I have been used better than here in a way because when we were in the lines we just had our work to do and no drill. But its drill, drill, drill, all the time and guard duty here. Oh well, it's the Army and I always wanted to be in it, but now we have done our bit, why not send me home.

Well Eva, I will ring off for now and will write soon.

Love to all,

Private 1ˢᵗ Class Raymond W. Maker

January 3ʳᵈ 1919

Dear Kip,

I received your letter ok and as usual I was glad to hear from you and know that you are all well. I just wrote to Dad and Eva a couple of days ago. As to the suit you said you had for me, Kip, I am very much obliged but when I get home I never want to have anything to do with an Army suit. I am sorry that you did not have a chance to go to school because I would like very much to give you a right high ball. I could almost see myself doing it when I don't give our own officers one, but they never mind. Kip, I would have liked to have you get a commission because you would have had a good time. I am sorry in a way that you were not with me here. You would have seen some great things about war, but you never missed anything because you might have gotten bumped off, and then what?

I came so darned near it that I thought I was dead for a few hours. I guess by the way things look now that we will be home soon now because they are all cleaning up all the records and things.

Do you see much of Folly? He fought a hard war over here, but he was game to come. Mullens, the poor kid, I don't know how he is. He got hit quite badly and I guess he will be on his way home soon. Did you ever hear from Harvey? Is he home yet? We had a bunch captured at the same time and one of them came back to the company and I guess they sent him home.

What did you think of the helmet? I wish I had gotten some more, but no chance now. They are worth about three or four hundred francs here now. That's about $35, so you see they are hard to get, and I think that I was where there were hundreds of them just to pick up.

Well, Kip, I don't know of much more to write about, so I will sign off for now.

Your loving brother,

Private 1ˢᵗ Class Raymond W. Maker

January 3ʳᵈ 1919
My Dear Dad,
I think that it is about time that I wrote you a few lines because you are still on my books, but Dad, somehow it is hard for me to write to you all, so when I write to Eva it is for you all. Well, Dad, I am feeling fine and dandy and I hope that you are also.

I had a fine time on my furlough, believe me. I was to have 7 days at La Bourboule and after they were up I took 9 more with a couple of fellows touring France and that was the time that I wish I had the Hudson. Well, when I got back the Captain never said a word to me, so I made up for some of the hard times I spent in the trenches. I was down to Monte Carlo for one place and I going to get a map and mark my trip on it and send it home.

I saw the talk that General Edwards made in Boston and believe me, Dad, he sure was some general, and it was tough that he was taken away from us when he was here in the lines and just before it ended and if he runs for governor of Massachusetts give him your vote and all you can get because I know what he is worth.   But you know how it was with him here. He was too smart for General P. You know who I mean.   And so, they sent him home because he was getting too much credit. It's all in the game. I think it won't be too long before we are home now because things look that way now and I guess that I won't be sorry.

We have rain here about every day and mud, Dad. Well its mud that's all. I suppose that you are working hard and believe me, Dad, I will have some great old stories to tell you when I come home and when I do come home I guess that I will never want to travel any more.

I have not heard from Mullens for some time, but I would not be surprised if he was on his way home. Poor kid, he got his just because one damned fool got cold feet. He got two holes in his back with a piece of shell and I hope he gets a medal, but all that they say is well it was in the line of duty. Never, no more Signal Corps for me. We did the work and the dugout rats got the credit in the war. Well, Dad, I will close now and to see you all soon. Love to you and all the folks.

Your loving son,

Private 1ˢᵗ Class Raymond W. Maker

January 8ᵗʰ
My Dear Dad,
Just a few lines to let you know that I am all ok and I expect to be home very soon now. We are to leave here about the 15ᵗʰ of this month for our sea port, but the Lord only knows when we will sail. We have been having fine weather the last couple of days and we hope that we will be out of the mud soon. I don't know of much to write about, but I have not too much to do so I thought that I would write you a few lines.

I wrote to you a few days ago and Eva too. I have not heard from home for quite a while, but I hope everything is all ok and that you are not working too hard. I suppose that Uncle Ed is still at the old job and that Mr. Charles and the Honorable C. C. Etsy are about the same.

Gee, Dad, but won't I be glad when I will be able to put on my old clothes and be free once more and can sleep so long as I want and have something to eat. I also wanted to be a soldier and I have had my chance and did my bit, too. So now, never again. I have had enough. I mind it more now after the war is over because it is so still and its drill all day (but not for me). When we were at the front we had about our own way, but here it's all different. Well, Dad, I think I will ring off this time and as I said before, I hope to be home very soon. So please keep the home fires burning because I will see you very soon.

Love to all the folks.

Your loving son,

Private 1st Class Raymond W. Maker

January 9th
Odival, France
My Dear Sister,

Well, today, I heard some very good news that is that we are to leave here in a very few days. We have turned in our guns and a few other things and tomorrow we turn in all of our signal stuff as that means something and all we talk about now is when do we get on the boat.

We have been having fine weather here for the last few days, but this afternoon it has started to rain, and I suppose that it will keep up now until after we move from here because every time we move it rains, but I shouldn't worry just as long as we move out of here.

Don't you think I am doing fine with this typing machine, so far? It sure does take some time to pound it out. I have not got anything else to do. Well, Eva, I have got to stop now because the mail just came in and I will have to get on the job. I will write some more later.

Well, here I am again, only it's another day and it has started to rain. I had to start this on a big typing machine as I think I put the little one on the bum. Well, today they are packing up things and getting ready to move out of here.

Gee, Eva, won't I be glad when the day comes to move out. I think that we are going to a place called Le Mons, but I am not sure. It is a very large place and they have been using it for a replacement camp during the war.

I hope that everything is going on fine at home with you all and that you are not working too hard. I suppose that it is very cold there now and that there is a lot of snow. We have not had it so cold here this year as it was last year.

Well, Eva, I don't know how I will get home and get good old civvies on once more. I think that I will miss the old leggings and I suppose that I will be giving everybody I meet a salute and saying "Qui, Qui" to everything that is said, but believe me Eva, I can now talk war with Uncle Ed and I can tell him what he missed in the Civil War.

Well, Eva, I cannot think of anything more to write about, so I will ring off and give my hands a rest.

So, love to all the folks and the best of love to you.

Your loving brother,

Private 1st Class Raymond W. Maker

January 13th

Odival, France

My Dear Sister,

Well, here I am again, but to tell the truth I don't know what to say as I have written to you very often these last few days. Well, Eva, everything looks fine for our move so far and I hear that we are going to move out of here by the 29th of this month for s place called Le Mons and I hope that the dope is right.

We have about everything turned in now and about all there is doing now is fixing up the paperwork and a few other things. I wrote a letter to Dr. Joyce as I did not have anything else to do and I was thinking of him all last night for some reason.

I hope that this letter finds you all ok and that you are not working too hard. I have not heard from you since December 22nd, and so I am wondering if any of you folks were sick or anything. I hope not, Eva, because it is no time to be sick because I am coming HOME tout suite. Do you get that? Believe me, Eva, I can rattle off the old Français.

I should be fairly well off for money for a while. Don't you think that I have done a good job being over here for so long and not sending home for any money and making sure I save it? Well, Eva, I am sure feeling fine and I hope that you all are too. I suppose that Uncle Ed is still on the old job and that Dad is working very hard these days at his old job and that Kip will be out of the Army very soon, now.

Well, Eva, we will have one good old blow out when I get back and it will be in the Hudson. I hope that when you get that shell that I sent home it will be ok, and I have a few other things that I will bring home myself because I am afraid I will lose them. Don't you think that I am doing fine with my typing?

Well, Eva, I don't know of too much more to write about at this time, so I will close the books this time and I will write again very soon.

So, love to you and all the folks.

Your loving brother,

Private 1st Class Raymond W. Maker

January 22nd
My Dear Sister,

Well, Eva, here it is a few days later. I think I wrote to you a couple of days ago. I guess that we move out this time all right because the Captain and 17 men are leaving today, and we are to leave the 29th, so if you do not hear from me for a while don't worry because we will be on the move and may start any time.

We are having quite cold weather here now and we have no fire in our barracks. Oh, this is a great Army now. I found out yesterday that I had my name in the battalion history for a couple of things I did in the lines. I have not heard from Mullens, so I think he is on his way home, poor kid. Be sure, he is a brave lad, but what he did he get, the same as all of us, and we have a couple of guys in our company who got the DSC by asking an officer to put their names in for one.

I have no idea, Eva, how long we will be at our next place, but we are on the way home any way and may be home by the 22nd of February, I hope so.

I hope that you are all well and everything is going on fine at home. I heard that the state money was being paid again – the $100 a month. I hope so because we sure can use it. We have quite along hike to the train from here and I suppose it will be in box cars when we will ride. But what is the use of kicking, the war is over. I was surprised to hear that Erma was married, but it did not hurt my feelings any. Just think, Eva, I am about the only one in my company I guess that has not got a girl, but you have taken the place of three of them since I have been over here.

I don't know of much more to write about, Eva, at this time, but I will try and get one more letter in before I move from here.

So, love to you and all the folks.

Your loving brother,

Private 1st Class Raymond W. Maker

January 23rd
My Dear Sister,

I thought that I would try and write you a few lines today, as it will be about the last time that I will write here. What I wanted to tell you about was that I have a list of some pictures that were taken while we were on the lines by a moving picture man for the War Department and you can send to Washington and get some of them, so I will send you the paper with the numbers on them and what they are.

As I wrote to you yesterday, there is not very much to write about today. We will continue to have cold weather here, but we do not kick on that as we would rather have cold weather than a lot of rain and mud. I think that I told you that we were to leave here on the 29th of this month, thank the Lord. I went up to Nugent last night and had a fine feed of French fries and they went right to the spot with me. We had a lot of mail come in yesterday, but I did not see any mail from you. Did I tell you that the fellow that was with me when I was gassed was sent home and I think that if I wanted to stall them off at the hospital that I could have been sent home, too. But, Eva, I came over here to do my bit and ride it out and not to be sent home just because I was sent to a hospital and Eva, I think that I have done by bit and it's the truth too, but to tell the truth, I think that I would stop at the next war as I have played soldier all I want to and every word weighs a pound at that.

I hope that you folks are all well and that you are not working too hard these days as I sure am not, and I do not believe in it here. I hope that we will not have to stay at the next place very long and that they send us right home from there, but nobody seems to know anything about it here.

So, the only thing to do is to wait and to trust on good luck that's all that I know of to do. I wonder what Kip will do now that he is out of the service and I wonder what I will do myself, when I get out. But, it is a sure bet that I will have a good rest before I go back to work.

Well, here I am after dinner, so I will start all over again. You see that I can get along fine now with this typing machine. That is, I think I do, but it only takes me an hour to find one letter, but I don't think that I am too much in work that I can't stop and write a few lines to my Sister.

It started to snow since I began to write this letter and now there is about an inch of snow, so you may be able to tell about how long it takes me to write a few lines. I wish that that I could be at home now and sit down and have one good fed and tell you folks a few good war tales. Oh, Eva, I can make Uncle Ed take a back seat when I start and tell a few stories.

I wonder if he was walking along a road and all of a sudden, a Boche machine would fly almost right down on top of us and open fire on us with a machine gun or drop a few bombs, or if he had to go through a gas attack for about 8 hours. Oh, Eva, we had a great war over here and in a way, I wish that you could have seen some of it.

I think that Mullens must be on his way home by this time because I have not heard a word from him for quite a long time. I did get a letter from a fellow that went through quite a barrage with me and he got hurt and he is now home. He is the guy that was with me that we had our names put in the battalion history. I guess that I was sure lucky when I pulled through this war and not get used very badly.

I sure would like to see Aunt Lucy and I suppose that she looks about the same as she always did. I suppose that Dad is working very hard these days and that he has one fast horse just to pass away the time with. I was sorry to hear that Dad and Mr. Charles were sick with the flu and it was a wonder that you did not get it again.

I suppose that you folks have a lot of snow there by now and that kids are sliding down School Street. I have never seen a sled or a sleigh over here yet, and Eva, they are so far behind the times here that it will take them about 10 years to get a stove in some of their homes. I would like to see you trying to cook dinner in a fireplace. It sure gets my goat to wait for them to cook me something to eat.

I have never heard from Joe Barette since he left the States, if he ever did. I have always thought of him because one day, when we went over the top, I saw 8 tanks that were stuck in the mud and the Boche were sure shooting the hell out of them, so I could not get over to see who they were.

I am sending you a couple of newspapers that I want you to keep. One is an order about a French General praising the 104th and the other one is an order about General Edwards being sent home and I would like to keep them for a keepsake. I have another paper that I took off of a Boche lieutenant stating that he was given an Iron Cross and it is a dandy, too, with a picture on it. But, I don't think that I will send it home because I may lose it. I was offered 100 francs for it, but nothing doing, and I was broke at the time.

I see that I will have to start another page. I did not intend to write as much as I have but as I said, I have time and I am doing this as I am not doing anything else. I will ring off for now. Love to you and all the folks at home.

Your loving brother,

Private 1st Class Raymond W. Maker

FEBRUARY 1919

February 7th
Brette, France

My Dear Sister,

Well here we are, Eva, all moved but we had quite a time getting here. We left Odival on the 30th of January and got to a place called Mulsanne after riding for about 55 hours in a box car with 31 men in it and after we got there we had a hike of 20 kilometers because we were lost and got into Mulsanne and got all fixed up fine and we had a room, three of us, and a nice fire place and two beds, and then we had to move out of the place because we did not belong there, and so it was "get out" and we hiked again 9 kilometers to here. We have a room here and have been having some good eats. We got 5 dozen eggs $1.40 a dozen or 7 francs, and cocoa and stuff like that. We have a fine place but must steal wood to get by.

We are 12 kilometers from Le Mans and about 65 kilometers from Paris. I don't know how long we will be here. The town is not much good and that makes it hard. We are drilling about all day and this noncom has to do guard duty, east and west, in the a.m. now and take care of the mail in the p.m. I am going to can the job now because they are trying to put it over on me. I had a letter from Mrs. Farmer a day or so ago, but none from you in some time. They are going to give us U.S. rifles to drill with now that the war is over. I suppose they want us to bring them home instead of having to ship them.

Oh, it's a great war all right, but thank the Lord it won't last much longer. I suppose that we will start home sometime in March. I am feeling fine and I hope that you all are too, and that you are not working too hard. I see that quite a lot of fellows that were in our company are home from the hospital, but we know these numbers and they played the game all okay. We have a good bed in our room.

Well, something funny just happened here. A Frog came in and said that he was going to send his eggs away, so we bought 4 dozen more. Can you think of paying $10.40 for 9 dozen eggs? We are getting ready to make some cocoa and then hit the hay because I am just a wee bit-tired tonight. As I said before, I hope that you are all well and not working too hard. I will sign off for now and will write in a few days, so love to all the folks and the best to you.

Your loving brother,
Private 1st Class Raymond W. Maker

February 8ᵗʰ
My Dear Sister,
Well, today, I broke the ice and got your letter dated January 15ᵗʰ and I sure was glad to get it, too, because it has been so long since I have heard from you.

I glad that you are all well and happy and I am sorry that I am not with you yet, but please keep the home fires burning. I'll be there soon if things go right, but I guess by the way they look now that it will be over a month before we start because they are giving furloughs again and for 14 days and I put my name in to go to Tours.

As I wrote yesterday, I don't know if I ever told you about my pal, Dupont. I call him Dup. He was with me about all of the time and can talk the Frog stuff, so we get by very well when the getting is good and when we get home I am going to bring him with me.

You tell Kip that it is about time that he got a job because the both of us cannot be hanging around at the same time, and that he will have to keep me in money because I am broke. I had to laugh when I heard about Uncle Ed and I do hope that Jap makes out all ok. Keep right on writing to me Eva, because I am still here, and the Lord only knows that we stand for God's country and must do our duty.

I have not heard from Gladys for some time and I have wondered if she was sick or not. I must write to Mrs. Farnum after this letter as I owe her a letter. The place where I was on my furlough was about 50 kilometers from Clearmont, so if you look on the map you may see it. It is called La Bourboule which is next to Mt. Dore and it was sure in the mountains, too.

But, Eva, I sure had a great time after I left the gang, or the gang left me. I told you in a letter, but I will tell it again. After the gang left, I left the next day and went to Clearmont and from there to Nevers and from there to Rouen, and then to Lyon, and to Marseilles, and on to Nice, and then to Monte Carlo, and back to Marseilles, and to Avignon and then back to Lyon, and to Dijon, We started for Paris but our money gave out and when I got back to my company, they never said a word after being gone for over 9 days. Well, Eva, I will close now and send my love to all the folks and the best of love to you.

Your loving brother,
Private 1ˢᵗ Class Raymond W. Maker

February 8ᵗʰ
My Dear Dad,

Don't be surprised when you see that I am writing to you, but I don't forget the old timers, so don't you forget it. I wrote to Eva last night and again tonight because I received her letter today and I was glad everything is ok.

I hope to be home with you in a little while and when I get there I suppose that you will feel damn glad to have me home and, Dad, believe me I will be damn glad to get home.

I had to laugh at the YD that Eva made in my letter. They are like

this and we wear them on the left shoulder. The diamond is OD cloth and the YD is blue. I suppose, Dad, that when I told Eva I was going into cafes and drinking that you did not like it, but to tell you the truth, Dad, we had to do it sometimes because we could not drink the water and all of the Frogs have a canteen of red wine and there we were going around getting the dead Frog's canteens to get the wine and it was rotten stuff at that. The wine is an "issue" in the French Army and when they go over the top they have given them rum and it is the same with the English. You might think that it is wrong, but let me tell you, Dad, when you stand there on a firing step and they are sending gas and big shells over and you are waiting to go over, a good stiff drink of rum makes a fellow feel well.

I don't know how to tell you this, but they say that they dope the Boche when they send them over the top and by God they ought to, because it sure was hell. I'll tell you all about it when I get home and you can think for yourself if I am right.

Well, I'll change the subject. Why don't you write to me; but never mind, Dad, I'll be home soon and then we can make up for it.

I suppose that you are taking life cozy. I hope so, and I hope that Uncle Ed is well, too. Give my regards to Mr. Charles and Charles Esty and to Mr. Joyce and last, but not least, to Uncle Ed. We have a good place to live in as I told Eva, and just now we are getting ready to have some dropped eggs on toast. Well, Dad, I will ring off for now and hope to see you all very soon. Love to you and all the folks.

Your loving son,

Raymond W. Maker

February 9th
My Dear Sister,
Brette, France

There is not too much to do, so I thought that I would write you a few lines. I have a nice warm fire in our fireplace and I was just trying to figure out how much money I have saved, or in other words, have earned. To start with, I had a bond for $50.00 and the State pay was $60.00. I sent you $150.00 and my allotment was $120.00. That is $380.00, and I heard that they passed a Bill to pay the rest of the State pay and if that is right it will be up to the month, or $120.00 more, and that is $500.00 and Uncle Charlie is $50.00 and I hear that the Mother's Club in Boston, has about $100.00 or more for each one of us in the old Battalion. That makes it $660.00, and they say the government is going to give each of us six months' pay when we muster out and that would be about $235.00, so all in all, it would be close to $900.00, so I think it pays to go to war once in a while.

I wrote to Dad last night and have written three letters to you since I have been here, so I think that I have done very well and believe me Eva, I sure will be glad when the time comes to be able to talk to you and not have to write.

I see in the newspapers that if we land in Boston you will not be able to see us until after we get to Camp Devens because we will all have to go through a lousing machine and I guess it's right because I never want you folks to get as lousy as I have been and, in fact, I am. It is impossible to get rid of all of them. Eva, you can take a bath and change your clothes and they are in our blankets and if we are rid of them, we can get them for somebody else. So, the only thing to do, as we say, is to read your shirt. That means to look it over and pick them off and I found some once, that could carry a rifle on their shoulders.

It has been quite cold here today and being Saturday, all we had was an inspection and the rest of the day was off, so I had a good wash and I have hung close to the fireplace the rest of the time. It is 4:30 and I think that we will go to supper "se soir" (tonight). We are going to have some French fries and fried onions before we hit the hay. We are sick of eggs for a day anyway, as we have had dropped eggs on toast for breakfast and I am the head cook.

I hope that they will give us a third service stripe before we come home. We were supposed to get it April, but we will be on foreign service pay on the 20th of March and that will make it 18 months, but if they don't I will wear mine because they are not going to cheat me out of it for just a couple of days because 18 months in this country is no joke.

Well, Eva, supper time is at 5:00 pm and so I must cut this out and get my beans, but they are not the white ones, they are the old cheap red ones and are no good, but we have to eat. Well, my love to you and all the folks and please keep on writing and I hope to see you all very soon.

Your loving brother,
Private 1st Class Raymond W. Maker

February 9th
Dear Eva,
I did not put the above letter in the mail as you see, so I thought I would write a little more. I have just eaten my breakfast – dropped eggs and coffee and I am waiting for the water to heat up to wash up and have a shave.

I hope that you won't think, by the way that I write, that I am living the life of a king, because I am not. What we eat here is on the side and to tell the truth Eva, we have to steal most of the stuff because it is so hard to get every night. We go over the top for wood and other things because they change so much so we make up for it. So, I don't think that you can blame me.

I do hope that Mr. Charles is better now and please tell him to get a little fat on because I will take a few rounds out of him soon. I am going to try and have my picture taken before I come home and see if I have changed any.

I have not seen Ed Collins but once since we left Verdun. I have got a dandy little Medal of Verdun for you and I wear it around my neck with my dog tags. I have a dandy little silver chain that I keep them on. You know that we have to wear two tags around our necks with our names and numbers on them. My service number is 199223 and I wish that you could see some of the draftees' numbers.

I would like to see you cook a feed in a fireplace like we do here. I have some cards of Nugent that I will send with this letter. Nugent was the next town to Odival where we were for nine weeks. I would have rather gone into the army of occupation and have seen the country than have hung around here the way we have, but we are on the last lap now and we expect to leave here in March sometime for HOME.

Well Eva, I will close for now and will write again soon.

Love to all,

Private 1ˢᵗ Class Raymond W. Maker

February 10ᵗʰ
My Dear Sister,

Well, here I am again. I made a mistake in the date in my last letter and dated it one day ahead. I am here all alone by my fire and feel so lonesome that I thought you might like to know how and what our company was and what it has done.

Well, first of all, they called it the outpost company. When we said for France we had 75 men from a depot and on January 16ᵗʰ we received

116 men from Fort Leavenworth and in a few days more we received another 75 men from a depot battalion. That makes 266 men and we were to have a company of 285 men and 4 officers and they were to send out 65 men and one officer with the 104th infantry regiment and Mullen went with the 101st and J. Nelson and I were to handle all telephones and telegraphs from the company PC to the regimental PC. So, you see how it was. I was with D Company of the 104th most of the time and where they went I was with them because they had to have service (service first). B Company, in our battalion, ran from Regiment to Brigade Headquarters, to Division Headquarters, and A Company handled all the wireless at Division Headquarters. So, you can see who did the work, A, B or C Companies in a battalion. B Company had one man killed and the Lord only knows how many were wounded. We were getting replacements all of the time.

I went with the 101st at Verdun but did not want to let you know because Eva, I never expected to come back because Verdun was hell. That's all a Frog soldier told me. We never saw war until we were at Verdun and now I know he was right! Oh, Eva, I can have some great stories when I get home and it won't be any bull at that.

My pal Dupont is on guard duty tonight and my pal Bill Reardon is going to the hospital. He has a bum side or something and he is going to have an x-ray on it.

We had a great feed this am. Hayden gave us a couple of cans of what they call Kickapoo Hominy and all you have to do is warm it up and put milk and sugar on it. We never go to breakfast now because we get cans of milk and other stuff from Hayden, but the hardest thing is to get up for roll call in the morning. We have to get up at 6:00 am and it is quiet dark then. Oh, won't I have a good sleep when I get home.

Don't think for a minute Eva, that we are living great here just because we steal a few things and have a bed, because nothing doing. But it sure is something different from the lines. I wish you could see the trenches once and see the way we had to live. You would think that it was impossible to live in them, but I guess that we fooled them, and I think that I cheated you and Kip out of $5,000.00 that's where the joke comes in.

Well, Eva, I think that I will ring off for the time and I will write again soon.

Love to you all,

Private 1st Class Raymond W. Maker
PS: I hear that we are to sail on the 15th of March.

February 11th
Dear Kip.

Just a couple of lines to you but to tell the truth, Kip, I don't know what to write as I have written home so many times in the last week – every day, I think.

I am glad to hear that you are out of the service and now it's up to you to find a good job because you are old enough now to know what you are up to and that you will not be able to hang around home all the time. Don't get sore Kip, this is no hard talk, but you must realize now as I said, we are not always going to have a home and so it's about time that you and myself as well started and do something worthwhile and start in and save up some money to make a home for ourselves. So, keep an eye out old kid and jump to it. It's your own war and it's up to you. That's all.

Well, Kip, I am fine, and dandy and I hope to be home very soon now and when we do we will have one good old blow out. We are getting some rifles tomorrow to drill with. They want to make soldiers out of us now that we fought the war. But, we are only having them for just a couple of weeks.

We are having cold weather here now and I hug the fire every chance that I can get. Well Kip, I will close now and to see you all very soon.

Love to all the folks,

Private 1st Class Raymond W. Maker

February 15th
My Dear Sister,
Brette, France

Just a few lines as I have my pen filled up and it has been a couple of days since I have written. I have been living alone for a few days, but Jack Nelson is here with me now. Today we have what they call a bunk inspection and we have to lay out all of our things on our bunks, but I laid my stuff on my bed.

We were paid on the 13th and I had quite a few names to pay out and when I got all squared up I had about 40 franc and then I got into a crap game and made another 360 francs, so that makes about 400 francs I have now and if I get my second furlough I hope to have a good time because it takes a lot of money to live here.

I paid 30 cents for a box of sardines and there were only 7 in it. That's the way things are and when you kick they say it's the war (C'est la guerre), and it makes a fellow sick. But, thank the Lord, we will be out of this country soon.

We have rifles to drill with and they wanted me to drill some of the boys as I know how with a rifle and I said nothing doing, let the guts who are getting the money do it.

I don't know Eva, how it was that I never got a non-com job, but I guess I did not fit and be a back-biter. They offered me a corporal's job about a couple of months ago and I would not take it. I said that if I could not have it when they made them in Camp Norman prince, then I did not want it at this late time, so in a way it makes me feel a little sore to see so many of the fellows in the old company with stripes and me without, but by God, Eva, I did my bit and that's more than a lot of them can say.

I hope that you are all well and that you are having good weather there. We are here, and it's like spring here now. I am fine and dandy and so is Jack Nelson. I have not heard from Mullens and so I think that he must be on his way home or at home by now. I have never heard from Frostie and I don't know how to find her. Dr. Glass is at Division Headquarters and that's too far from here to try and find out from him. I would like to know because it would give me a better chance to get a furlough then because I could go and see her.

I wrote to Kip and Uncle Andrew the other day and I wrote a fine letter to Uncle Andrew. I hope he gets it all ok. Jack Nelson sends his regards to all and he will write to you soon.

General Hale came here on the 13th and he was very much pleased with our battalion and said that our company was the best drilled and looked the best in the Division – how's that! He made an inspection while we were in Odival. I hope to see General Edwards at the head of our 26th Division when we get home and I think he will be.

Oh, Eva, we've got some Division, or we did have, but we have lost a pile of men and most of the men now are all replacements and never saw the front lines. We have about 278 men in our company now, and it's quite hard to try and find the older fellows, but it's the war as the Frogs say.

Well, Eva, I will ring off for now and wait around for our bunk inspection.

Love to all,

Private 1st Class Raymond W. Maker

February 15th
My Dear Dad,

I don't know how it is, but I have had a writing spell for some weeks now and I have written to almost everybody. This is my second letter to you in about a week. I wrote to Eva this am and now it is after 5:30 pm and I am waiting for Hayden to come up and we are going to have a feed that would knock your eyes out. We are going to have some steak and French fries and onions and cocoa and toast, but the only trouble is we have to use a fireplace and it takes a lot of time.

I am well, and I am getting hog fat here and I hope you folks are all well and fine. We have rifles to drill with now and I have a new one and I wish I could keep it, but we turn them in in a few days.

We are in hopes of leaving here by the first of the month and if the Germans mind their own affairs we will be home by sometime in March, and how I will feel Dad, the Lord only knows. Won't I be happy when I can come and go when I please and the best part of it all is to be home and talk English? I get along fine alright with the French words, but it takes about an hour to get what you want, and they are so slow. It is no wonder that the war went on for four years. They move so slow and are half dead.

I often wonder what I will do when I get home and in the last few days I was thinking that I have been knocking around enough and that it was time I settled down, so I was thinking of doing work on the trees. There is money in it and I made a lot of money, but never knew enough to save it, so I think I will try it again or I might get a chance to get Stalker's job. He has had it long enough and knowing the work and being over here and having done by bit, I think I could get it. Don't you think so?

Give my love to Uncle Ed and Mr. Charles, Charlie Esty, Mr. Joyce and all the folks. Before I forget it, I wish Dad, that you could have seen some of the war and you see for yourself what we had to go through and see a field after a barrage had hit it and you sure would wonder how the boys lived through it. But some of them did and the Lord only knows how it was.

I am glad that Kip never got here. I mean in the Army that des the fighting. He sure had a bomb-proof job and I'm glad he did too. I wish that I had one myself at times, but now that is all over. I would not have missed it but at the same time I would never go through it again and I am not alone, believe me.

They say that we are to leave France by the middle of March and I hope that everything turns out all right. I am sending a couple of newspapers with this letter and I hope that you will get them ok. They are fine papers for us, but you might not get interested in them. Well, Dad, I think that I have written enough for now and I will close. Hoping to see you all very soon.

Love to you and all the folks.

Private 1ˢᵗ Class Raymond W. Maker

February 17th 1919
Brette, France
My Dear Sister,

Just a couple of lines before I go to bed. I have a YD shoulder patch that I thought you might like to have, so I will send it in this letter. I went to the next town yesterday and it is a bum place. I am sending a couple of cards too, that I got there. This is another day, the 18th. I started this letter and could not write any more last night, as I could not think of a thing to say.

Well, tomorrow is a big day. We got up at five and have breakfast and leave here with our packs at 6:15 for Le Mans and we are to parade before General Pershing, and Eva, we sure have a finely drilled company. I will let you know how it was. We are lucky we are not going to have to hike it. We ride in trucks for a wonder. If you knew what I am doing now you would laugh. It is now 10 minutes before three and the boys are all at drilling and I have a nice fire going and I have a bunch of onions, (I forgot how to spell them) and anyway, I am frying them, and I hope that nobody comes in until after I have them all eaten.

I saw in a Boston newspaper that a lot of our 26th Division boys came home on the Canada and landed at Boston. I wish that I was one of them, but we will be there soon. I had a great dream last night all about our home coming and Oh, what a welcome we had and the feeds, I can taste them now. I guess that is what made me so hungry. I have to pay a franc a day for our little room, and the Frog woman next door does our washing, so we have a kind of clean place compared with what we had before. But, Oh, Eva, I sure have been covered in lice more than once and I will feel lost without a few big cooties. They are regular pers.

My pal Bill is back from the hospital and so is Jack Nelson and Bill and myself are keeping the house and in fact I do the cooking and house-keeping and I am going to give up that job. They pass the buck to me all the time. Well, Eva, my feed is almost done, so I will close and hope to see you all very soon. Love to you and to all the folks.

Your loving brother,
Private 1st Class Raymond W. Maker

February 20th 1919
Brette, France
My Dear Sister,
Well, here I am Eva, and I have the blues for sure tonight, and I have a little bit of home sickness. We had a very hard day yesterday. I got up at 4:30 and left here on trucks and we got to a place and we walked a couple of miles and it rained all day and it had rained the day before. Well, Eva, we got to the parade where we were to be received at about 8:00 am, and the place was ankle deep with mud and water and we waited almost in one place until about 3:30 or 4:00pm, and the General Pershing came to our company and he inspected us, and when he passed by me he saw my wound stripes and he asked me where I was wounded and I told him that I was gassed at Chateau-Thierry and wounded at Verdun, and he said, "I'm glad you were able to be in the company." I wish that you could have seen it, Eva. It was something that I will never forget. I It took him from 12 noon until 5 pm to go over the Division, walking. And then we all paraded by him and what a mob. I never saw the whole Division together before and it all turned out fine and they say he was very much pleased and gave us credit at last! You may see the pictures of it in the newspapers. They took some photographs, but it was a rotten day all right. I met Ralph Harvey there and also Ed Collins, both were POWs. They are both in the same outfit. Harvey does not look very well, and he said that the Germans did not use him very well and Ed Collins looks the same as ever.

I took a bath this afternoon and have new underwear, so I feel so much better but for some unknown reason I have that home sickness. I have not had it but a couple of times. We had the day off today and Saturday is another day, the 22nd of February. I have not heard from Gladys for some time. I hope to hear from you again soon. Our chaplain is leaving us tomorrow and he is giving a farewell talk tonight. We have a YMCA tent here and we have a lot of stuff here, but we run it ourselves. No YMCA for us. We don't believe in them over here anymore.

I understand that the Mother's Club have a bunch of money that they are going to give to us when we get home and a big banquet. I hope that you are getting all of my letters all right, Eva, because I sure have written quite a few in the last month. I'll tell you, Eva, what hurts me the most of all is that there is no Mother waiting there for me, Eva. I have felt it more since I have been here and at times I wondered what there was to live for and the time that I was at Chateau-Thierry and at Belleau Woods where I went through the barrage, I was praying to be hit and put out of the way, but I know why it never came. It was because she was watching out for me. Well, Eva, I will close as I want to hear the chaplain's farewell talk.

Your loving brother,

Private 1st Class Raymond W. Maker
PS: I hear that we are to leave here about the 15th of March.

February 24th 1919
Brette, France

My Dear Sister,
Just a few lines today as I am waiting for the mail to come in. We drilled all morning and after we came back they read the order about us going home. We are to be the first Division to leave in April, so by that word we should be home by the middle of April. They say that the order will not be changed, and we all hope so. I wrote two letters yesterday and would have written to you, Eva, but I could not think of a thing to write about.

The time goes by very slowly now and we have started to have the rainy season here, again. I hope that you received my letter telling you all about our great parade for General Pershing and also the YD shoulder patch that I have sent to you in the mail.

We are still drilling with the rifles and hope to turn them in in a couple of weeks now that the war is over. The YMCA and the Knights of Columbus are giving us quite a lot of stuff. I guess that they had so much stuff left over that they had to give it to us now, but not when we were on the front lines.

I started this letter in our canteen and now I am at the office. I will write a longer letter in a day or so.

Love to all and I hope to see you all very soon.

Your loving brother,

Private 1ˢᵗ Class Raymond W. Maker

February 26ᵗʰ 1919
Le Mans, France

My Dear Sister, Well, here I am at Le Mans. I am here on a 24-hour pass and I am at the YMCA. It is raining hard outside and it is also quite early in the morning. I left Brette at 5:30 and came here on a little narrow sample train and talk about your slow rides. It is only about 8 miles to Brette and it took the train 1 hour and 45 minutes to get here. It is quite a large place, but as I have not been around it yet, I cannot tell you much about it. I had some free hot coffee and some cookies, but I am waiting until the places open up for a good feed at 11:00 am.

I think I told you that we will be the first Division in April to leave France and we hope to be home about the 19ᵗʰ of April and then I will be happy once more. We will get our third overseas stripe, I guess, but I do not want to wait to get it. I want to get out now. I will try and have my picture taken here if I can find a place.

They have a good YMCA here. I have to be back in Brette to move at 6am, so in order to get back in time I will have to leave here at 5pm tonight because that's the time the train goes back, so you can see a 24-hour pass is not much good under those conditions.

I hope that you folks are all well and happy and that you are having good weather there and please tell Dad to get the Hudson all cleaned up and fixed up at my expense because Eva, I sure do think that I have earned the right to have a good time for at least a month. Am I right?

This place is quite old here and I will send you some post cards of it. Did I tell you that I saw Ed Collins and Ralph Harvey at the review? I hope you get my letters telling you about it. It was a great thing, Eva, and I wish you folks could have seen it. It was something that I would not have passed up.

I am here with the 1ˢᵗ Sergeant of our company. He is quite a pal of mine and he is living with us in our room and he sleeps on a cot so now

I have quite a family to look out for. Jack Nelson is sick in bed. His legs are all stiff and he has bad headaches and Bill Reardon is all in so astride of that everything is fine with me and believe me Eva, I have never felt better, but I have the blues quite a lot lately, but I am better now. I often think of Pete and wondered why he has never written to me, but I'll be home soon and won't have to be thinking of letters then, anymore.

I hope that you will be able to read this all ok because I have a Frog pen and they are as different as the Frog people are. I am trying to hate them now that we won the war for them and it's all over. They are much different. They want to suck us in with everything but when they do we try and get square with them.

This is the place that Wilber Wright came to from the USA to first try out his flying machine that he brought over. It is a very old place and some of the buildings are very old. It has stopped raining now, so I think that I will take a little walk and find a barber shop and have a shave. Have you heard from Mrs. Farnum yet? She said that she was going out to see you. Please tell Uncle Ed that he wants to have the old fishing line ready because we will try out the fishing grounds. I suppose he has a smile when he hears this, and that Dad says "Huh." Tell Kip that he wants to be at work and push out a few francs to help a worn old war veteran out to a blow out and tell Dad that I will promise not to run the machine up and into Mrs. Gordon's hedge but, but I sure gave Kip the ride of his life and I drove that old machine better than Jap could, even if I was a greenhorn.

As I am waiting for Andie to get through with a story, I might as well keep on with this letter. I have a nice $20 bill and if I have good luck I will keep it and buy myself a suit of clothes when I get home and I also have about 60 cents in silver that I have picked up. I have about 140 francs and payday will be in a few days now, as we will sign the payroll roster tomorrow. I mean the 28th and they say we will be paid early this next time on account of having all the pay records all fixed up. So, I won't have to spend my $20 unless I buy some things to bring home. But, I don't know what to buy I'll get you something, Eva.

I lost about all of my good things at Chateau-Thierry and when I was on furlough even that kit roll you gave me and the watch that Dad gave me are gone. I had them all together in a gas mask bag and a Frog stole the bag on a train when I was out for a feed at a station and I had my gun with me and I would have blown his head off if I could have found him. The watch was broken, and I was keeping it in the bag with the rest of my stuff to have fixed when I got to Lyon, but there it goes, so what's the use of kicking. I have another watch and it's an Elgin and a dandy watch, so I'm all ok.

So, don't you think I have done well in writing home to you and the best of all not asking for any franc, but sending them home? Well, Eva, I am all done, so I will cut it out and I will write later and tell you about this place.

With love,

Private 1ˢᵗ Class Raymond W. Maker

February 28ᵗʰ 1919
My Dear Sister,
Brette, France

Well, as it is the last of the month I will close up the books and tell you about my trip to Le Mans. I wrote you a letter from there and maybe you will get it before this letter, or maybe you won't, but Eva, it was some trip. What I mean is the walk that I told you that I was going on was to have my picture taken.

Well, we found the place and went in and it started off well and when it came to the price the Frog said it was 35 francs a dozen. Well that was the one time that I wish I could speak French and tell him what I said in English. I always knew that my face was not worth much, but not when it comes to paying almost $8.00 for a dozen post card pictures. So, I am off that stuff for life. So, the way it looks, Eva, you get no pictures of me from Le Mans.

Well, we hung around for a while taking in the different things and when we set out to get back to our train, we learned that it had left at 4pm and it was 5pm, so we decided to stay a while longer and we might get a ride part way. We did all right. We left the place at 9 pm and started to walk and none of us knew the road and to make a story short, we walked until we about gave it up and at 2:15 we strolled into the great town of

Brette. We were tired, well a little more than tired, and tried to find out how far we had gone, and the main road map says 15 kilometers and the Lord only knows how many extra miles we had gone.

Well, we went to bed aching and I never knew anything until Bill woke us up for supper today, and I am taking life a little soft because my feet are so sore. I went on sick call this morning and was marked "to quarters" so that our try to get to Le Mans was never to be done again unless we have a ride both ways.

Jack Nelson is all okay now and as I have said before, the time goes by very slowly, waiting for the world to leave us here. For some part I think that we will sail home from Brest, but I am not sure. I suppose things are a little more on the go at home now and that the war is over and that the prices are getting cheaper. I hope so, but I never saw such a place as this country for high prices. There is some talk about Captain Hobbs becoming a major and the commanding officer of our battalion and I hope that he gets it and as for me I still hold down the 1st post job and I don't expect anything more from this company, but believe me Eva, when I get home and out of the service, I can talk plain English and tell off a few people about a few things, but if a guy looks sideways here he is put in the jug and given about 10 days and 2/3rds of three month's pay, but they have never gotten me, yet, for some unknown reason.

Well, Eva, I don't know of much more to write about this time and every day I am looking for a letter from you. Well, I'll close for now and will write again soon.

Love to all,

Your loving brother,

Private 1st Class Raymond W. Maker

MARCH 1919

March 1ˢᵗ, 1919

Brette, France

My Dear Sister,

Well, Eva, I started this letter on a Saturday night, but I think that I will finish it by tomorrow, but I have just been to a show, so I must tell you all about it. It was run by the boys in our company and it sure was fine. We have a YMCA tent here and they fixed it all up with a stage at one end and we have a 6-piece orchestra which was great. Two fiddles, a snare drum and a base drum, and a trombone, cornet and a piano, and they only started playing about a week ago with the orchestra. The play was taken from "Seven Keys to the Baldpate" and it was fine. We had footlights and the lights for the music were made out of blinker lights we used in the trenches.

They had another show while we were in Odival and they played at the different regiments and at the Division Headquarters before the general and we are in hopes of putting them on at home just like we do here with the same things. They got the clothes from the Frogs and they looked great.

Now, I must tell you about our soccer team. We have a team here, Eva, that has played 6 or 7 games and we have the champions of the 52ⁿᵈ brigade and they will play the 51ˢᵗ brigade soon, for the championship of the Division. If they should win that game they can go to Paris and play of the championship of all of the Allied Expeditionary Forces. What do you know about that? You see, Eva, we have 285 men in just our company and they are from every state, so we have some good stuff to pick from.

Well, Eva, sad news. I have lost my mail job after the hike I had from Le Mans. I stayed in bed all of the next day and the Captain did not like it very well and when I started to work the next day after, he said that I was fired, and I asked him if he would fire me from out of the army, too.

But, now that I am out of a job, I may get a little time off once in a while. I never did have much time off when I had the job, so I don't really care. I may have to go on guard duty, now, but I've done that before, so I guess it won't hurt me any. And, the best part is that it will be all over very soon, now. Just this month then homeward bound and then Eva watch out for me because I am wild, just wild, and I'll do things for a sister that I have done before, because Eva, when a fellow is over here, and he has gone through it all, he has thoughts of the things that he could have done and all the mean little tricks he has done.

I don't know how it was, Eva, but the nights I have been in the lines, I have thought ok, I will make up for all the things I have done and I guess all the boys were the same way, because Eva, we would sit around and talk of home and talk of things that we would never have talked about before we came over here, and to tell you the truth, I think that I know that I am a better man than I ever was. This may sound strange to you Eva, but it's the truth.

I suppose that some people think that when we get home we will be wild and all that stuff, but Eva, this war has made more than one fellow a man, because it's the things that he has done and the love for his fellow brothers and above all, a value for life and friendships.

Now, don't think Eva, that I am an angel now. I have done things that have been wrong over here, but nothing great. No one is perfect. I don't know how I happened to write this way, Eva, but it had to be said and I did not intend to write so much as I have, but I guess it won't hurt me any.

I have a fine fire going in the fireplace and some nice hot cocoa and I am waiting for Andie to come back from the office and then we are going over the top. What I mean by that is we are going out on a little raiding party to bring back "wooden Boche" to get some wood and the zero hour is 10 pm, for by then, all the Frogs will be asleep.

My pal Dupont is coming back tomorrow. He has been away at a rifle range working on the telephones. They have a range there with just 100 targets, some range that. I hope that you get my letters telling you all about our review for General Pershing and my trip to Le Mans. Well, Eva, I will close for tonight and I will write again tomorrow.

Well, Eva, here it is on Sunday and first of all I must tell you how we got fooled bright and early this morning. After going over the top last night with good luck, we sat by the fire until late thinking because tomorrow was Sunday. We could sleep an hour later (as we normally do on Sundays) and this morning as were sleeping away, the guard came in at 5:45 and said "get up" because it was 6:45 and we looked at our watches and it was only 5:45, so we had a great time with the guard and then he said they changed the time at midnight one hour ahead. It was some joke on us, but we did get dinner earlier anyway. They start their daylight savings time on the 2nd of March.

Well, Eva, I just had a good bath and with all clean clothes, and I feel great, with a shave, too. I have had quite a few baths while I've been here, and I am rid of the cooties for a while, but there are still a few left in the blankets yet, and I hope to be rid of them soon.

Eva, you don't know how long this month is going to be with us, but there is nothing to do but to stick it out. I'm glad in a way because it will give me my third service strip, spending 18 months in a place where the people are all different and going through hell, too, but as I said before nothing to do but stick it out and wait for the better days to come and when they do Eva, well I don't know what to say. I wish that you could have a look at me now, and at our room. We have rain here almost every day but thank the Lord there is no mud. I will never forget the mud in France as long as I live. I was looking at that lucky piece you sent to me a while ago and I know that there sure was luck in it all right. I am waiting for dinner now and I will have to leave this for a while, but I will try and write another page by and by.

Here it is about 10pm at night and they repeated the show again tonight and so I had to take it in and after it was over I went to a Frog dance. I sure wish that you could have seen it. They had a thing that looked like a piano and you put in a 2-cent piece and away she went but talk about your noise and all the Frogs do is go around and around. Well, Eva, I think that I will close the book now and go to bed because it's early tomorrow for me. Well, Eva, I hope to be home soon, and they say we will leave around the 6th of April. Well, love to all the folks and I hope to be home soon.

Your loving brother,
Private 1st Class Raymond W. Maker

March 4th 1919

Brette, France

My Dear Dad,

Just a few lines to you to let you know that I am in the best of health and I hope that you all are, too, and I am also hoping to see you all very soon. Eighteen months to spend over here is quite a while to be away and to go through what we have been through. They say here that we will leave Brette about the 25th of March and that we may sail by the 1st week of April and if that is straight we had ought to be home by the 19th with good luck.

A year ago today, I was up near Soissons in the Chemin-des-Dames Sector and I was about one half mile from the front lines and when we left that sector the Boche started their drive on Soissons and we came down through the area of Chateau-Thierry and we started a drive that stopped the Boche from getting into Paris and Dad, it was the old 26th Division that won the hearts of France. Well, Dad, there are some great stories that I can tell you about - that fight and many others.

Remember the time that I wanted to become a soldier and I had to have you sign a note before I could get into Company E? Well, I have been one, Dad, and thank the Lord I was not drafted. If you know how much love we have for Mr. Wilson. They have all the best jobs in the Army and they don't know anything. Can you think of being in a company and going through the fight and then after the fighting is over to have the damn drafter come to your company and he never heard a shell or saw a real trench, and then boss you around. I wonder what you would do. But, they could not make any more noncoms because they had to use many from the replacement camps that they had, and that is how it is with us. But, as I said before, we are about all done and I have had enough of the part of soldier, believe me.

We have had rain here about every day and it sure makes the time go by very slowly. Don't you think that I have done very well in writing some since I have been over here? We get our third service stripe on the 5th of April, so I will be fairly well fixed for stripes. I can wear two wound stripes to brag about, if I want to. Well, Dad, it is very near supper time, so I will ring off for now and send my love to all the folks. Hoping to see you very soon.

Your loving son,

Private 1st Class Raymond W. Maker

March 11th 1919
Brette, France

My Dear Sister,
Well, Eva, I broke the ice at last and received that long-delayed letter and one from Mrs. Farnum, at the same time. I was very glad to hear that you are all well and I guess that you are there with a typewriter. I gave that up quite a while ago. They say that we will leave here around the 20th, and I hope so. I am glad to know that Kip is working and that things are going on just fine. I am sure waiting to get a look at the place once more, Eva, and as the time drags by it makes me want to get home all the quicker.

We have quite a place here now for shows and movies and so we are all set up with lights and we have two great hand-painted curtains that the boys made, and we have some kind of a show every night.

There is a great Division field meet going on at the Division Headquarters and it lasts for three days. I am sending you a little drawing that we use for our trade mark and we are having the goat painted on our helmets. I guess we are the goats all right.

I am writing this before dinner, so I will have to cut it short. I will write a longer letter tomorrow. As I did not get this letter mailed I will try and write a few more lines. I wrote to Nucker this afternoon and tomorrow I am going to the Field Day. My pal Bill goes on a furlough the 13th and Dupont left on his furlough on the 9th, so there are only two of us here now.

I have had so many baths and I have had my clothes washed and boiled so much that I am rid of the cooties at last, and it sure is some job to get rid of them and they won't let anybody go home who has them, and I don't blame them. I don't know what you folks would do if you had them, but you see Eva, sleeping in the places we have had to, and on old straw, we never had a chance before to get rid of them. We had flapjacks for dinner and they were great, but what I am longing for now is a big dish of ice cream and some good home-made food. I think the ice cream comes first, that is after I get home and if old Taylor will set them up. I will have to put him over the top.

I was wondering if Fisher ever got over here and I am glad that I beat Captain Sullivan's crowd over here. They only got here a little while before it all ended, and I don't think they ever saw any action. I would like to know where cousin Frostie is because if she wrote to me I could get a pass and go to see her, but that is the only way she would have to write to me. That's army stuff for you. I guess she's done her bit all right because she was only about 12 miles from the front lines. I saw her near Chateau-Thierry.

I have a nice scar and I hope it does not go away before I get home to show you how near I came to getting it, but it is going away fast now. Well, Eva, I will close now and write some more in a day or so.

Love to all,

Raymond

March 13th 1919
My Dear Sister,
As it has been a few days since I have written, I must get on the job. The Division field meet is all over and we lost with our soccer team and the 104th won the meet and the D Company that I was with most of the time, made more points than any one Regiment, how's that? They had some great boxing and there was some mob there. You would think it was the Brockton Fair, if it were not for the uniforms.

I have a new job. I am running the fire that we have to boil all of the clothes in to get rid of the cooties and I have every other afternoon off. It looks as though we will leave here soon, now, as we are getting our things all checked up and turning in all of our extra gear. I have often wondered if Mullens was home. I never heard from him but once since he went to the hospital. Poor kid, he sure got his and it was all because another fellow got cold feet and was afraid to do his bit. We have quite a lot of them hanging back in the SOS (Services of Supply) and now that we are going home they are starting to come back. If I was the captain of the company I would send them back and the worst part of it is they are mostly sergeants. Can you beat it? I see in the newspapers where they are ready to give us quite a time and as for me, I am sure ready to get it.

The first trees are starting to blossom out and the little spring flowers are all out, so you see spring is here with us. Last year, at this time, I was up in the Chemin des Darns sector and I received two letters from you. I have it all in my little diary book and I put down that I have eaten soup so much that I am a soup bone and March 11th 1918, I was up in the gun pit with some Frogs and those damned fools set fire to the grass and the stuff they had over the top of the gun. I started to run and just as I got to my dugout the shells flew up and a large piece of shell fell right in front of my door. That's the truth.

The diary book that Bessie sent me sure comes in handy. I kept it for a whole year and we were not supposed to have such things in the lines, but we all take a chance once in a while. There is not too much to write about, so I have to tell you about some of the things that have passed to make a letter and I hope that they will all pass out of my life soon and forever because some things, Eva, send the creeps up your back when you think of them.

I am sending you some post cards that we were given. I have not sent you the pictures of the goat yet, as I said I would in my last letter, as the fellow who is or was painting it has not gotten it done yet. But, I will send it to you.

I hope that this letter finds you are all right and as for myself, I am fine and dandy. We put on our third service stripe the 21st of this month and I am going to send you my two old ones because they have seen something believe me. Well, Eva, I will close for this time and please tell Dad to have the machine at Camp Devens to bring me home. Love to you all.

Your loving brother,
Private 1st Class Raymond W. Maker

March 15ᵗʰ 1919

Brette, France

My Dear Sister,

I received your letter last night and it came in a good time. Only 14 days to get to me. Well, Eva, I think will be my last letter to you from here because we have good news. We are to be already to move out at any time now and we turned in our rifles and this morning we had a field inspection by the AEF embarkation officers, so things are going on just fine. But the days, Eva, they go by so slowly. I don't know if I will write again or not as I said before because we will be on the move and if we stay at any base or port for any time, I will write, but we hope to be home by the 10ᵗʰ of April anyway.

Here's hoping that all of the inspections come out all OK and that will get us home all the quicker. Yes, Eva, I guess that Ed Collins and yours truly are the only ones that come from the outfit that saw anything and we would not take anything for it, now that it's all over and we came through it OK.

It must have been a good sight to have seen Joe Collins in that fix and I see where you and I are going to have a little argument when it comes to suffrage. Here, us guys are over here doing the fighting to make the world safe for you women to live in and the likes of Joe Collins and a few more try to run the works. Please don't get sore, Eva. We'll have it out, later.

As for that insurance, I did not mean it in the way you took it. It was only a joke. Well, Eva, we are going to have a little feed here Ce soir (tonight). We have 2 dozen eggs (oeuffs) and four of us are going to put them out of the way. Seven francs a dozen ($1.40) can you beat it?

I hope that I can ring in for one of those suits they are giving away, but I should not worry as I don't have to suck around to anybody, believe me. Oh, for the sight of my home town and last but not least, you, all so with great courage and cheer. We will have to stick it out for a couple of more weeks. I have got so many places to go to and visit when I get back home. It will take some time. You are right, Eva, when a fellow soldier with a bunch of fellows, he knows who his pals are, and they are not forgotten very easily. I was with a pal at Chateau-Thierry and well I remember. I said to him (Ike), his name was Westley Reed, if you and I ever hit the States you are coming home with me. He lives in California, and he sure is, and only tonight we were talking about it. Well, Eva, I will ring off for now as I must start cooking the eggs. Love to all.

Your loving brother, Raymond

March 18th 1919
Brette, France

My Dear Sister,
I did not think that I would write from here again, but somehow the inspection we had last Sunday did not go well with the embarkation men as we have another inspection tomorrow and General Hale is to be here. General Hale is strong for our outfit and he said that he did not believe that we were so bum that he would see our next inspection (tomorrow). I have something now breaking out on my face; something like barber's itch and there are quite a few cases of it here. The doctor said it was from eating too much grease. I do hope to get rid of it soon.

The time is going by just as slow as ever with me, but we do hope to be out of here this week. We are to go to Brest and then we leave here in American cars and they sure are some different vehicles than what the Frogs have. They have big engines and box cars here and I wish that you could see the little cars that the Frogs use and the way that they have them chained together, and all of them are painted 40 hommes and 8 chevaux (40 men and 8 horses). I will never forget it, as they put about 50 men in them.

I hope that Mullens is home by now, because I have not heard from him, only since he first went to the hospital. There was a real game kid, Eva, and he sure got hurt badly. Jack Nelson is doing fine and in fact all the boys are OK. We have about 290 men in our company now. They are all coming back from the dugouts now that we are going home. They say we will be home by the 19th of April and I hope so. And, I hope that they won't keep us long after we get there. I have never been so sick of the Army as I have been since I hit this place. The town of Brette is alright, but somehow things don't seem to go right and there are so many men in the companies that it is hard to get the things that A and B Companies are getting. But we will be home soon and that's all I want to happen.

I hope that things are going on well and that you are all feeling fine. And, just a little whisper, Eva, if you should see a nice girl who is looking for a nice little soldier boy, just tell her that I am there. I guess that I am getting old and so I will have to leave it up to someone else to do my match-making for me.

Dupont and Bill are out on furlough and I expect to see them all back here as we are to leave, and they want us all here with the companies and regiments before we leave this area. We will leave all of our cooking ranges here and turn in all our machines the day before we leave. It seems good to be without rifles and we have just our belts so that makes it even better.

Well, Eva, I will close, and I don't want you to look for another letter from me, as I may be home before I know it. My love to all.

Your loving brother,

Private 1st Class Raymond W. Maker
PS: Dupont just came in.

March 19th 1919
Brette, France
My Dear Sister.
Well, Eva, our inspection is all over and we got 100% on it this time so we are all set and just waiting for the word to start. The General was here today, but I have not heard what the latest dope is yet. We have had lots of rain here, about all day long, and it is getting quite cold. Dupont came back last night, as I was addressing your letter and he said that he has sent you a couple of post cards from the place where he was and he said that he hoped you don't think he has a bit of nerve sending them to you, as he has never met you, but he thought you would like to have them and see what the country looks like here. So, I guess that it's all right because I said it was. When a guy like him stayed eight days in the Belleau

Woods with me and goes through hell like we did, he sure is my pal for life and that's the truth.

Eva, we always thought of home because we never knew when it was our turn to get it. We never had any sleep during the whole time we were there and oh how they shelled those woods and there was some one getting killed all of the time. It was just pure hell, if it was anything, and when the lines got blown he would never see me go out alone, nor I him, and so, Eva, you see what it means to have a pal like Bill Reardon.

I don't believe that I have ever told you about him. He is a guy who is 43 years old, and his father was a great harness man. Ask Dad if has ever heard of the Reardon collar. Well, Bill and I never were together in the front lines, but we were always with each other when we were out, so that's how I happen to pal around with him. He did his bit at Beaumont. He was a sergeant, but he went to Paris and overstayed his time and he got busted so he is a high buck private in the rear rank. Dupont got gassed at Verdun. Now, Reed went through the whole war and he never got a mark on him and a nicer guy never lived than he, and he did his bit several times. So, you can see, Eva that I have three pals that never showed yellow and I know that they will stick by a fellow whenever he needs help and that is worth more than money can buy.

I am flat busted, Eva, as I lent money to fellows going on furlough and we won't have another payday in France, so I will have to lead a simple life and smoke the makings, but I should not worry. I will be home soon and then, oh boy. Well, Eva, don't look for another letter after this one because we will leave here in a few days, so I will close now, and I hope to see you all very soon.

Your loving brother, Raymond

March 21st 1919
Brette, France
My Dear Sister,
Just a few lines to let you know how nice the YMCA has been to us during this last week. They promised to give us a show one night and we had our stage all fixed up and we waited for two hours for them and

last night they were to come, and they never came and tonight the same thing all over again. And, all the hard work the men did to fix the stage and the long wait, and they never came. That's how they use us here. That's our case, but now if they do come, we are all going to let them start and then after they start we will give them the razz.

We have started our cootie cleaning and we have a bath house and every man has got to take these baths and have all of his clothes boiled and his blankets steamed and them hot irons applied to them. So, your truly rang in for the job. I am working in the dry house that is to start tomorrow.

I haven't heard from you for some time now, Eva, but I do trust that you and all of the folks are well and fine and that the weather there is good. Putting the clock back an hour here makes it dark again when we get up in the morning, but I guess that I can stick it out. I have so far, but, Eva, if you only knew just how slow the time goes by with us waiting here. I am sending you a little piece that a fellow made up over here, Eva, and I will close now and hope that this letter finds you all doing okay.

You loving brother,

Private 1ˢᵗ Class Raymond. W. Maker

March 23ʳᵈ 1919

Brette, France

My Dear Sister,

Well, Eva, we are still here, and the Lord only knows how much longer we will be here. In my last letter to you, I thought we would be out of here by now that the inspection came out okay, but I guess we are booked up here until the last of the month. But, we will be home sometime. Some of the regiments have left this area and I guess they are in Brest waiting for the boats.

Bill Reardon came back from his furlough last night. He said he was up to a fine place called St. Milo, up near the English coast. We are all ready to move and we have been for some time now. We have the lists all made up to go on the boats and we are all set. There is no news of any kind, so I don't hardly know what to write about.

I have not heard from Gladys for 3 or 4 months and so I don't know what the trouble is. She spoke about getting married some time ago, so I would not be surprised, but I should not worry. We never were in love, that is, I was not.

I suppose that you folks are having fine weather there and that it must be getting warm there by now. We have been having fine weather, but it rains about every day for about an hour. Do you ever hear from Grandma since she went up to New Hampshire?

I suppose that I will have quite a time going around and see my friends after I get home and I will have to take a month or so off and do a little running around and thank the Lord I won't have to go and ask for a pass or get in wrong, if I beat it away. We are to wear our third stripe today, but we have not gotten the order yet, but anyway we have been away from home for 18 months as of yesterday, and believe me, Eva, it seems like 18 years.

I am writing this letter in the morning and I am supposed to be at work, so I am going up and see that the fire is all ok, and I will write some more after dinner. Well, here I am, again, and I have just seen Bill Morrow. He told me that we were going in the same boat with them and that we were to leave here on the 27th of this month. I hope that he is right. I have taken off my old stripes and I am sending them to you in this letter. Keep them, Eva, because they have seen some service.

Well, Eva, I can't think of much more to write about, so I will close for now and I don't know if I will write again to you or not.

Your loving brother,

Raymond

March 24th 1919
My Dear Dad,
Just a few lines to let you know that I am still waiting to leave France and that I hope to see you all very soon. So, if you have the machine, keep her oiled up because I want you to drive up to Camp Devens and bring me home.

I wrote to Eva yesterday and told her about all the news that there was to tell. I am fine, and I hope that you folks are all doing well. I do not think that I will write another letter over here as we leave here in just a few days.

I suppose that Uncle Ed is still on the job and I am wondering what you are doing. I can see you sitting in that old chair and falling asleep or reading the horse newspaper. I am in a little hurry because I have got to have this letter in by retreat if I want it to go tonight and the post office is moving in a day or so. You will have to excuse this short letter, Dad, but there is no news to write about, but I can tell you lots of stories when I get home.

I hope you heard General Edward's speech, as Eva said you were going to hear him. Well, I will close now, and I hope to see you all in a couple or three weeks. Love to you all.

Your loving son,

Raymond

March 26ᵗʰ 1919

Brette, France

My Dear Sister,

Just a few short lines before supper. We had our last cooties inspection today and we are all ok, and we are to leave here Friday, the 28ᵗʰ for Brest. For sure, this is the last letter we can write from here – this town – and I do hope to beat this one home.

They say that the boats are all ready for us and that there are five of them. There were only two in the company that had cooties and they just got fixed up and are now all ok. I just found out that we could not write anymore, so here I am in a big hurry to get this letter into the post office.

So, keep the home fires burning for I will be there tout suite. It rained here all day and it is cold here. No news outside of what I told you, so I will close now with the best of love to all and I will see you all soon.

Love to all.

You loving brother,

Private 1ˢᵗ Class Raymond W. Maker

APRIL 1919

16 April 1919
POSTCARD

Ocean Transport Service

Hello, Dad,

Don't know if I will see you before this card gets to you or not, but we are to land on the 17ᵗʰ and go to Camp Devens, so if I don't get home, come up quick and see your old soldier boy that has come back with bells on.

Raymond
PS: I will try and call up from the camp but come up anyway.

16 April 1919
POSTCARD Ocean Transport Service

Dear Sister,

Expect to land on the 17ᵗʰ and I hope that I will be home by the time you get this. Had a great trip over and fine weather.

Raymond

18 April 1919
8:22 PM

Western Union Telegram
Will be home early tomorrow morning.

Raymond

CASUALTIES IN BATTLE OF THE 26TH DIVISION

Killed:	Officers	Men	Total
	78	1,652	1,730
Wounded	100	11,977	12,077
Gassed	113	3,250	3,363
Missing	10	273	283
Prisoners	9	127	136

The division returned to the United States and was demobilized on May 3, 1919, at Camp Devens, Massachusetts.

- 26th Division Summary of Operations in the World War
Prepared by the American Battle Monuments Commission – 1944

THE KEY TO VERDUN

KEY TO A LOST GATE OPENS OLD MEMORIES

By William A. McNamara

The Providence Sunday Journal, December 2, 1956

If diplomacy is a respecter of memories, Suez-strained Franco-American relations have been bolstered by a Providence ceremony that bridged an ocean, 40 years and a sea of precious memories.

The ceremony, which ended quietly the other night in an art gallery, started last June when a souvenir-rich World War 1 veteran from Cranston read a newspaper story about a Europe-bound "minister without portfolio" from Providence.

Raymond W. Maker, a veteran telephone company employee who is fond of old friendships and memories as long as they don't interfere with the proprieties, was prompted by the story to call Mrs. Charles A. Post, president of Alliance Française, with a request.

He asked her to drop a key off at Verdun, France.

NO LITTLE THING

This may sound like a little thing, but it isn't. The key, besides being more than seven inches long and heavy, has the added value of belonging to the historic North Gate of the Verdun Citadel where the German advance was squelched 40 years ago.

It is true that the great Citadel no longer has the enormous North Gate who key clanked into doughboy Maker's pocket as something to remember the war days in France by, but the key still has a place of honor.

This was the assurance of Mrs. Post, who at an Alliance meeting Friday night presented to the soft-spoken Cranston man an official certificate from the senator-mayor of Verdun for this unexpected addition to the battle site's historic collection.

KEY, BUT NO GATE

Mr. Maker, my merely closing his eyes, "can still see as plain as day" the big North Gate that Mrs. Post says is no longer there – nor apparently, obtainable. The idea that the French can't find the historic gate, as big as it was, but have found the key is an engaging one for the principal's in the little drama, including the French.

So, the keepers of the "elegant' memorial hall at Verdun, said Mrs. Post, has placed it in exhibit "with the choicest things." And a certification of that fact, made by Francois Schleiter, senator-mayor of Verdun, was given to Mr. Maker at the Faunce House Art Gallery, at Brown University.

Mrs. Post said she took her "diplomatic" mission seriously and that the Hotel-de-Ville officials in Verdun took it no less seriously. At a 40th anniversary celebration had by the citadel, she was invited to speak on the return of the key and was decorated with the Verdun Medal.

UNEXPECTED HONOR

Though she had included Verdun in her planned itinerary, Mrs. Post had not expected to be so honored a guest. Her main objective was delivery of a friendship book from Rhode Island to the president of France – an outgrowth of France Comes to Rhode Island Week a year ago.

Mrs. Post, a recent recipient of the French Legion of Honor, showed Mr. Maker her Verdun Medal the other night and observed lightly: "You lost something, you see, and I gained something."

But Mr. Maker is not so sure. He thinks his grandchildren will be more impressed by the official declaration in French from "le senateur-maire" than they would be by the worn old key.

THE FINAL CHAPTER

During a visit to Rhode Island in October 1992, my mother brought out a box from within her closet and said, "I have some things I want you to have. Here are all of your Grandfather's letters from World War I, and this is the key to the North Gate of Verdun, France, the one that Daddy mailed back to Aunt Eva. In 1956, your grandfather gave a key to a lady, a Mrs. Post, who was traveling back to France and she presented that key to the mayor of Verdun, but what she did not know was the key that Daddy gave to her was an ornate iron key a friend of his had made by the Providence Casting Company in North Providence."

On November 15, 2018, my wife Helen and I had just returned from a trip to France. Having never before been to Europe, I had no preconceptions of what to expect once we arrived. Fortunately, Helen had visited France several times in the past and was conversant in French.

Of equal if not more importance was the GPS I borrowed from Major Greg Dyson, USMC, who had recently been stationed in Frankfurt, Germany, and was happy to program his GPS to the places we wanted to visit. After landing in Paris, on November 5, we drove west to the small fishing harbor of Port-en-Bessin on the French coast. Our first stop on the morning of the November 6 was Pointe Du Hoc, the fabled site where U.S. Army Rangers of the 2nd Ranger Battalion, scaled ninety-foot cliffs to assault and capture that German gun position. The strategic point is the highest elevation between Utah and Omaha Beaches. Located nearby is the Normandy American Cemetery and Memorial in Colleville-sur-Mer, on the site of the American St. Laurent Cemetery, established by the U.S. First Army on June 8, 1944, and the first American cemetery on European soil in World War II. It is the most visited cemetery of the American Battle

Monuments Commission, receiving more than one million visitors each year.

Leaving Port-en-Bessin, on we traveled east to the town of Ermenonville, where we had arranged to stay at the Château d'Ermenonville, a fifteenth century castle which was a popular place for the French kings to visit. King Louis XI often stayed here, as well as Henry IV and our first ambassador to France, Benjamin Franklin.

Departing Ermenonville, on November 9, we drove east to visit Belleau Wood and visited the Aisne-Marne American Cemetery and Memorial. The cemetery lies in a sweeping curve on 42-acres of ground and is the final resting place of 2,289 Americans who died fighting for France. Near the entrance to the cemetery is a small stone church that was destroyed during the war. General Edwards, commanding the 26th Infantry Division, had promised the local villagers that he would ensure the church was rebuilt and in October 1929, their church was dedicated to the memory of those men of 26th "Yankee" Division.

Our next stop was Château-Thierry, where we walked the ground where Raymond had fallen victim to a gas attack launched by German artillery July 22, 1918. Two miles west of the village is the World War I Château-Thierry American Monument, which commemorates the sacrifices and achievements of the Americans and French before and during the Aisne-Marne and Oise-Aisne offenses of 1918. The thousands of white crosses at these American National Cemeteries are a sobering reminder of the price paid by American infantrymen to secure the future of France. Overall, in roughly six months of combat, the American Expeditionary Force suffered more than 255,000 casualties, including 52,997 battle deaths, as well as more than 50,000 non-battle deaths, mostly due to the influenza epidemic.

On the morning of November 10, we arrived at the Verdun War Memorial at 11am and were cordially met by the Director, Monsieur Thierry Hubscher, and his assistant, Gabrielle Perissi. After introductions were made we went to an upper-level conference room in the War Memorial and were met by the Memorial's Chief Archeologist and Collections representative, Ms. Natacha Glaudel, and Monsieur Frederic Plancard, a news reporter for L'EST Republicain Newspaper. With

"Gabby" Perissi, translating, I related Raymond's story and his acquiring the key to the North gate of Verdun, taken as a souvenir of his eighteen months of service in France.

Both Monsieur Hubscher and Ms. Perissi were excited to discuss an article written by Greg Norman, a reporter from Fox News, which had appeared that morning on the Fox website. Mr. Norman had contacted the staff at the War Memorial in preparing his story about Raymond W. Maker and my returning of the key to appropriate place in Verdun.

Monsieur Hubscher was most appreciative that the key would be presented to the War Memorial, where it will be included in an upcoming exhibit depicting the participation of American Expeditionary Forces in Verdun. The Verdun War Memorial has the ability to conserve and display the key professionally, more so than any other government memorial facility.

I believe that the most memorable event of this trip was the arranged visit to the citadel, the walled fortress inside of the city. The citadel was built around 1624. From 1890 to 1914, a seven-kilometer underground tunnel system was built beneath the citadel and served as the headquarters of the French Army during the first battle of Verdun in 1916. According to one description, "the citadel of Verdun is strongly lowered and covered with heavy masses of soil. Therefore, it is more than barracks, it is a casemate; it is the point of contact between the front and the rear. All reliefs end here, they all start from here – it is the switchyard between War and Peace." (Gaston Gras, *Douaumont*).

At 8:15 am on February 2, 1916, the German army launched its major offensive at Verdun. The first shells fell on the citadel. As intended, the staff and civil services found shelter in the tunnels, which were dug under sixteen meters of solid rock.

From that point on, the citadel was organized as a small subterranean city with ceaseless activity; offices for the staff, immense dormitories for up to 2,000 troops, powder and ammunition depots to supply the front lines, a bakery equipped with nine bread ovens capable of producing 21,000 rations per day, a chapel, a theater, equipment dedicated to the breaks and amusement of the soldier, a switchboard system, a hospital, and an electrical power station. As they were never reached by the tremendous enemy bombardment, the tunnels played a crucial moral and logistical role in the survival of the soldiers and civilians inside. As the citadel symbolized the resistance of an entire nation, it was the setting for numerous ceremonies during and after the war.

To appreciate the significance of the citadel, visitors experience an electrical motorized ride (*nacelle*), taking up to six passengers at a time, through the vast dank and dark tunnel complex. Raymond W. Maker and his fellow soldiers of the 104th Infantry Regiment lived inside these tunnels during the month of October 1918, and he commented on them in his diary entries and letters to his sister on the 8th, 11th, 12th and 16th of that month. It was an incredibly humbling moment to realize that I was in the exact same place that he was, a hundred years later, and almost to the month.

We left Verdun on November 14 with a far greater appreciation for what the Doughboys of the 26th Infantry Division had experienced during their eighteen months of service in France.

Following a severe heart attack and stroke, my grandfather was hospitalized in the spring of 1964 and was given no chance of recovery. Upon learning of his worsening condition, a letter written by Raymond's closest friend and fellow war veteran Ted Wilson offers a wonderful tribute to Raymond's selfless character on the battlefield:

Abington, Massachusetts
Dear Marge,
June 9/64

Many thanks for writing to me and informing me of existing conditions. The news of your father's set back has left me in a daze and the feeling of helplessness is almost too much to take.

We seemed to become attached to each other from our first meeting in Camp Norman Prince in 1917 and the friendship between us increased as the first year passed. No matter what the situation was, his first thought was always, "Are you OK, Ted?" On one occasion, he threw himself on top of me in a shell hole to protect me as much as possible, explaining this to me later by saying "You've got a mother at home waiting for you and I haven't." To quote the Good Book – "Greater love hath no man than to lay down his life for his brother."

Such is the type of man you can proudly call your father.

It really hurts deeply to realize that I cannot help him in any way at a time when he needs it. His fate appears to be in God's hands and in my humble way, I'll pray to Him to spare your Dad to his family and to me. You certainly are having much to be concerned about with your mother and father both disabled at once. Again, I am unable to offer any help except my sympathy. My wife has only met your mother once or twice, but already has a very fond regard for her, as I do myself.

Please let me know if you think a visit at the hospital would be advisable, and if so, when I can do so as I have no phone, Marge, but my son has, and he is quite near my home. His number is 617, Triangle, 89078. Feel free to call him and I'll get the message.

Thanks again for your letter although its contents have taken a lot out of me. Remember me to your Ma, Jack, and all the rest.

Your Dad's Buddy,
Ted Wilson
392 Plymouth Street

With his wife Gladys admitted to the same hospital, having been diagnosed with breast cancer, Raymond, surrounded by his family, passed away on June 15, 1964.

THE MAKER FAMILY

Raymond's Sister - Eva M. Maker

(Visiting Nurse of Holbrook, Massachusetts)

Eva and her buggy in 1919

Holbrook – A Nurse or all Seasons

In 1918 the Spanish Influenza epidemic hit hard in Holbrook, Massachusetts. Whole families were stricken. Mrs. Alva Southworth, R.N., made home visits with local doctors to help where she could in the town of 3,000 residents. Mrs. Southworth saw the need for a district nurse for the town. To her home she invited a group of influential citizens who that night organized the Holbrook Visiting Nurse Association.

A young lady from Framingham, Miss Eva M. Maker, took the job of district nurse in 1919 and filled the position with great distinction for 41 years thereafter, until her retirement in 1960.

Townspeople first saw Nurse Eva Maker travelling house to house by foot, then by horse and buggy. The team was donated by Hooker's Ice Cream Company in 1919, after they bought their first truck. By 1920 the nurse had learned how to drive a Model-T Ford purchased from donations.

In 1929, Eva Maker married James Sullivan, who became Chief of the Holbrook Fire Department. He often helped his wife make emergency calls at all hours of the night and in all kinds of weather.

Eva Maker Sullivan assisted doctors at home births and helped with minor surgeries at a time when the kitchen was often the operating theatre for a tonsillectomy. A whirlwind of energy, she often tended the entire family of a bedridden mother, feeding the children and even doing the family wash. Through the years she often distributed clothing to the needy and collected toys to be mended by the Fire Department men for charity.

Carrying on the Tradition of Carry

The Holbrook Visiting Nurses Association (VNA) grew to a staff of four nurses and a physical therapist. The agency was incorporated in 1964 and received Medicare certification in 1966.

In 1979, the Holbrook VNA formally merged with the Braintree VNA, forming the Visiting Nurse Association of the South Shore, Inc. The needs of the town for home health care services could be met only by a larger, progressive agency.

Today, the VNA of the South Shore continues the tradition of service to the townspeople of Holbrook begun by Eva Maker Sullivan. Under a contract with the Board of Health, the VNA provides Well Child, immunization, and senior citizens clinics as well as cancer, diabetes and other screenings. And school nursing services continue at St. Joseph's School. As in all the South Shore towns served, the VNA of the South Shore provides a comprehensive program of home care in Holbrook for anyone who is ill or disabled.

[*Minutes of the meeting of the Weymouth VNA, March, 1933]

The Maker Family - 1900

Raymond's Father - Winfield Scott Maker (1853-1924)

Rosalba Harriet Maker (Raymond's Mother) - 1870

The Maker Family (circa 1900) Left to Right: Clifford, Raymond, Eva, Harriet, Rosalba, Winfield Scott and George Whitney Maker

Clifford (Kip) Maker (Raymond's Brother) - 1918

**Clifford (Kip) Maker (L), Eva Maker, (C)
and Raymond W. Maker (R) - 1915**

The 1917 Hudson

**Pictured above is "Uncle" Edward Maker, standing second on the left,
wearing his Union Army uniform. Edward, and his brother, "Uncle"
Andrew, to his right. Both men served in
the 19th Maine Regiment during the Civil War. - 1898**

**Private 1st Class Raymond Whitney Maker
Company C, 101st Field Signal Battalion,
26th "Yankee" Division, AEF - 1918**

Raymond - 1925

Raymond Whitney Maker - 1960

(Photo by Marceau, Boston)

MAJ. GEN. CLARENCE R. EDWARDS,
Commanding 26th Division, July 25, 1917-October 25, 1918.

**Major General Clarence R. Edwards,
commanding officer, 26th "Yankee" Division – 1918**

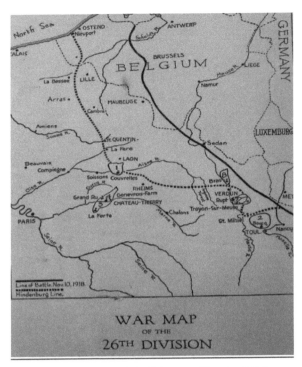

Military map of the Western Front - 1918

U.S. Army infantrymen in the trenches - 1918

Going "Over the Top" – 1918

Base Hospital #31, where Raymond was hospitalized after being gassed

Base Hospital #31 - 1918

American Red Cross Nurses - 1918

104th Infantry Regimental Band – 1918

Horse and handler with gas masks – 1918

Two field signal soldiers with gas masks - 1918

Yankee Division Soldier with rifle, bayonet and gas mask- 1918

The Yankee Division shoulder patch WW1

No man's land, Château-Thierry – 1918

A Battalion of Infantry en route to the ceremonies at which the Croix de Guerre was conferred on Lieut. C. R. Holmes and Sergeant Murphy.

Men of the 26th Yankee Division marching to an awards ceremony - 1918

View of the ration dump of the 101st Field Signal Battalion, located at the crossroads leading to " Death Valley," which was constantly under shell fire, at Samogneux, France, Oct. 27, 1918.

101st Field Signal Battalion Supply Dump - 1918

No man's land, Verdun - 1918

Victims of gas attack - 1918

Verdun – 1918

The bakery inside the Verdun citadel - 1917

26th Division Boys return on the Mt. Vernon, April 4, 1919.

**The 26th Yankee Division Returns Home
to Boston from France – April 1919**

Raymond's trench knife

Raymond's Colt .45 ACP (Note - Serial # 274084 with leather wrist strap and clip with lanyard ring)

Raymond's lamp (Engraved with his name and unit, and with his "101st Field Signal Battalion Goat mascot painted on center. At the base of the 75mm shell are four .45 shell casings he saved, after killing four German infantrymen at Belleau Wood).

Raymond's mess kit with the nicknames of fellow soldiers

The bottom half of Raymond's mess kit.

Raymond's mess kit lid inscribed with places he had been.

Raymond's mess kit set

Raymond's knife (clipped to fit his mess kit) and GI issued fork and spoon.

Verdun - 2018

The author, presenting the key to Monsieur Thierry Hubscher, Director of the Verdun War Memorial, November 10, 2018.

The Key to the North Gate of Verdun – 2018

**Helen K. Norton, Verdun Mayor the Honorable Samuel Hazard, and Maj.
B. H. Norton USMC (ret.) - November 11, 2018**

CPSIA information can be obtained
at www.ICGtesting.com
Printed in the USA
LVHW070916260121
677358LV00029B/2749